AD

ARCHITECTURAL DESIGN

GUEST-EDITED BY
BRADY PETERS AND
XAVIER DE KESTELIER

COMPUTATION WORKS
THE BUILDING
OF ALGORITHMIC
THOUGHT

02|2013

ARCHITECTURAL DESIGN
MARCH/APRIL 2013
ISSN 0003-8504

PROFILE NO 222
ISBN 978-1119-952862

AD

ARCHITECTURAL DESIGN

GUEST-EDITED BY
BRADY PETERS AND
XAVIER DE KESTELIER

COMPUTATION WORKS: THE BUILDING OF ALGORITHMIC THOUGHT

32

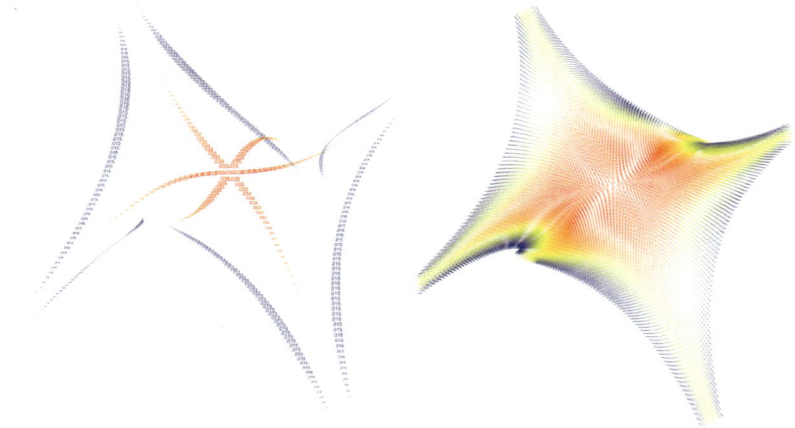

Computation augments the intellect of the designer and increases capability to solve complex problems.
— *Brady Peters and Xavier De Kestelier*

42

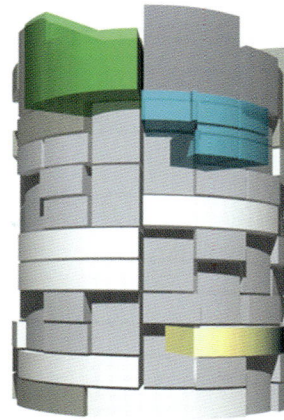

110

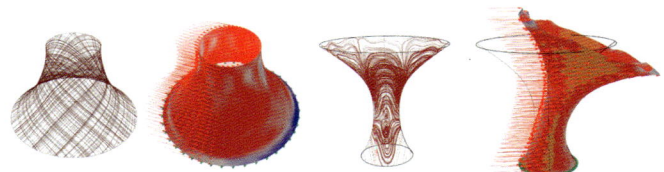

ΛD

ARCHITECTURAL DESIGN

MARCH/APRIL 2013
PROFILE NO 222

Editorial Offices
John Wiley & Sons
25 John Street
London WC1N 2BS
UK

T: +44 (0)20 8326 3800

Editor
Helen Castle

Managing Editor (Freelance)
Caroline Ellerby

Production Editor
Elizabeth Gongde

Prepress
Artmedia, London

Art Direction and Design
CHK Design:
Christian Küsters
Sophie Troppmair

Printed in Italy by Printer Trento Srl

Sponsorship/advertising
Faith Pidduck/Wayne Frost
T: +44 (0)1243 770254
E: fpidduck@wiley.co.uk

Subscribe to ΛD

ΛD is published bimonthly and is
available to purchase on both a
subscription basis and as individual
volumes at the following prices.

Prices
Individual copies: £24.99 / US$45
Individual issues on ΛD App
for iPad: £9.99 / US$13.99
Mailing fees for print may apply

Annual Subscription Rates
Student: £75 / US$117 print only
Personal: £120 / US$189 print and
iPad access
Institutional: £212 / US$398 print
or online
Institutional: £244 / US$457
combined print and online
6-issue subscription on ΛD App
for iPad: £44.99 / US$64.99

Subscription Offices UK
John Wiley & Sons Ltd
Journals Administration Department
1 Oldlands Way, Bognor Regis
West Sussex, PO22 9SA, UK
T: +44 (0)1243 843 272
F: +44 (0)1243 843 232
E: cs-journals@wiley.co.uk

Print ISSN: 0003-8504
Online ISSN: 1554-2769

Prices are for six issues and include
postage and handling charges.
Individual-rate subscriptions must be
paid by personal cheque or credit card.
Individual-rate subscriptions may not
be resold or used as library copies.

All prices are subject to change
without notice.

Rights and Permissions
Requests to the Publisher should be
addressed to:
Permissions Department
John Wiley & Sons Ltd
The Atrium
Southern Gate
Chichester
West Sussex PO19 8SQ
UK

F: +44 (0)1243 770 620
E: permreq@wiley.co.uk

Front cover: Foster + Partners, Detail of
construction of Masdar Institute of Science
and Technology, Masdar City, Abu Dhabi,
2010. © Nigel Young/Foster + Partners

Inside front cover: Concept Sophie Troppmair,
CHK Design

EDITORIAL
Helen Castle

In recent decades, computation has become an established driver of architectural exploration – perhaps only rivalled by sustainability. This was most conspicuously the case in the late 1990s and early noughties with the rise of Blob Architecture, which optimised the use of computer-aided design (CAD) in the creation of new geometries and amoebic, cellular-like forms for iconic buildings. (The trend for blobs and NURBS coincided with a construction boom and a raft of high-profile cultural buildings, such as Frank Gehry's Guggenheim Museum Bilbao and Foster + Partners' The Sage Gateshead.)

Architecture now is certainly less noisy and ostentatious in its display of the digital, no longer wearing its processes so evidently on its surfaces. With each cultural and technological shift, though, computation continues to take on a new focus for its invention and innovation. Four or five years ago, excitement centred largely on the emergence of new fabrication and manufacturing techniques (see, for instance, Bob Sheil's △ *Protoarchitecture*, July/August 2008). Now, however, as Brady Peters and Xavier De Kestelier, the guest-editors of this issue, observe in their introduction, the onus on architects lies in the application of computation 'to simulate building performance, to incorporate performance analysis and knowledge about material, tectonics and parameters of production machinery in their design drawings'. This emphasis on simulation and prediction unleashes computation from being merely a generative tool to being at the heart of building and practice, and even beyond to the monitoring and assessment of completed structures.

This issue is thus dedicated to the application of computation in a practice setting. Despite the increasingly necessary application of algorithmic thought for large-scale and complex architectural projects, computation rather than just the use of off-the-shelf software remains a specialist area standing apart from mainstream practice. As described by Peters and De Kestelier in the introduction, computational experts are largely concentrated in standalone teams – whether internal research units or external consultancies. As Hugh Whitehead, the former head of the Foster + Partners Specialist Modelling Group, has stated, scripting remains 'an isolated craft'. Peters' and De Kestelier's ambitions for 'an integrated art form' remains an aspiration for a further computational shift in architecture. △

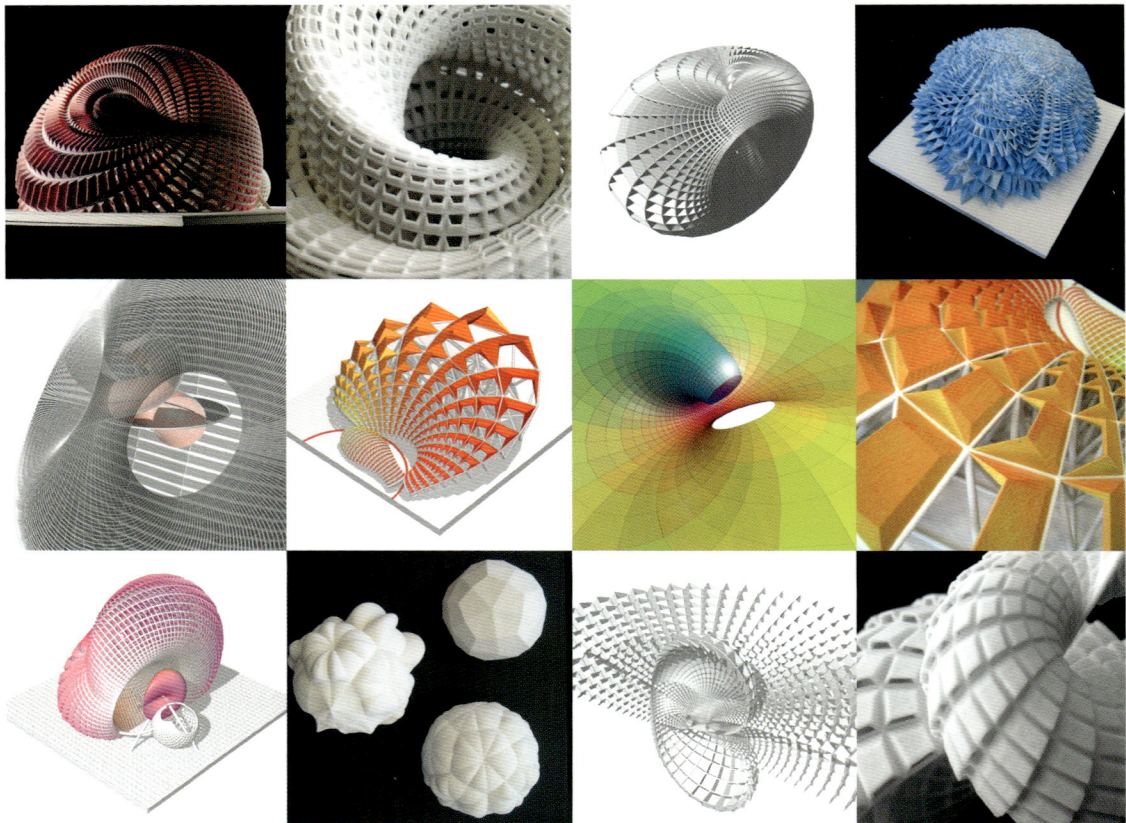

Foster + Partners' Specialist Modelling
Group (SMG) with John Pickering, *15
Inversion Studies*, 'Beyond Measure:
Conversations Across Art and Science'
exhibition, Kettle's Yard Gallery, Cambridge,
UK, 2008
These 3-D printed models were developed
during a series of experimental workshops in
which the artist John Pickering and the Specialist
Modelling Group participated. They explored
new geometrical territory through the use of
mathematical formulae, computer programming
and parametric software. *15 Inversion Studies*
explores the mathematical concept of the
inversion principle and suggests a possible
relevance to architecture. The resulting
mathematical surfaces were populated with
adaptive structural and cladding components.

Architects Brady Peters and Xavier De Kestelier have extensive practice-based experience in the use of digital design including parametric modelling and computational techniques, performance-driven design, and the communication and construction of complex geometry. They have collaborated in various capacities since 2003. Through their positions in practice and at academic institutions they promote the use of computation as a design tool and as a way of extending the potentials of the designer. They met while working in the Specialist Modelling Group (SMG), the internal research and development consultancy of internationally renowned architecture practice Foster + Partners. Working on the design of complex building projects from conception to completion, they have demonstrated the use of computation to develop designs and communicate architectural solutions. Within SMG, they were also responsible for conceptualising and coordinating exploratory research efforts, establishing, for example, Foster + Partners' in-house rapid-prototyping capabilities, and developing full-scale rapid manufacturing technologies through their collaboration with Loughborough University. They taught digital design and fabrication at the University of Ghent in Belgium, and are active members of the Smartgeometry organisation, where they coordinate and build this international network of digital designers and computational thinkers.

Brady Peters uses computer programming to design architecture, and has written hundreds of programs that have been used in many Foster + Partners' projects including: the Smithsonian Courtyard in Washington DC (2007), Thomas Deacon Academy in Peterborough, UK (2007), the Elephant House in Copenhagen (2008), Arc Table for Molteni & C (2010), Khan Shatyr Entertainment Centre in Astana, Kazakhstan (2010), and the Hydro/Scottish National Arena in Glasgow (2005–). His current research develops algorithmic techniques for the design of performance-driven architecture. He has integrated environmental analysis with architectural design, developed structural form-finding tools, and written acoustic simulation programs. He has recently completed research projects with the Center for Information Technology and Architecture (CITA) at the Royal Danish Academy of Fine Arts in Copenhagen, with Rensselaer Polytechnic Institute in New York, the Acoustic Technology Group at the Danish Technical University (DTU), and with the Spatial Information Architecture Laboratory (SIAL) at RMIT University in Melbourne, which have resulted in the development of design tools and architectural surfaces for acoustic performance. Originally from Canada where he gained a BSc and MArch, he is a PhD fellow at the Royal Danish Academy of Fine Arts School of Architecture. He has taught architecture in Denmark, Belgium, the UK and Canada, and has published book chapters and academic articles on computational design in architectural practice. He has been a tutor at Smartgeometry workshops since 2006, and, with Terri Peters, is the co-editor of *Inside Smartgeometry: Expanding the Architectural Potential of Computational Design* (John Wiley & Sons, 2013).

Xavier De Kestelier is a partner at Foster + Partners where he is co-head of SMG. Recent projects include: Kuwait International Airport (2009–), the National Bank of Kuwait Headquarters (2007–), and Kai Tak cruise terminal in Hong Kong (2013). Originally from Belgium, he gained an MArch from the University of Ghent and an MSc (Urban Design) from the Bartlett School of Architecture, University College London (UCL). He has initiated and overseen two major research projects, the latest of which is funded by the European Space Agency and focuses on the application of additive manufacturing for lunar habitation. In 2010 he became a director of the Smartgeometry organisation. He has been a visiting professor at the University of Ghent and at Syracuse University in New York. He is now a teaching fellow at the Bartlett where he leads a research cluster in the Graduate Architectural Design programme that focuses on advanced digital fabrication. He has been a visiting critic and guest speaker at a wide range of universities and organisations including the Architectural Association (AA) and Royal Institution in London, Cooper Union and Syracuse University in New York, and the Berlage Institute in Rotterdam. ⌀

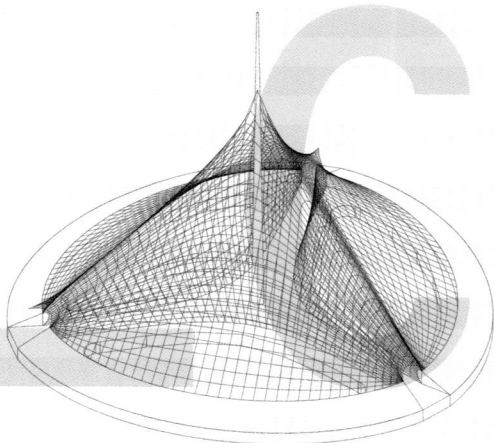
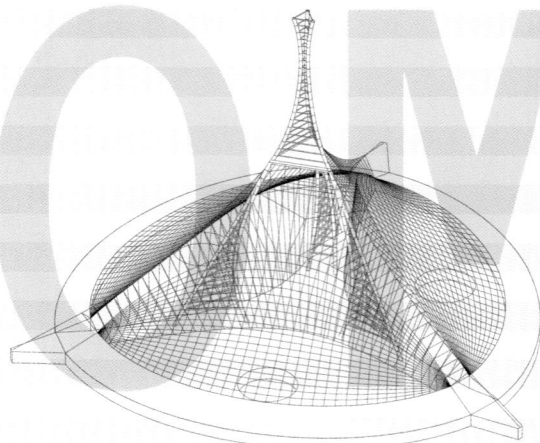
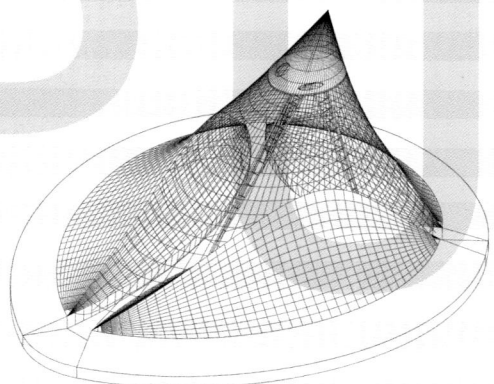
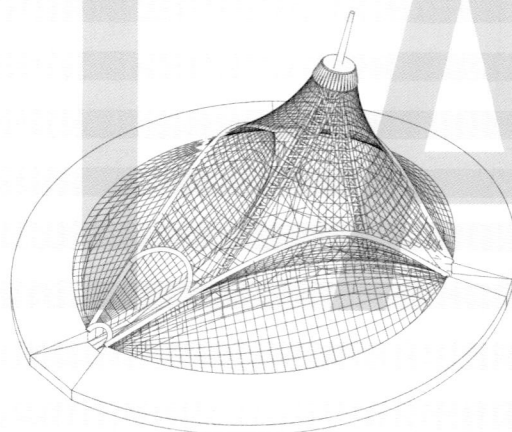
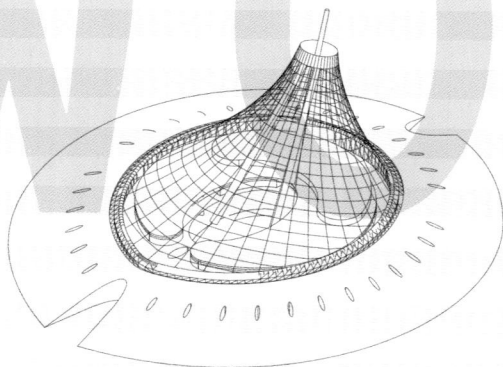
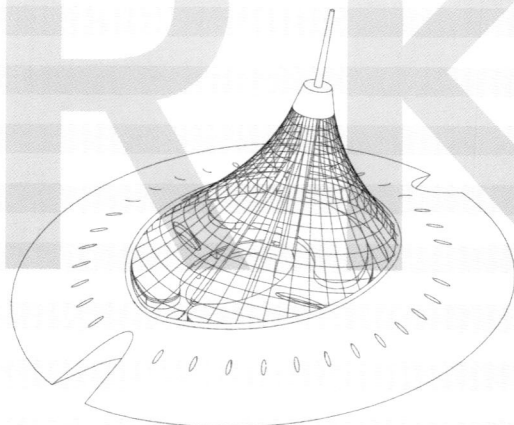

THE BUILDING OF ALGORITHMIC THOUGHT

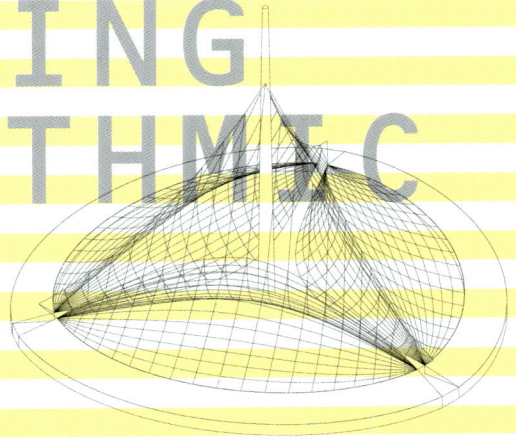

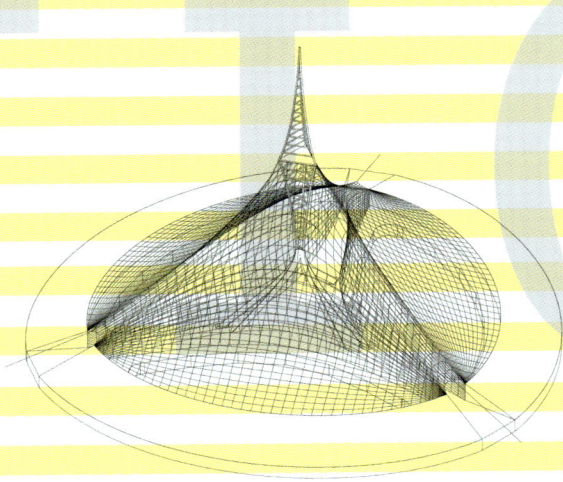

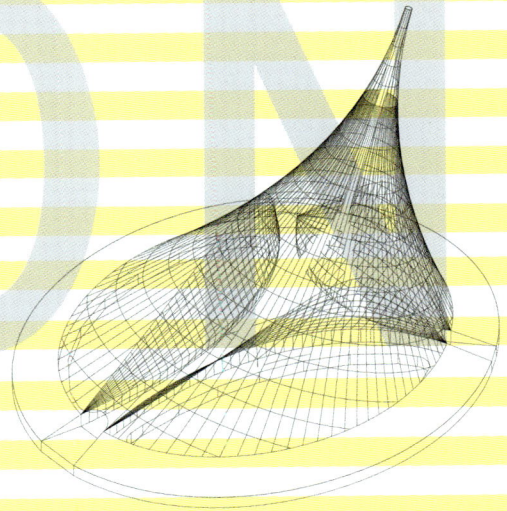

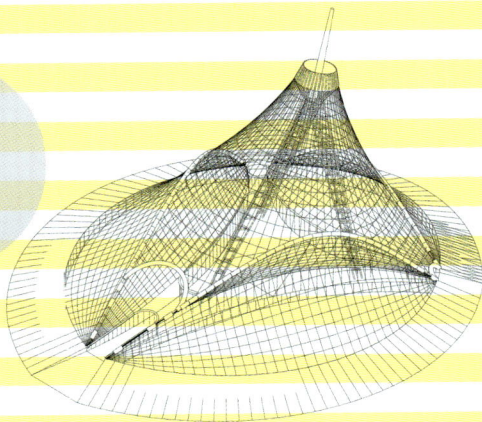

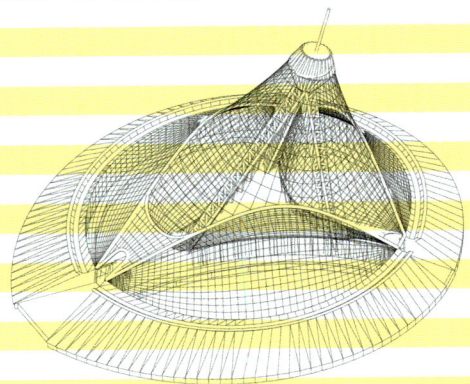

Computation is redefining the practice of architecture. Architects are developing digital tools that create opportunities in design process, fabrication and construction. Using built architectural projects, this issue of ⌀ provides insight into emerging design approaches that use computation as a design method. While this issue aims for a balance of ideas, scales of work, and types of practices, it is not a cross-section through all of architecture, but rather a presentation of state-of-the-art uses of computation.

But what do we mean by computation? Most architects now use computers, but usually to simply digitise existing procedures with entities or processes that are preconceived in the mind of the designer. For example, architects use the computer as a virtual drafting board making it easier to edit, copy and increase the precision of drawings. This mode of working has been termed 'computerisation'.[1] 'Computation', on the other hand, allows designers to extend their abilities to deal with highly complex situations. Sean Ahlquist and Achim Menges define computation as 'the processing of information and interactions between elements which constitute a specific environment; it provides a framework for negotiating and influencing the interrelation of datasets of information, with the capacity to generate complex order, form, and structure.'[2] In this issue of ⌀, the term 'computation' means the use of the computer to process information through an understood model which can be expressed as an algorithm. This then allows the exploration of new ideas: computation augments the intellect of the designer and increases capability to solve complex problems.[3]

As illustrated here with new building projects by some of the world's most forward-thinking practices, computation also has the potential to provide inspiration and go beyond the intellect of the designer, like other techniques of architectural design, through the generation of unexpected results. For example, when an architect writes a computer program to solve a design problem, further options can then be explored through modifications to the program – sketching by algorithm.[4] An algorithm is a particular set of instructions, and for these instructions to be understood by the computer they must be written in a language the computer can understand, a code.

Architects designing many of the projects featured in this ⌀ have used scripting languages such as RhinoScript or Visual Basic for Applications (VBA) in Bentley Systems' MicroStation™ to write programs to customise their design environments in their existing architectural design software. While other computer languages are used, and indeed have been used since architects have first used computers (see Daniel Cardoso Llach's 'Algorithmic Tectonics' on pp 16–21), the power and availability of these scripting languages, and now also Robert McNeel & Associates' Grasshopper® visual programming language, have propelled the increased usage of computation in practice. Algorithmic thinking means taking on an interpretive role to understand the results of the generating code, knowing how to modify the code to explore new options, and speculating on further design potentials. We are moving from an era where architects use software to one where they create software.[5]

Foster + Partners, Khan Shatyr Entertainment Centre, Astana, Kazakhstan, 2010
above and previous spread: A form-finding algorithm was used by the design team to quickly generate design options for the cable-net structure. The algorithm formed part of the parametric model that was used to develop and define the building form.

10

COMPUTATION IN ARCHITECTURAL PRACTICE

Computational designers construct 3-D models and create design tools, but their expertise goes beyond these tasks. They generate and explore architectural spaces and concepts through the writing and modifying of algorithms that relate to element placement, element configuration, and the relationships between elements. In this important way, their role also goes beyond simply making digital tools for designers. Critically, the making of these custom tools takes place within the design process, and becomes integral to the design itself. These two points are key in understanding the possibilities of computational design and the role of the designer in architectural practice. For computational techniques to be useful, they must be flexible – they must adapt to the constantly changing parameters of architectural design. The design environment, of which the architect is now part author, must be flexible and have the ability to accommodate change (see Brady Peters and Daniel Davis's 'Design Ecosystems' on pp 124–31).

The structure of architectural firms is changing in response to the work of computational designers. Looking at the offices represented in this issue of ∆, there are four ways in which these designers are organised: the internal specialist group, the external specialist consultancy, the computationally aware and integrated practice, and the lone software developer/designer.

The most common approach is to have computational designers working in internal specialist groups largely separate from the design teams. These groups act as internal consultancies and designers integrate with the design process to varying degrees depending on the needs of the project. They exist in practices such as Foster + Partners (pp 22–35), Herzog & de Meuron (pp 56–61), Grimshaw (pp 104–9), Aedas|R&D (pp 42–7), UNStudio (pp 82–7) and Skidmore, Owings & Merrill (SOM) (pp 48–55).

A second approach to integrating computational design expertise into the design process is to have a consultancy of computational designers. These practices tend to be technical and specialised, either in engineering or software development. They can be hired by architecture firms who can therefore take advantage of computational techniques without actually having to internalise the expertise. Examples include Buro Happold SMART Solutions (pp 62–5), Knippers Helbig Advanced Engineering (pp 74–81) and Gehry Technologies (pp 36–41).

Computation can also be fully integrated into the practice and the actual design process. In these firms there is no separation between design intent and computational technique, and computation is used in a natural or unconscious way. Examples are MOS (pp 96–103) and Facit Homes (pp 88–91).

The fourth approach relates to an emerging model of hybrid software engineers/architects. Empowered by advances in scripting interfaces and knowledge of computer programming, these designers are actively creating their own design software. While these small offices have not yet built many projects, they are, for their size, very relevant to architectural practice as a whole. Examples included here are: David Rutten (Grasshopper®/Galapagos – pp 132–5), Daniel Piker (Kangaroo – pp 136–7, Andrew O Payne and Jason Kelly Johnson (Firefly – pp 144–7), Giulio Piacentino (WeaverBird – pp 140–1), Thomas Grabner and Ursula Frick of [uto] (GECO™ – pp 142–3), Arthur van der Harten (Pachyderm Acoustical Simulation – pp 138–9).

But do all architecture firms need to have an internal specialist group to develop computational approaches? Perhaps not, as networks, both digital and social, now allow for the access to knowledge generated by others. Events such as Smartgeometry,[6] and online forums such as the Grasshopper community,[7] allow designers to gain knowledge of digital tools and codes, workflows and algorithms that they can then use or adapt to their own design. Computation and the use of the computer facilitate the sharing of codes, tools and ideas. This accumulation of ideas is one of the ways in which we can refer to a *building of algorithmic thought*.

Foster + Partners, Beijing International Airport, Beijing, 2008
bottom: Computation is a necessary component to design and deliver the biggest building projects in the world. Beijing International Airport is more than 3 kilometres (1.9 miles) long, has 735,000 square metres (7.9 million square feet) of floor area, and serves 43 million passengers a year. The roof was constructed from 60,000 beams, and covers a total area of 360,000 square metres (3.9 million square feet). The project was designed and built within five years.

When architects have a sufficient understanding of algorithmic concepts, when we no longer need to discuss the digital as something different, then computation can become a true method of design for architecture.

Foster + Partners, Smithsonian
Institution, Washington DC, 2007
opposite: A single computer program,
written by Brady Peters, an architect on
the design team and a member of Foster
+ Partners' Specialist Modelling Group
(SMG), generated the geometry of the
roof. The computer code was used to
explore design options and was constantly
modified throughout the design process.
It was also used to generate the final
geometry and additional information
needed to analyse structural and acoustic
performance, to visualise the space, and
to create fabrication data for physical
models.

Gehry Partners, Fondation Louis
Vuitton Museum, Paris, 2005–
below: The building information model
of structural and enclosure systems
was developed through parametric
scripting driven by system performance
constraints, and used to fabricate and
install all aspects of the project.

COMPUTING PERFORMANCE AND SIMULATION

Architects are increasingly experimenting with computation to simulate building performance,[8] to incorporate performance analysis and knowledge about material, tectonics and parameters of production machinery in their design drawings. These new custom digital tools allow for performance feedback at various stages of an architectural project, creating new design opportunities. Using these tools, structural, material or environmental performance can become a fundamental parameter in the creation of architectural form (see Sawako Kaijima, Roland Bouffanais, Karen Willcox and Suresh Naidu's 'Computational Fluid Dynamics for Architectural Design' on pp 118–23, and Clemens Preisinger's 'Linking Structure and Parametric Geometry' on pp 110–13). The development of computational simulation tools can create more responsive designs, allowing architects to explore new design options and to analyse architectural decisions during the design process.

Stan Allen suggests that meaning in architecture is constructed as an encounter between architecture and the public.[9] If so, then it does not matter what design tool or technique was used in the design of a building; however, the choice of tools does have an impact on the design. Throughout history, the work of an architect has been linked to the use of drawing as a design tool.[10] Like drawing, architects working with computers and with computation still work through a medium of representation. However, with its increasing simulation capabilities, the computer lets architects predict, model and simulate the encounter between architecture and the public using more accurate and sophisticated methods. In this way, computation makes possible not only the simulation and communication of the constructional aspects of a building, but also the experience and the creation of meaning.

Skidmore, Owings & Merrill (SOM), Infinity Tower, Dubai, 2012
The lateral stepping of the perimeter columns for the Infinity Tower became a driver of the building's exterior architectural expression, and were designed in a close collaboration between the SOM architects and structural engineers. The use of finite element (FE) algorithms was critical to the success of the collaboration, providing analysis and visualisation of the structural forces for the various structural design options that were considered for the building's twisting form.

COMPUTATION FABRICATION AND CONSTRUCTION

In architectural practice, computation not only works, but has become necessary, to build the largest projects in the world. Given the complexities of form and the compressed timescales of construction today, groups such as Foster + Partners' Specialist Modelling Group (SMG) have become essential aspects in the construction of many projects. As Mouzhan Majidi has said: 'This hasn't simply transformed what we can design – it's had a huge impact on how we build.'[11] One example of the impact of computational design is in component design. Unlike in Modernism, where the design effort often went into the perfection of a single detail, the computational approach currently tends to be the development of parametric families of components and in the requisite control of data. Here, what is relevant is the relationship between the parts, and the management of this change in response to local performance requirements. As new design tools are developed to link the virtual design environment with the physical environment, architectural designers will increasingly have the capacity to explore building systems and building environments (see Andrew O Payne and Jason Kelly Johnson, pp 144–7) This could lead to a future where an architect´s digital model could continue to be relevant during the occupation of the building, where feedback between users, building and environment is updated in the digital model and reflected in changes in the building and its performance.

Computational design linked to computationally driven manufacturing requires a new interpretation of the design and construction process (see Jan Knippers's 'From Model Thinking to Process Design' on pp 74–81). This invention of new techniques and technologies has, and will continue to cause shifts in our discipline's definition and boundaries. Jan Knippers notes that this is the point for significant innovation. Similarly, Dennis Shelden writes that these computational tools and techniques will even more significantly affect the processes of design and delivery, the definition of the discipline of architecture, and the connection of the work to us and to society (see his 'Networked Space' on pp 36–41).

COMPUTATION AS AN INTEGRATED ART FORM

Computational designers are more than just creators of complex 3-D models or the developers of digital tools – they distil the underlying logic of architecture and create new environments in which to explore designs and simulate performance, both physical and experiential. Their roles and skills are currently evolving with technology and the needs of the particular project and practice. While there are many ways in which they integrate with practice – as lone guns or integrated designers – it is clear that computation enables new ways of thinking. Through computation, the digital architectural design environment has both the ability to construct complex models of buildings and give performance feedback on these models. In a similar way that the pen or pencil can be used to either draw building details or create conceptual sketches for buildings, computational tools can be used to increase efficiency and allow for better communication, as well as for conceptual sketching of algorithmic concepts.

When computation is integrated as an intuitive and natural way to design, then perhaps collections of essays like this ∆ will no longer be necessary. However, we are not yet at this point; these concepts must be tested in practice through designing and building. The results must be communicated and reflected upon. Architecture is currently experiencing a shift from the drawing to the algorithm as the method of capturing and communicating designs. This computational way of working augments the designer's intellect and allows us to capture not only the complexity of how to build a project, but also the multitude of parameters that are instrumental in a building's formation. When architects have a sufficient understanding of algorithmic concepts, when we no longer need to discuss the digital as something different, then computation can become a true method of design for architecture.

Hugh Whitehead, the former head of the Foster + Partners SMG, observes that 'at present scripters tend to be of the "lone gun" mentality and are justifiably proud of their firepower, usually developed through many late nights of obsessive concentration. There is the danger that if the celebration of skills is allowed to obscure and divert from the real design objectives, then scripting degenerates to become an isolated craft rather than developing into an integrated art form.'[12] This issue of ∆ promotes the idea of computation in architecture as an integrated art form. ∆

Notes
1. Kostas Terzidis, *Algorithmic Architecture*, Architectural Press (Oxford), 2006, p XI.
2. Sean Ahlquist and Achim Menges, 'Introduction', in Sean Ahlquist and Achim Menges (eds), *Computational Design Thinking*, John Wiley & Sons (Chichester), 2011.
3. Douglas C Engelbart, *Augmenting Human Intellect: A Conceptual Framework, Summary Report*, Stanford Research Institute (Menlo Park, CA), 1962, p 1.
4. Brady Peters, 'The Smithsonian Courtyard Enclosure: Computer Programming as a Design Tool', in Brian Lilley and Philip Beesley (eds), *Expanding Bodies: Art, Cities, Environment. Proceedings of the ACADIA 2007 Conference*, Riverside Press (Waterloo, Ontario), 2007.
5. Mark Burry, *Scripting Cultures*, John Wiley & Sons (Chichester), 2010, p 8.
6. Brady Peters and Terri Peters (eds), *Inside Smartgeometry: Expanding the Architectural Possibilities of Computational Design*, John Wiley & Sons (Chichester), 2013.
7. www.grasshopper3d.com/.
8. Branko Kolarevic and Ali Malkawi (eds), *Performative Architecture: Beyond Instrumentality*, Routledge (New York), 2004.
9. Stan Allen, *Practice: Architecture, Technique and Representation*, Routledge (New York), 2008, p XIV.
10. Jonathan Hill, *Immaterial Architecture*, Routledge (New York), 2006, p 33.
11. David Jenkins (ed) *Norman Foster Works 4*, Prestel Verlag (Munich), 2004, p 28.
12. Mark Burry, op cit, p 252.

Massimiliano Fuksas and Knippers Helbig Advanced Engineering, Bao'an International Airport Terminal 3, Shenzhen, China, 2012
The airport's space structure is covered on both sides by a perforated cladding consisting of 60,000 different facade elements and 400,000 individual steel members. A parametric data model controlled the size and slope of the openings, which were adapted to meet the requirements of daylight, solar gain and viewing angles, as well as the aesthetic intentions of the architect. The nearly 1,400-metre (4,593-foot) long terminal building is designed to serve 45 million passengers a year.

ALGORI TECTON

HOW COLD WAR ERA RESEARCH SHAPED OUR IMAGINATION OF DESIGN

DANIEL CARDOSO LLACH

THMIC
ICS

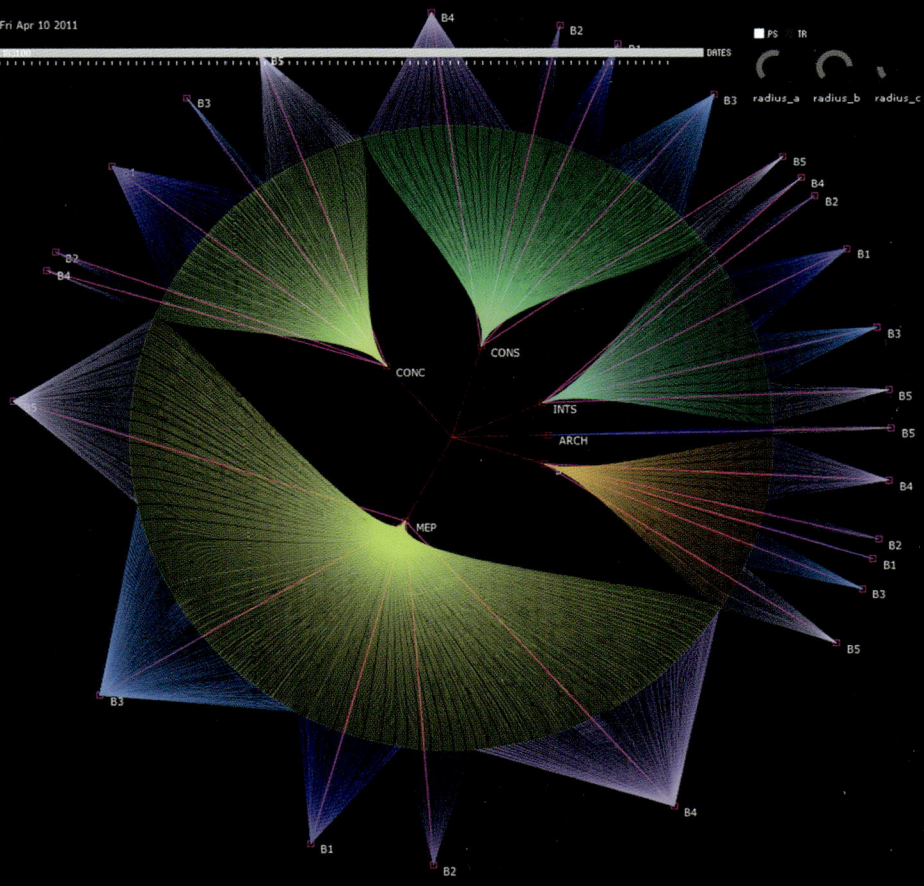

DATES

PS   IR

radius_a   radius_b   radius_c

30447
Date opened: Sun Jan 18 2011
Status: OPEN
Building: B1. Level L01. Zone: N
Location in grid: 7, 7 / U, U
Discipline: 1, Trade: GT.
Responsible organization: ARCH
Responsible person: Cedric Eric

1) Thickness of material and fireproofing may
clash with bulkhead 2) Steel elements clashes
with ceiling.

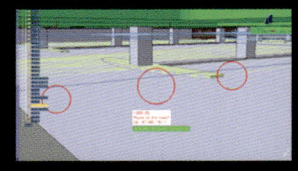

ARCH: 12	CONC: 262
B1: 12	B1: 98
B2: 0	B2: 16
B3: 0	B3: 121
B4: 0	B4: 20
B5: 0	B5: 7
INTS: 185	MEP: 860
B1: 39	B1: 177
B2: 48	B2: 249
B3: 67	B3: 101
B4: 17	B4: 65
B5: 14	B5: 268
CONS: 343	STEL: 169
B1: 25	B1: 45
B2: 100	B2: 36
B3: 46	B3: 7
B4: 35	B4: 21
B5: 137	B5: 60
	Total: 1831

Between 1959 and 1967, the Massachusetts Institute of Technology (MIT) hosted the pioneering Computer-Aided Design Project, funded by the US Air Force. Engineers, researchers and students were brought together to re-imagine 'design in the language of the machine', and one of the most renowned students on this programme was Ivan Sutherland, the inventor and programmer of Sketchpad – the first interactive graphics system. Here, **Daniel Cardoso Llach**, an architect and researcher based at MIT, traces the influence of this Cold War project on the culture of building design and production today.

Within the vibrant culture of research and development taking place at the Massachusetts Institute of Technology (MIT) during the Cold War era, a group of engineers re-imagined design in the language of the machine. Such redefinition rests on a series of technical and epistemological supports: on one hand, the encoding of perspective geometry in matrix form, the development of the first programming languages, and the indexical combination – in the computer – of data and graphics, enabled these engineers to make distinctions between traditional and 'computerised' design practices. On the other, a philosophical view of design as a kind of generalised problem-solving led them to articulate a cybernetic discourse of design as the iterative performance of a 'man–machine' problem-solving engine. Creative design was, under their view, a repetitive cycle of representation, analysis and materialisation, where a 'creative' moment was always followed by a 'mechanical' one: a symbiosis where 'a designer and a computer can work together as a team on design problems requiring creative solutions'.[1]

The collective of engineers, researchers and students behind these technical and discursive innovations worked under the umbrella of the Computer-Aided Design Project, a research operation active at MIT between 1959 and 1967 and funded by the US Air Force. Do their innovations underpin the contemporary ethos of building design and production?

DEPARTING FROM DRAUGHTSMANSHIP: A NEW CRAFT

Despite the Computer-Aided Design Project's military intent, the engineers followed what they thought was the most general approach possible to design. Instead of developing specialised applications to solve particular problems (such as systems for designing missiles or aircraft), they sought to develop abstract languages able to describe 'any' design problem.[2] In contrast to paper drawings, the engineers realised, the symbolic world of the computer allowed for different forms of description to coexist and interrelate. For example, in a computerised description of a house, shapes could be used as indexes for information about materials, prices, structural calculations and other attributes. Steven A Coons, one of the MIT project's leaders, nicely captured this idea of design as a multivariable endeavour in a 1963 paper:

> In the design process the designer is concerned with a large set of variables [some of which are] continuous, like the weight of a certain part [and some are] discrete 'point sets' (like material: steel, brass, lead, plastic).[3]

One of Coons's students, Ivan Sutherland – who famously programmed the first interactive graphics system, the Sketchpad[4] – thought that the production of computer-generated representations was essentially different from (and perhaps superior to) traditional drafting: 'An ordinary draftsman is unconcerned with the structure of his drawing material. Pen and ink or pencil and paper have no inherent structure. They only make dirty marks on paper,' he wrote.[5] Notably, Sutherland's claim was premised on the projection of tectonic qualities onto computational representations. The capacity of computers to index multiple layers of information[6] suggested a topological resemblance between representations and physical artefacts. Thus, the key challenge for the new practitioners of computational design, Sutherland thought, was to not think of computer-generated graphics as drawings of a design, but instead as computerised descriptions: things that are built instead of drawn. By identifying a new craft of building representations, Sutherland anticipated a contemporary culture of integrated approaches to project description and delivery:

> One should think of computer-aided design as producing not only graphical outputs but also material lists; labor estimates; floor area computations; heating, lighting, and ventilation simulations (to demonstrate the adequacy of the design); as well as many other auxiliary outputs. Only when the computerized version of the design is the master document from which all auxiliary information is derived, preferably with computer assistance, will a complete computer-aided design system have been created.[7]

ENCODING THE THIRD DIMENSION: ROBERTS'S 'PERSPECTIVE HACK'

It was Sutherland's colleague, Lawrence Roberts, who developed the technology to display objects in perspective on the computer screen. As a student and summer research assistant at MIT, Roberts shared with Sutherland the TX-2 machine, the computer where the two would develop some of the earliest computer graphics applications. While developing his doctoral thesis – a program to generate a 3-D object from digital descriptions of photographs of planar solids[8] – Roberts found that there was no known way of representing perspective on the computer. He thus hacked it by studying the mathematical methods for perspective geometry from German textbooks from the 1800s and then 'translating' them into the matrix form used to program computers.[9] His method made it possible for the computer to display a 3-D object from any given 'camera' point, and his algorithm continues to run in most modern 3-D software. Modestly, Roberts recalls that during this period of discovery they 'were picking up old things that people had done … and applying it to the real world'.[10] Modesty notwithstanding, Roberts's 'hacking' of perspective is a crucial moment in the establishment of our age's distinctive representational tradition: an indexical combination of Albertian perspectivalism, and data processing.

Daniel Cardoso Llach, Data visualisation of a contemporary building's design and construction coordination, 2012
above and previous spread: In line with the aspirations of the early CAD pioneers, contemporary design and construction projects rest on an intricate network of digital flows. This data visualisation traces the coordination process of a large project during four months of its development.

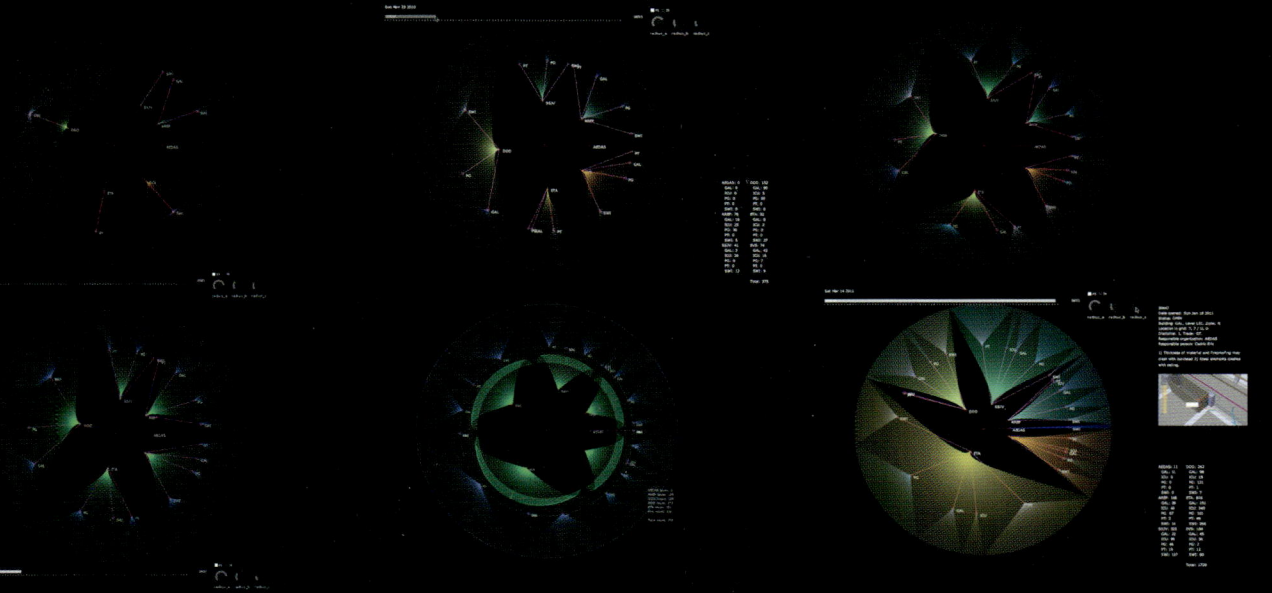

One should think of computer–aided design as producing not only graphical outputs but also material lists; labor estimates; floor area computations; heating, lighting, and ventilation simulations (to demonstrate the adequacy of the design); as well as many other auxiliary outputs.

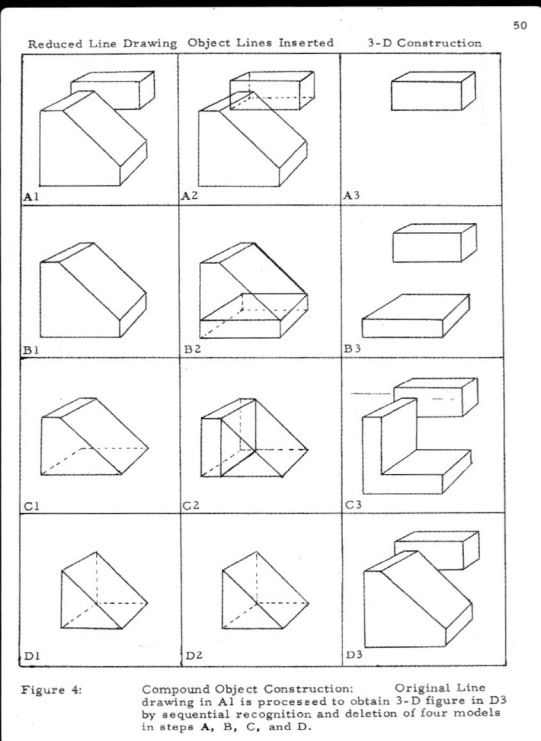

Figure 4: Compound Object Construction: Original Line drawing in A1 is processed to obtain 3-D figure in D3 by sequential recognition and deletion of four models in steps A, B, C, and D.

IMAGING MECHANICAL ARCHITECTS: NEGROPONTE AND THE CAD PROJECT

In the spring of 1966, Nicholas Negroponte, then a Masters of Architecture student, attended Coons's Computer-Aided Design course. The course introduced Coons's pioneering method for the computational description and manipulation of parametric 3-D surfaces,[11] as well as Roberts's methods for perspective representation.[12] The young Negroponte asked Professor Coons to become one of his academic advisors, and went on to write a thesis on the computer's capacity for 'simulating' perception.[13] In his early career as a faculty member at MIT, he further sought to use the theoretical and technical framework developed during the Computer-Aided Design Project years to re-imagine architectural and urban planning practices as technologically enabled participatory endeavours, bypassing what he construed as the elitist sensibility of architects and planners.[14]

To the disappointment of these pioneers, during the decades that followed the MIT Computer-Aided Design Project, the CAD software industry was dominated by systems seeking to 'simply' automate traditional drafting procedures. However, the technical and discursive innovations of the project anticipate the infrastructural role of software in building design today. While Negroponte's techno-idealistic conceptualisation of human–machine design interaction has offspring across many different fields, the discourses of design and representation engineered by Sutherland, Coons, Roberts and others underpin the current trends towards increasingly synchronous, networked and collective 'building information models'.

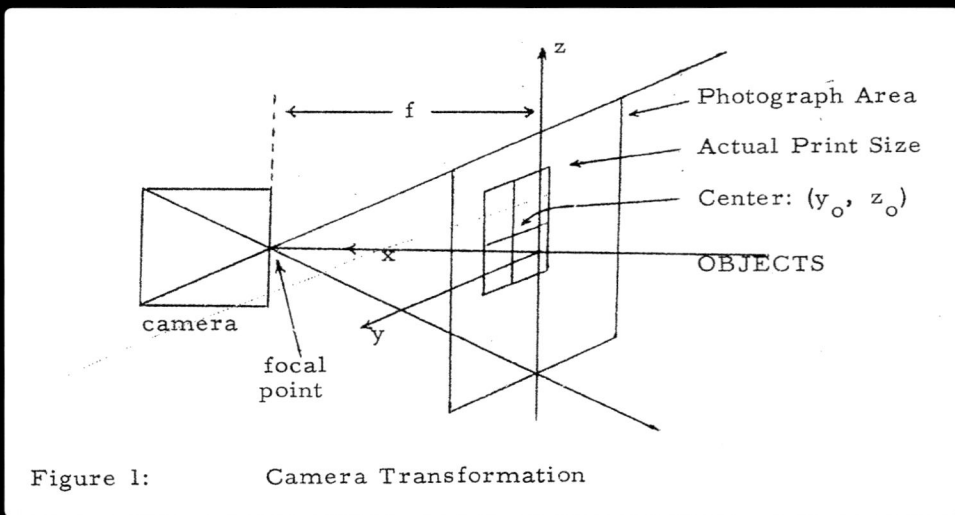

Figure 1: Camera Transformation

POSTSCRIPT

Reminding us of the inevitably material dimension of architecture, historian and architectural theorist Kenneth Frampton conjures the Greek voice 'Tekton' to redeem the structural articulation of architecture as the discipline's fundamental vector.[15] A similarly constructionist sensibility can be used to understand how, within the vibrant cultures of technology production that evolved at MIT during the Cold War era, engineering students and researchers formulated technological discourses of design premised on the structured character of computational abstractions. This brief overview has highlighted how, by construing computational representations as a form of building, these engineers gave new meanings to the words 'design' and 'representation', inaugurating a technological imaginary of design and creativity. Through its influence on nearby researchers like Negroponte, and on popular discourses about design, this imaginary had important effects on architecture and urban studies, illustrating a crucial moment in the ongoing building of algorithmic thought. ∞

Notes

1. Douglas Taylor Ross, Steven A Coons and John E Ward, *Investigations in Computer-Aided Design for Numerically Controlled Production: Combined Interim Engineering Progress Report, 1 June 1965–31 May 1966*, MIT Report ESL-IR 2. Douglas Taylor Ross, *Computer-Aided Design: A Statement of Objectives*, MIT Electronic Systems Laboratory (Cambridge, MA) 1960.
2. Steven A Coons, *An Outline of the Requirements for a Computer-Aided Design System*, MIT Technical Memorandum ESL-TM-169, MIT Electronic Systems Laboratory, (Cambridge, MA), 1963, p 300.
4. Ivan Edward Sutherland, 'Sketchpad, a Man-Machine Graphical Communication System', PhD thesis, MIT (Cambridge, MA), 1963.
5. Ivan Sutherland, 'Structure in Drawing and the Hidden-Surface Problem', in Nicholas Negroponte (ed), *Reflections on Computer Aids to Design and Architecture*, Petrocelli/Charter (New York), 1975, p 75.
6. Ibid.
7. Ibid, p 76.
8. Lawrence G Roberts and Peter Elias, 'Machine Perception of Three-Dimensional Solids', PhD thesis, MIT, 1963.
9. Ibid.
10. J Hurst, JT Gilmore, LG Roberts and R Forrest, 'Retrospectives II: The Early Years in Computer Graphics at MIT, Lincoln Lab, and Harvard', *ACM SIGGRAPH '89 Panel Proceedings*, ACM (New York), 1989, p 56: http://doi.acm.org/10.1145/77276.77280.
11. Steven Anson Coons, 'Surfaces for Computer-Aided Design of Space Forms, Mac-tr -41', MIT Project MAC (Cambridge, MA) 1967.
12. Roberts and Elias, op cit.
13. Nicholas Peter Negroponte, 'The Computer Simulation of Perception During Motion in the Urban Environment', Masters thesis, MIT (Cambridge, MA), 1966, p 99.
14. I critically discuss Negroponte's technological reconfiguration of design elsewhere. See Daniel Cardoso, 'Inertia of an Automated Utopia: Design Commodities and Authorial Agency 40 Years After the Architecture Machine', *Thresholds*, No 39, July 2011, pp 39–44.
15. Kenneth Frampton, *Studies in Tectonic Culture: The Poetics of Construction in Nineteenth and Twentieth Century Architecture*, ed John Cava, MIT Press (Cambridge, MA), 2001.

top: Ivan Sutherland working on Sketchpad, 1963.

Steven A Coons, Computer-generated surfaces, 1965
bottom: Coons's method for surface representation, published in 1965, is the origin of parametric surface descriptions.

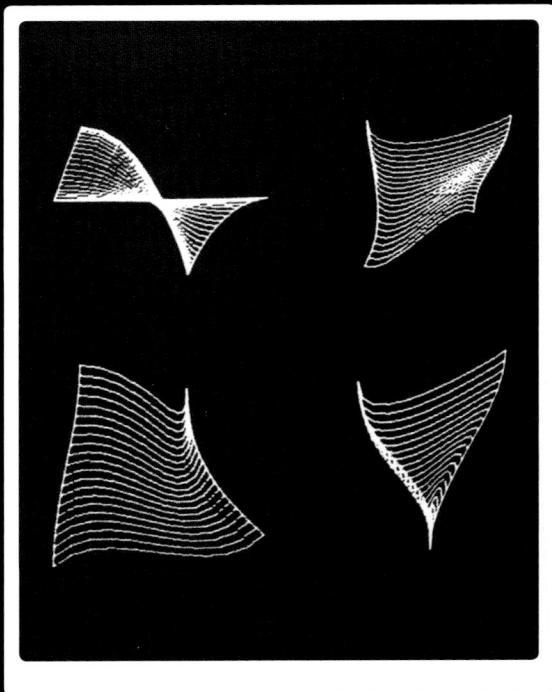

XAVIER DE KESTELIER

RECENT DEVELOPM AT FOSTER + PARTNERS SPECIALI MODELLIN

Foster + Partners, Molteni Arc Table, Milan, 2010
Numerical representation during simulation run-time
displaying changing thicknesses at every node point
along the table's surface. The design team was able to
access the changing thicknesses and determine ways
to influence its behaviour.

ENTS

ST

G GROUP

Established 15 years ago under the leadership of Hugh Whitehead, the Specialist Modelling Group (SMG) at Foster + Partners has an unrivalled reputation internationally as an in-house research group. It provides Fosters with expertise in computation, geometry and fabrication, as well as in environmental analysis and simulation. **Xavier De Kestelier**, co-head of SMG and partner at Foster + Partners, describes how the group has developed and expanded over the last few years, growing the range of its specialist knowledge that informs projects as diverse as the YachtPlus Boat Fleet (2009), Kuwait International Airport (2009–) and Masdar Institute of Science and Technology (2010).

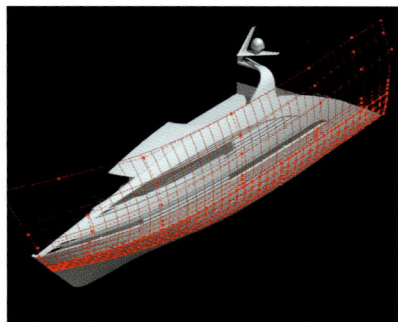

Foster + Partners, YachtPlus Boat Fleet, 2009
The geometry of the yacht was derived from one parametric surface that defined both the overall form and the smallest details.

Hugh Whitehead set up Foster + Partners' Specialist Modelling Group (SMG) in 1998 as the practice was starting to harness the potential of computational design to achieve ever more energy-efficient forms. The group's objectives were to develop the techniques and expertise that would enable the practice to design and build a new type of geometrically complex, environmentally responsive architecture.

SMG's early work was described by Whitehead in his seminal article 'Laws of Form',[1] illustrated with projects such as London's City Hall (2002) and Swiss Re Headquarters (2004), and the Chesa Futura residences in St Moritz, Switzerland (2004). These buildings were pioneering in their scale and complexity, and in the pivotal role of parametric and digital design in their realisation. This article and the three project texts that follow it are intended to complement Whitehead's original essay, describing how SMG's structure and approach has evolved over the last few years.

Over the past decade the group, like the Foster studio, has significantly expanded, growing from a handful of people to a team of more than 20. To reflect the changing needs of the practice, SMG has diversified into two teams, one dealing with computation, geometry and fabrication, and the other with environmental analysis and simulation.[2] Although each team has a different focus, many of the office's projects combine the expertise of both.

The group has also seen a diversification in the skills and backgrounds of its members. In the early days, most staff were architects with strong digital skills. While some still come from an architectural background, in recent years they have been joined by specialists from other disciplines: fine art, mathematics, industrial design, mechanical engineering, building physics, physical computing, fabrication and acoustics. The creation of a relatively small team with broad-ranging expertise is a deliberate strategy to encourage the unexpected connections and fresh perspectives that characterise the studio's open, collaborative approach. This interaction between

different fields has generated design solutions that may not have emerged within a more traditional, homogeneous group. Illustrating the crossover between mathematics and creativity in practice, mathematician-geometer Kristoffer Josefsson describes the issues of symmetry that have influenced Foster + Partners' design for Kuwait International Airport (2009) – see pp 28–31. Despite their seemingly opposing cultures, it is surprising how easy communication and collaboration can be within the team. This process is helped by sharing a common language, as everyone uses computation and digital tools to explore and communicate their work.

Foster + Partners' early SMG projects were designed before the current generation of ready-made parametric design tools such as Robert McNeel & Associates' Grasshopper® and Bentley Systems' GenerativeComponents™ (GC) existed. Early design work was often done through heavily misusing existing computer-aided design (CAD) software, by hotwiring incompatible pieces of software together and by modifying workflows with custom computer program scripts. At this time, only one or two members of SMG were proficient in developing these platform-specific scripts. However, over the last decade the skills to create parametric models and write computer scripts have become much more widespread, with scripting even forming part of the curriculum at some architecture schools. This shift is reflected in the group's skills, as now almost every member is proficient in a range of scripting languages and parametric software on different platforms. There is no longer a division between the team members who write the scripts and those who use them. Everyone is able to develop their own workflow, often from a combination of parametric constructions and scripting. A recent development is for SMG team members to have developed their own software before they join the studio, as with Daniel Piker and his Kangaroo plug-in for Grasshopper (see pp 136–7), and Arthur van der Harten with Pachyderm, an acoustical plug-in for McNeel's Rhinoceros® (see pp 138–9).

The majority of projects undertaken by SMG at the end of the 1990s and early 2000s were located in the UK and Europe where the studio had a very good understanding of local construction and fabrication capabilities. Many of the later projects described here are in less familiar geographical contexts, and are not restricted to buildings. As a result, SMG has had to rethink the way that digital information is delivered for construction. The computational model's ability to describe the project for fabrication has therefore become a central concern.

One such non-building project was the YachtPlus boat fleet. In 2005, Foster + Partners was commissioned to design a series of 41-metre (135-foot) luxury yachts. The design sought to articulate the thrill of sailing with a dynamic, singular form in which the interior walls follow the rounded profile of the hull and the owner's suite at the prow points to the course of the yacht. The geometrical complexity in visually fusing the superstructure with the predefined geometry of the hull led to SMG's involvement in the project. A parametric model was created to define the complete superstructure and the blended surface. Both the superstructure and the hull were manufactured from aluminium profiles and aluminium sheets, and the overall surface was doubly curved. In order to fabricate this, the shipbuilder subdivided the surface into a set of parts that could be manufactured through twisting and bending aluminium sheets. The patchwork of sheet panels matched the overall design surface to a few centimetres, and to fully match the design with one continuous surface, a naval plaster was applied then sanded down with a 7-axis robot.

Both the hull and the superstructure of the YachtPlus boat are constructed with prefabricated curved aluminium panels.

To create a perfect smooth finish on the exterior of the yacht, a fairing compound was applied and robotically sanded off until it perfectly matched the parametric design surface.

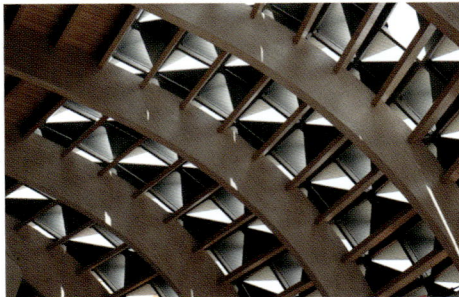

Early design work was often done through heavily misusing existing computer-aided design (CAD) software

The Knowledge Centre, part of the Masdar Institute of Science and Technology, has a double-curved roof that provides shading and regulates daylight.

In supplying digital data directly for fabrication, the YachtPlus commission was rare; even when SMG delivers precise geometrical data, the contractor will often still make their own data and drawings. The Arc Table for Italian furniture manufacturer Molteni & C (2010) was similarly unusual in providing an opportunity to deliver direct manufacturing information. Architect and associate partner at Foster + Partners Jethro Hon describes this process and its workflow in more detail on pp 32–3.

For the Knowledge Centre of the Masdar Institute of Science and Technology in Masdar City, Abu Dhabi (2010), SMG again explored the link between design and fabrication. The library forms part of the first phase of the Masdar City masterplan, which aims to create the world's first carbon-neutral desert community. The building's main feature is a large roof structure that shades the interior and integrates an array of energy-generating photovoltaic panels. The roof's primary structure is formed of curved Glulam beams, and here SMG aided the design team in the rationalisation of its geometry.

The roof surface was set out as a series of identical curves that were repeated to form a translational surface. With this type of surface, the fabricators were able to use one large formwork from which all of the primary beams could be made. Although the size of each beam is different, all were constructed from one mould: the largest beam would use the full length of the formwork, whereas a smaller one would only use part of it. Such embedded rationalisation is possible only when the architect has an in-depth understanding of the technical capabilities of the fabricator. Projects such as this demonstrate the importance of controlling the geometry from the initial design concept all the way through to fabrication. Foster + Partners' design systems analyst Dusanka Popovska describes how the geometry for the National Bank of Kuwait Headquarters (2012) has been controlled throughout each stage of the process (pp 34–5).

Over the past 14 years, SMG's expertise has become an important part of the Foster studio's research-based

Foster + Partners' Specialist Modelling Group, 2012
The Specialist Modelling Group at Foster + Partners specialises in computation, digital design and simulations, and is made up of people with backgrounds in architecture, mathematics, industrial design, engineering, building physics, physical computing, fabrication and acoustics.

methodology. As the group has grown, it has become more flexible, working both as an independent unit and embedding its members within the design teams. It also functions as an in-house technology consultancy. For example, SMG initiated the development of a rapid-prototyping facility for the model shop, and regularly collaborates with the engineering groups, applying their skills to enhanced environmental analysis and complex modelling challenges.

To remain at the forefront of advances in technology, SMG frequently trials new systems and equipment, yet visitors to the studio are often surprised to find that it is the only team working solely on laptops. This is because in a studio committed to innovation and collaboration, even SMG considers the computer to be just another tool, one of many, and believes that, like the architect's pencil, the technology is only as good as the people and ideas driving it. The strength of today's team lies in its unique combination of individual expertise and the creative synergies that derive from a broad skills base. In this way, the structure of the group reflects the Foster studio's integrated philosophy. SMG's continual and iterative participation in the design process helps to achieve outstanding levels of innovation – architecture that is technologically advanced, sustainable and beautiful. Δ

Notes
1. Hugh Whitehead, 'Laws of Form', in Branko Kolarevic (ed), *Architecture in the Digital Age: Design and Manufacturing*, Taylor and Francis (New York), 2003, pp 81–100.
2. The work of the environmental team is explored in Terri Peters, Δ *Experimental Green Strategies: Redefining Ecological Design Research*, Vol 81, No 6, November/December, 2011.

SYMMETRY AS GEOMETRY KUWAIT INTER– NATIONAL AIRPORT

Computer-aided design (CAD) software has often been associated with the limitations of Euclidean geometry. **Kristoffer Josefsson,** a mathematician and specialist geometer employed in the Specialist Modelling Group (SMG) at Foster + Partners, explains how the symmetry-encoded representation undertaken for Kuwait International Airport enabled the group to extend CAD tools for non-Euclidean use.

KRISTOFFER JOSEFSSON

Foster + Partners, Kuwait International Airport, Kuwait, 2009–
Example of a symmetry group encoding the symmetry of Kuwait International Airport. The dihedral group of order 6 consists of rotations of 120 degrees and mirrorings along diagonals.

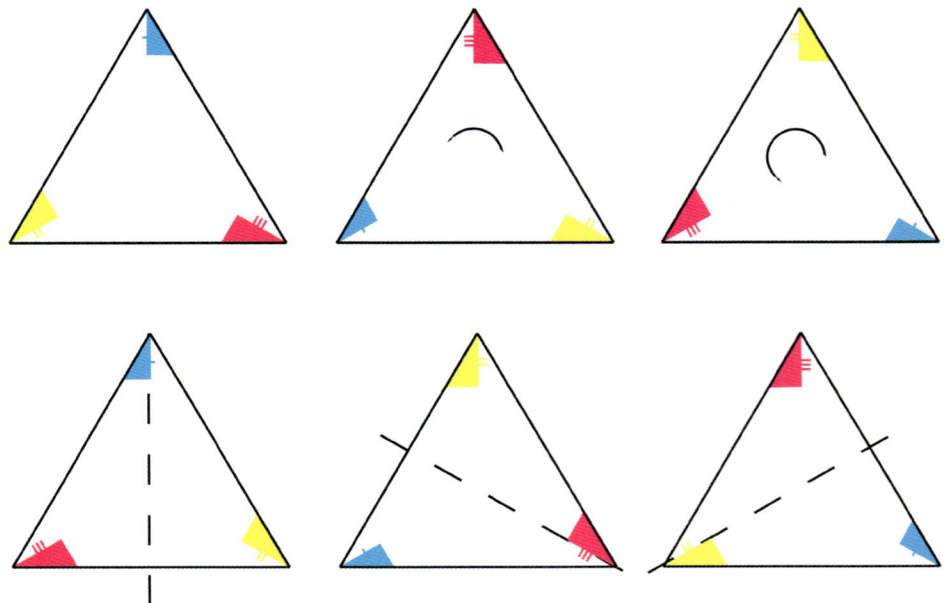

Since the launch of German mathematician Felix Klein's Erlangen programme of 1872,[1] the notions of symmetry and geometry have been tied together in an understanding of space that has changed the way in which we appreciate the universe. For example, together with Bernhard Riemann's ideas a few years earlier,[2] Klein's concepts were arguably a big part of the conceptual foundation of the physics that was necessary for Albert Einstein to describe his theory of general relativity.

Klein defines a geometry to be exactly the objects of a space that are invariant under – that is, not changed by – a symmetry acting on the space. A basic example is a circle that is invariant under arbitrary rotations, and an example with a subset of the symmetries of the circle is the equilateral triangle that is invariant under rotations of 120 degrees and mirroring along its three axes (the dihedral group of order 6, D3). A less evident example is any periodic planar pattern that is invariant under one of the 17 wallpaper groups (or plane symmetry groups) established in the 19th century.

For three-dimensional objects, we can look at the description of rigid bodies that are invariant under translations and rotations of space, or crystals that are invariant under a lattice symmetry that is determined by the energy configurations of the bonds of the molecules that constitute them. This conceptual notion of working on the smaller space where the symmetry is already built in is what will be expanded on here, within the context of architectural design and computer-aided design (CAD) systems.

p3   p6   p31m   p6m   p3m1

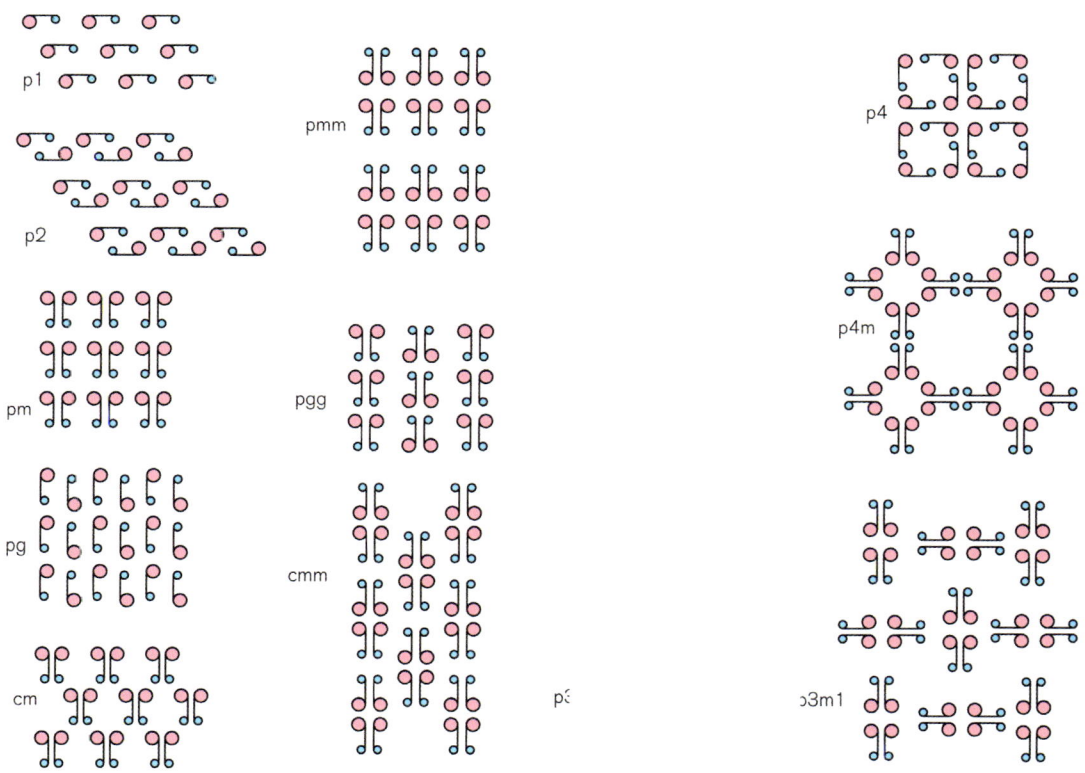

p1

p2

pm

pg

cm

pmm

pgg

cmm

p3

p4

p4m

p3m1

NO MORE CAD ON AN INFINITE PLANE

CAD software has always seemed to belong to the realm of Euclidean geometry. What is specified when opening a typical CAD software is an origin and a scale, and this is exactly what pins down the coordinates of the geometry to have meaning as Euclidean geometrical entities. But as the scale changes towards the small periodic substrates of the nanoscale, or to structures as large as the universe, the limits of Euclidean geometry become evident. As the domains of computational geometry expand, researchers are therefore extending CAD tools for non-Euclidean use.

The concept of topology is key to this expansion in computational geometry. In the modelling of complex topological spaces, while all of the local operations are Euclidean, it is how these local operations are glued together that contains the new topological relationships and what must now be incorporated into the CAD software. For the CAD user, this has implications for how the topological information is represented. Whether one models with meshes or smooth surface patches, the topological information is stored in the mesh itself or as the boundary representation (BREP). Research is therefore being carried out as to which triangulations and tessellations can incorporate periodic and other symmetry-induced geometries.

An example is the symmetry of facades and floor plans.[3] Facades have a natural symmetry of that of the different wallpaper groups, and the multitude of floor-plan arrangements may be enumerated and explored with the aid of symmetry groups. Recently the Autodesk® T-Splines® plug-in for Robert McNeel & Associates' Rhinoceros® software has incorporated symmetry information into the BREP. The geometrical quantities such as tangency, curvatures and so on are all represented in the control BREP of the surface, and hence there is guaranteed symmetry and continuity of these quantities.

top: Rotational and mirror symmetry. The T-Splines plug-in provided symmetry-encoded control points of the boundary representation (BREP) to ensure curvature continuity.

bottom: Smooth subdivision using the topology encoded in the mesh.

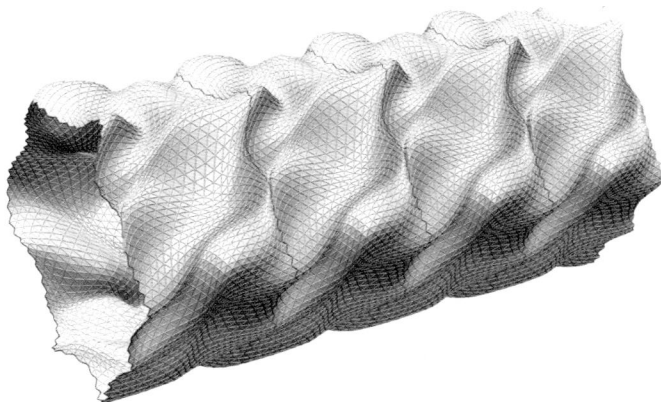

KUWAIT INTERNATIONAL AIRPORT

The Kuwait International Airport designed by Foster + Partners has a triple rotational symmetry around its origin. Moreover, each of its wings has mirror symmetry. This is thus an instance of the D3 group referred to above. Doing the geometrical computations using this group had some advantages. T-Splines was used to automatically give curvature matching of edges. The interfaces between the bays are highly complex in terms of curvature and benefited from the symmetry-encoded representation. In terms of the geometry method statement – used for communication with contractors – the notation that is given by the symmetric representation becomes clearer, more compact and less prone to errors.

Architects often work with objects of non-trivial topology, and it is now becoming possible to incorporate the topological considerations of a design using digital tools. This will lead to a simplified computational approach as the advent of new software that exploits symmetry and geometry opens up new design capabilities. ⌂

Notes
1. Felix Klein, *Vergleichende Betrachtungen über neuere geometrische Forschungen [A Comparative Review of Recent Researches in Geometry]*, 1872. An English translation can be found at http://math.ucr.edu/home/baez/erlangen/erlangen_tex.pdf.
2. Bernhard Riemann, 'Über die Hypothesen welche der Geometrie zu Grunde liegen' [On the Hypotheses which Lie at the Bases of Geometry], *Abhandlungen der Königlichen Gesellschaft der Wissenschaften zu Göttingen*, Vol 13, 1867.
3. See Jenny A Baglivo and Jack E Graver, *Incidence and Symmetry in Design and Architecture*, Cambridge University Press (Cambridge), 1983.

Architects often work with objects of non-trivial topology, and it is now becoming possible to incorporate the topological considerations of a design using digital tools.

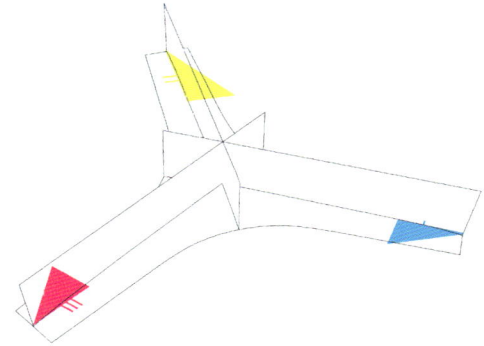

In the early design stage, the rotational and mirror symmetry was exploited to achieve maximal repetition for manufacturing the concrete bays.

above: Symmetry diagram of the airport.

MATHEMATICAL ENSEMBLE
MOLTENI ARC TABLE

Jethro Hon is an architect working in the Specialist Modelling Group (SMG) at Foster + Partners, specialising in computational methods with a particular focus on the optimisation of complex geometries, fabrication and building performance. Here he describes how a table designed for Italian furniture-manufacturer Molteni, inspired by tensile fabric structures, was generated through the group's experimentation with simulation software.

The free-flowing form of the Arc Table, designed by Foster + Partners for Italian furniture manufacturer Molteni & C, was inspired by tensile fabric structures and emerged through experimentation with digital simulations. The early adoption of this technique influenced the design of both the table and the software simulating its geometry. Throughout the design process, two fundamental guiding concepts were ergonomics and material efficiency. By developing the digital model for direct manufacturing, Foster + Partners' Specialist Modelling Group (SMG) challenged the level of control and accuracy of a simulated geometry.

SMG explored computational design processes for the Arc Table through sketching custom software to testing ideas.[1] The software created was engineered to form find towards an equilibrium state within a tensile structure given a set of forces and constraints acting on the input geometry.[2] With the intention of steering the form-finding processes, the need to visualise geometry in

JETHRO HON

Foster + Partners, Molteni Arc Table, Milan, 2010
Close-up of the Arc Table's finished and unfinished surfaces through the use of Ductal®, a lightweight fibre-filled concrete. The design team explored the use of this material due to its relative strength-to-weight ratio while allowing accurate control of thickness and detailing.

below top: From initial cross-sectional constraints used in the form-finding process, a surface then spans between these sections describing node and springs used for simulation. The colour-coded springs depict the gradual change of material thicknesses.

below bottom: Initial input for form finding the table's geometry using SMG's custom software. A cable-net made of nodes and connections describes the surface to be form found.

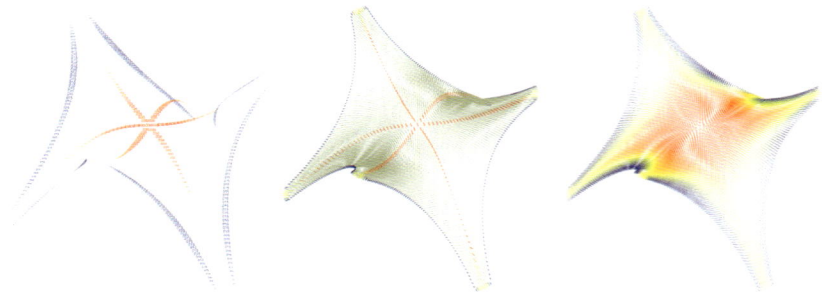

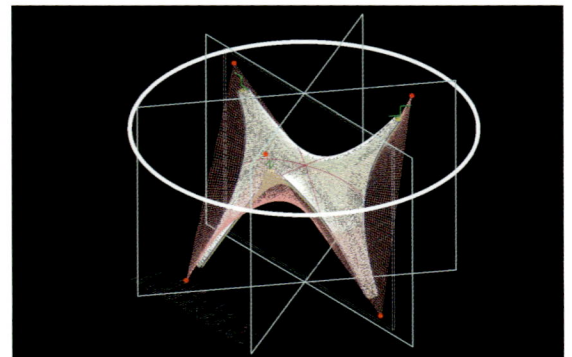

different modes during real-time formation became apparent. This allowed the designs to be interrogated for their ergonomics, the form of the edge profile, structural performance, fabrication strategy and manufacturing tolerances. SMG founder Hugh Whitehead has described such an approach as 'embedded rationale', where the geometry is armed with its downstream logic, and finds an efficient path to manage geometrical relationships upstream.[3] By doing so, the validation of the design occurs at simulation rather than by post-rationalising.

The initial geometry and corresponding forces acting on it were defined prior to each simulation. The initial geometry generally consisted of six alternating groups of low and high anchor points, and a surface that spans between them. The continuous surface was divided into mesh elements. Analogous to simulating a membrane surface, the mesh represented a cable-net consisting of nodes and connecting cables. These were modelled to approximate the bidirectional, or warp and weft, material effect of the mesh fabric. The form of the table is regarded as 'found' when the structural simulation is run on this initial geometry.[4] The configuration of the mesh network greatly influenced how the initial state reached equilibrium. For controlling specific node points, fixity conditions were assigned for tuning node movement in x, y, z, or 'surface normal' directions. Likewise, control of different cable tensions could be assigned. This enabled the team to influence the simulation and its final form.

As fabrication constraints were introduced, this increased the level of complexity as material thicknesses, edge profiling, structural specifications and mould release constraints required a complex management system that could maintain a high level of accuracy. Incorporating the engineers' 2-D specification into seamless 3-D free-flowing form is one of many challenges in achieving integration between design, performance requirements and construction techniques.[5] For the Arc Table, design options, from scale models to 1:1 parts, were regularly sent to in-house rapid prototyping facilities. The digital model was central within the production process as it enabled the fabricator for milling a 1:1 wooden prototype that was used to create the final steel mould.

The Arc Table design emerged through a deliberate intervention into how geometry behaves during simulation. The geometry was controlled through adding, subtracting and manipulating forces to influence the simulation, rather than through direct manipulation. Design intent and material logic were embedded in the digital model through the definition of mathematical rules. The computation of forces and digital management of material dimensions have therefore meant the designers can instead concentrate on experimenting and manipulating form. ◬

below top: The Arc Table complete with customisable glass top. The top end of the concrete base has three stainless-steel plates that are UV bonded to the tempered glass disc and secured to the base via small screws.

below bottom: Sectional rapid prototype model from a 3D Systems' ZPrinter, which allow full colour 3-D prints. An overlay with the 2-D structural specification shows Foster + Partners' design intent in parallel with the engineer's drawings.

Notes
1. Hugh Whitehead, 'Laws of Form', in Branko Kolarevic (ed), Architecture in the Digital Age: Design and Manufacturing, Taylor and Francis (Washington DC), 2003, pp 81–100.
2. MR Barnes, 'Form Finding and Analysis of Prestressed Nets and Membranes', Computers and Structures, Vol 30, No 3, 1988, pp 685–95.
3. Hugh Whitehead and Brady Peters, 'Geometry, Form And Complexity', in David Littlefield (ed), Spacecraft, RIBA (London), 2007, pp 22–33.
4. Axel Kilian and John Ochsendorf, 'Particle-Spring Systems for Structural Form Finding', Journal for the International Association for Shell and Spatial Structures, Vol 46, No 147, 2005.
5. Brady Peters and Xavier De Kestelier, 'The Work of Foster and Partners Specialist Modelling Group', in Reza Sarhangi and John Sharp (eds), Bridges London, Tarquin Publications (St Albans), Vol 1, 2006, pp 9–12.

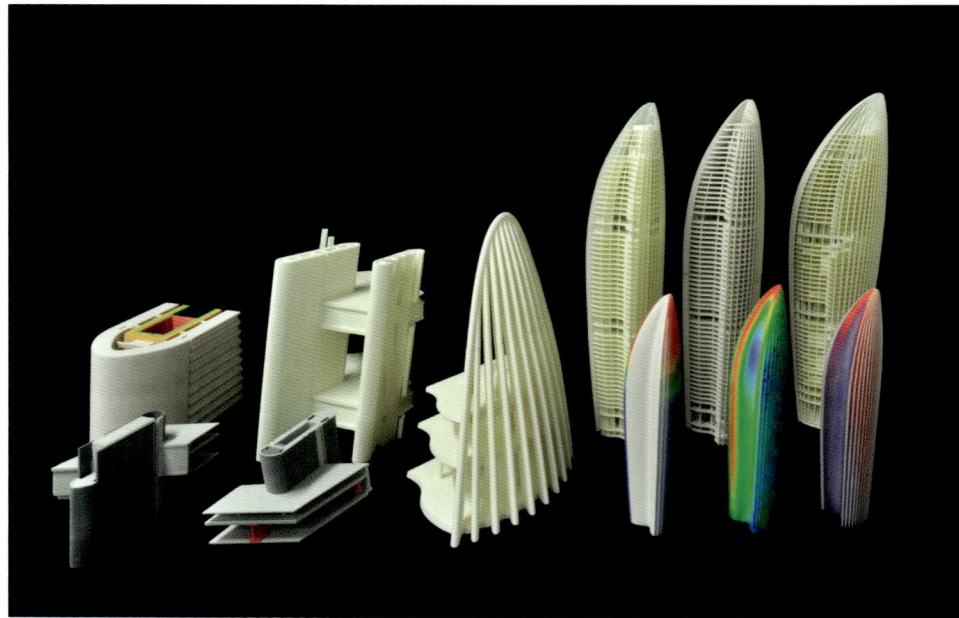

ARTICLE 02C

DUSANKA POPOVSKA

Foster + Partners' design for the National Bank of Kuwait Headquarters is for an environmentally responsive building and a complex geometry. **Dusanka Popovska,** a design system analyst in the Specialist Modelling Group (SMG) at Fosters, explains how the group was introduced at an early stage in the bank's design process to develop a parametric model that was capable of integrating various performance parameters while continuing to investigate geometrical solutions.

INTEGRATED COMPUTA-TIONAL DESIGN NATIONAL BANK OF KUWAIT HEAD-QUARTERS

Providing a unique addition to Kuwait's skyline, the geometry of Foster + Partners' design for the new headquarters of the National Bank of Kuwait is driven by a response to the local climate. The eastern and western facades of the tower are protected by vertical structural shading fins, while it opens up to the north to introduce natural light and views.

Foster + Partners' Specialist Modelling Group (SMG) was involved from the early stages of the design, assigned to develop a parametric model that would integrate different performance parameters and would be able to explore complex geometrical solutions for the building. Bentley Systems' GenerativeComponents™ (GC) was used as the primary parametric modelling software, supported with various scripted tools. In the early stages, the parametric model was used to quickly produce various options that were further developed by the design team. In the later stages, the initial design intents had evolved into a fully rational shape that embedded serious consideration of the various performance parameters, integrating the architectural aspirations, structural, environmental, functional and operational requirements. SMG collaborated closely

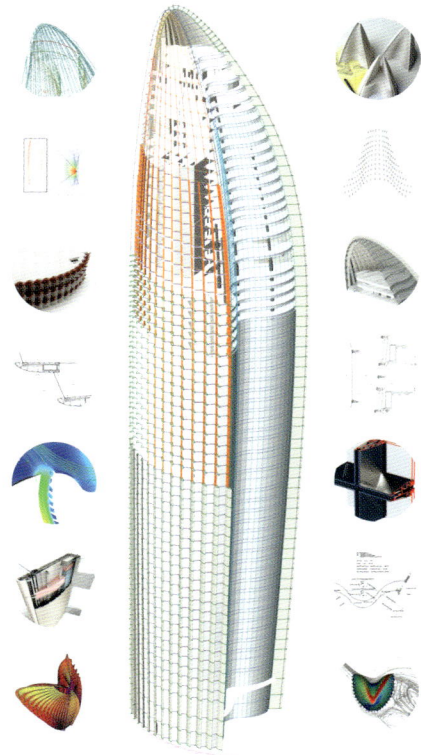

throughout the design process with the design team and engineering consultants Buro Happold.

The major elements that drive the overall geometry of the design are the orientation of the fins, profile of the edge fins, saw-tooth cladding between the fins, and the arcs that form the north facade. The fins are oriented to provide shading for the east and west facades, as well as structural support for the floor plates, and add to the experience of the internal space, dividing it and framing views back over the city. The parametric model contains a full geometric description of the construction build-up of the fins, and embeds engineering input through linking to a data spreadsheet. The sectional profile of the fins remains fully adjustable for various design investigations.

The fins were studied for buildability through testing the level of curvature of the elements and through the derivation of elements with possible repetition, all while maintaining the shape. The two edge fins on each side of the building come together to form continuous arches at the top of the tower, framing the view to the sky from the specially designed chairman's club. Where the arches meet the incoming

fins presented an interesting challenge in integrating the structural and cladding systems in an aesthetically pleasing solution. The glazing between the fins forms a saw-tooth in plan. This saw-tooth form is driven by structural requirements and its position varies according to a special rule, so that while it changes position between the fins, the glass edge is maintained in parallel so that all the glass panels are planar. The north facade has an undulating shape and the glazing is unobstructed for views and daylight. The undulating shape is simplified into three arcs that are scaled with the ratio of the distance between the two edge fins on each floor. This generates a scale-translational surface[1] composed of similar curves that further generate planar glass panels.

The design of the National Bank of Kuwait uses parametric modelling to tightly link the geometric relationships between its elements. The ease of using this type of modelling technique encourages the design and creation of complex buildings of this kind. Through the use of computational methods it was possible to extract all 59 floor plans and many sections that were used for further development such as space planning and details. The parametric

model was used to generate multiple variations of the building shape that were further developed for visualisation (rendering), and used to prepare models for calculations such as solar, wind and acoustic analysis, and also for rapid prototyping. ∆

Note
1. See Jorg Schlaich and Rudolf Bergermann, *Light Structures*, Prestel (Frankfurt), 2004, and James Glymph, Dennis Shelden, Cristiano Ceccato, Judith Mussel and Hans Schober, 'A Parametric Strategy for Free-Form Glass Structures Using Quadrilateral Planar Facets', *Automation in Construction* 13, 2004, pp 187–202.

NETWOR SPACE

DENNIS SHELDEN

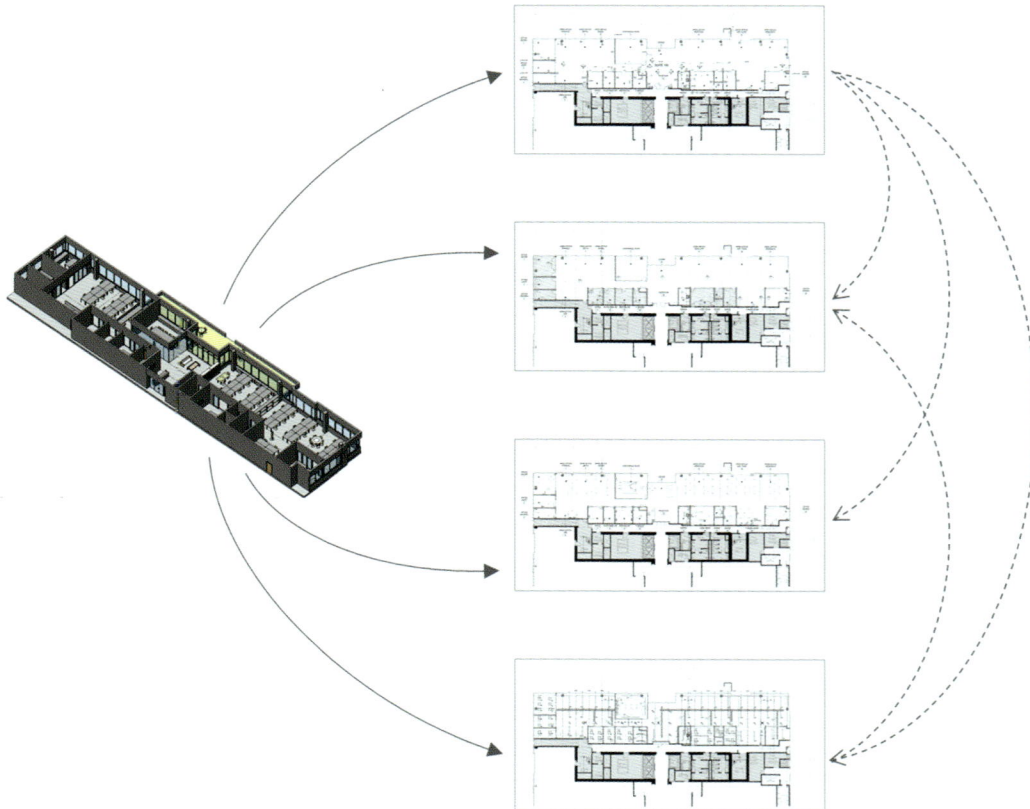

Michelle Lee/Gehry Technologies, Office Interior, Los Angeles, California, 2012
BIM technologies connect 3-D and 2-D views through continuous projection, but also support cross-referencing of domain-specific views through geometric and metadata mappings.

Dennis Shelden, Chief Technology Officer at Gehry Technologies, asserts 'a networked spatial approach to design informatics' that brings together a spatial understanding with a current knowledge of geometry, the digital and modern communications. This emphasises the connections between not only forms and objects in space, but also among disciplines in a collaborative practice context and of the Web itself. It is a connectedness that has been further facilitated by the adoption of 3-D building information modelling (BIM) that helps to streamline processes and facilitate better communication among disparate members of the design team.

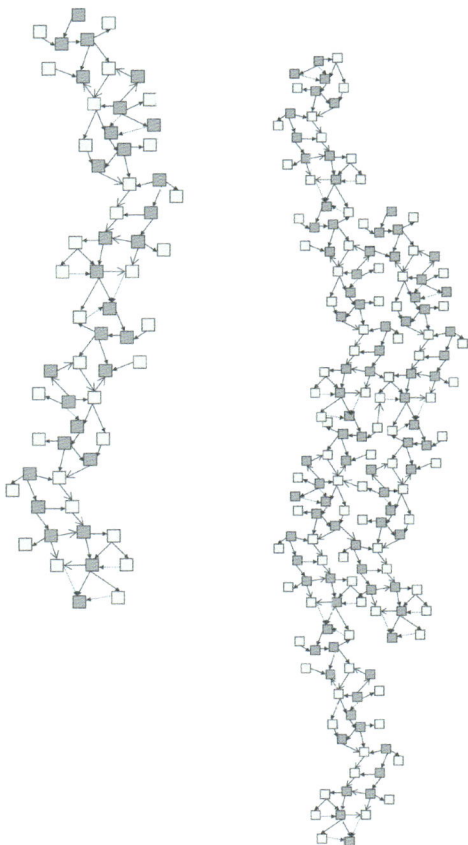

The past decade has seen an explosion in algorithmic and generative approaches to architectural form making. In the professional realm, building information modelling (BIM) has taken many of the advances in algorithmic computation and applied them to the practical realisation of form in space. Theory and practice have together validated the algorithmic approach to design and project execution, and much has been said on the topic in literature, academia and professional circles.

A topic of profound theoretical significance – implied both in algorithmic geometry and in professional application, but not fully understood as a central principle of design computing – is the notion of connected or networked space. Broadly, this is the interwoven fabric of spatial and epistemic structures that modern geometry, digital knowledge and 21st-century communication collectively define. Connectedness emerges pervasively from the synthetic project of architecture: the relations between forms in space, and the spaces generated from relations among forms; relations among the disciplines in collaborative practice, and the processes these relations establish; connections among spatial representations; between instruments of service and their worldly embodiments. And of course, there is the Web itself, which increasingly connects all places, things and knowledge digitally. From a computational perspective, these diverse phenomena and the connections between them can be viewed – and, more importantly, tractably traversed – as manifestations of essentially the same technical and theoretical structure of networked space(s): geometric, parametric, knowledge domains, and the digital and physical realms.

Architecture beyond Modernism has grappled with the opposition of continuity and disconnectedness, with localism and relativism. Difference and disjunction are central themes of Deconstruction.[1] Frank Gehry's work has been described as an architecture responding to the disaggregated experience of the modern urban landscape, breaking down form and using familiar building elements in non-standard contexts to create synthetic compositions of disjunct objects. However, prior to networked computation and digital geometry, this (dis)connectedness could be discussed only critically and anecdotally, and not in any formally operative manner.

Networks and networked space
Contemporary geometries are defined as mappings across distinct spatial structures, creating networked spatial systems of heterogeneous topologies. A new paradigm of networked space is emerging from the convergence of algorithmic geometry, knowledge systems and communications technologies.

The notion of 'network' implies a particular structure of (dis)connectedness – networks emerge as a structure among discrete entities, connected at distance. In software, a clear distinction is made between the private scope within an object and its public methods. In spheres of architectural concern, this division between 'within' and 'among' is blurred: nodes are spatially structured, but the network is in and of space as well. This bleeding from the space within to the space among engenders a richness, fluidity, dynamicism and, ultimately, a synthetic unity to the networks of architecture. This common structuring of geometry and space connects the multiplicity of architectural concerns and supports an increasingly computationally tractable traversal of them.

Geometry – the computational/mathematical discipline of spatial description – and its more worldly counterparts in shape, space and place are of course themes at the heart of architectural concern. From a semiotic perspective, geometry separates shape grammars[2] from more general structural linguistics,[3] enriching the arbitrary relationship between signifier and signified with similarities of isomorphism.[4] This connection between and among representations and phenomena is now expanded by the emerging persistence of networked computation. The classic operations among geometries – acts of projection and their inversions – are now maintained in parametric BIM technologies as ongoing connections between representations. These relations are no longer simply discrete transformational state operations among shapes, but comprise higher-order meta-spatial structures that bind views to objects and their aggregations. The more obvious advance proposed by BIM – from discrete plans and sections to a more homogeneous 3-D 'virtual space' representation – obscures the more radical proposition of persistent multi-modal parametric systems that are presented through domain-specific spatial views. In and among these networked views, discrete representations are portals into specific aspects of the behaviour of objects and configurations, filtered and tailored to the concerns of specific parties' domains of interest.

At a finer level of detail, the differential mappings between parametric and containing spaces of contemporary non-Euclidean curves and surfaces make explicit the alternative spatial expressions of geometries through differential mappings, transformations and embedding. And these parametric geometries themselves are members of higher-order spaces of possibility that capture possible geometries of a general class of spatial intentions. Parametric design is design of that parametric space whose structure reciprocally imposes a landscape on the further trajectory of design exploration.

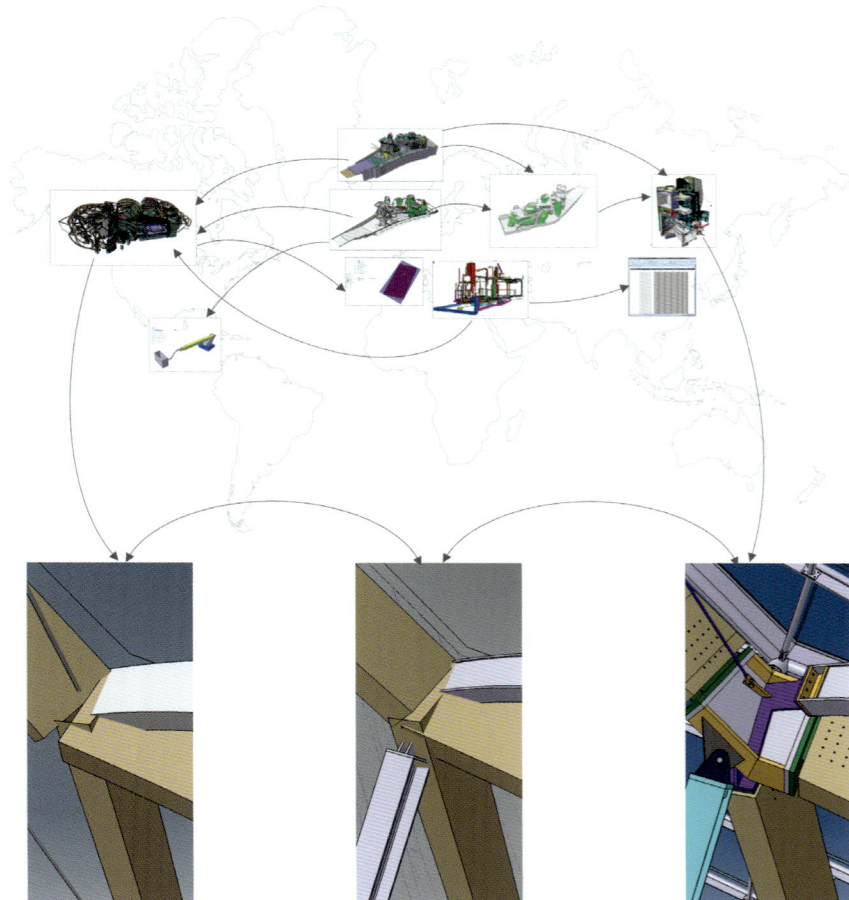

Gehry Partners, Fondation Louis Vuitton Museum, Paris, 2005–
Collaborative design is conducted by globally distributed networks of agents who transact against the global project information set through domain-specific views. Designed objects are themselves multi-representational, appearing in the context of domain-specific views as distinct but parametrically connected geometries.

NETWORKED DISCIPLINE

Connectedness of processes is at the heart of BIM, in which the use of intelligent 3-D digital models streamlines processes and helps facilitate better communications and better end results. Connectedness of disciplines relates to how architects, engineers and the other various building disciplines interact with one another and are now (in some aspects) converging. And the connectedness of process leads directly to questions of connectedness in temporality, as process depends on connections of time and space.

Historically, disciplines have been isolated from one another, with very simplified, limited transmission of information. This disconnectedness, partially a legacy of the mediums we have used in the past, protected by allocating responsibility to discrete players in the process while restricting the free flowing of information and intent between disciplines. Developments in practice have evolved to take advantage of this disconnectedness of medium, transferring it to a disconnectedness of responsibility and layering a control structure over that disconnected method of working together.

Multidisciplinary design implies a distance. The parties involved come to the collaboration from the perspectives of distinct professional domains – design as well as the multiple engineering and fabrication disciplines. The disciplines operate on the artefact through multiple lenses of distinct (spatial structured) instruments of service, signifiers with as yet no signified. The artefact calls collaborators towards it, but cannot yet itself be viewed even through its representations; the representations must themselves organise towards the artefact. Any coherency lent to this phenomenological proposition lies in the ways that the rules of engagement represented by the domains – individually and in concert – are defined as topologically structured spatial operations (grammars) on the design media topologies primordially, and only, by inductive proposition on the future artefact itself. Parametric BIM provides the technological capability to look at the symbolic and partially isomorphic mappings from one domain to another – mapping between disparate representations that also preserves encoded design intent.

NETWORKED AND WEB SPACE

The World Wide Web placed the notion of the network into the vernacular of contemporary culture. Its impacts on broader society have not as yet received much specific refinement by the concerns of architecture, but architecture is now poised to take on this agenda. Networked space points to the Web as an integrating technological and epistemic construct for architectural concern.

Beyond the discipline, the Web as a semantic structure has evolved considerably since its initial development. The basic structure of machine- and human-readable text, linking anchors and embeddable media were in place in its original development in the 1990s. However, the explosive success of the Web was due in no small part to its ability to embed media and objects of widely different types into an integrated, networked, and human-consumable structure. Media objects – images, movies and executable data types – were initially encapsulated as black-box objects, data blobs referenced within the overall web of textual hypermedia. More recent

Parametric BIM provides the technological capability to look at the symbolic and partially isomorphic mappings from one domain to another – mapping between disparate representations that also preserves encoded design intent.

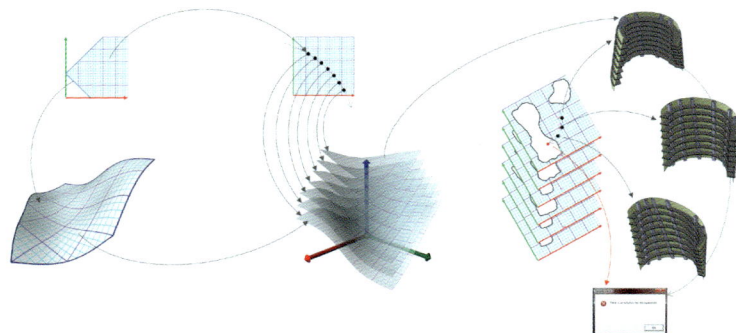

Networked spatial view of contemporary geometry
Contemporary mathematics describes geometry as a network of spatial mappings. At the lowest level, parametric surfaces are described as continuous mappings between 2-D parametric space and embedding 3-D space, while the surfaces themselves are points in higher-order state spaces. This chaining of lower-order parametric relations to higher-order state spaces extends to the definition of more complex parametric systems.

Architecture will, however, be uniquely impacted by spatial aspects – the ways that networked space and spatial structure weave their way through the Web and out into the world.

Present and future information/process structures
Project delivery remains a process of discrete, sequential operations and transactions. Authority and responsibility are organised around the distribution and acceptance of documents. The future of design process will be structured by direct and continuous connection among web service-based data, mediated through portals and devices directly into the physical environment.

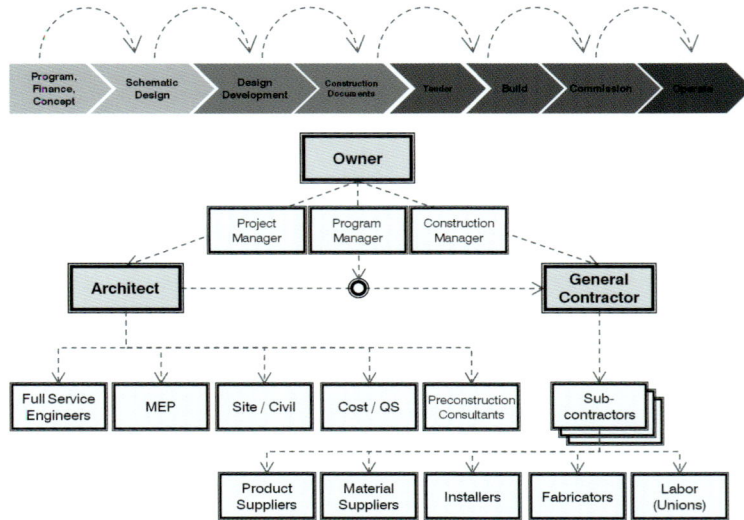

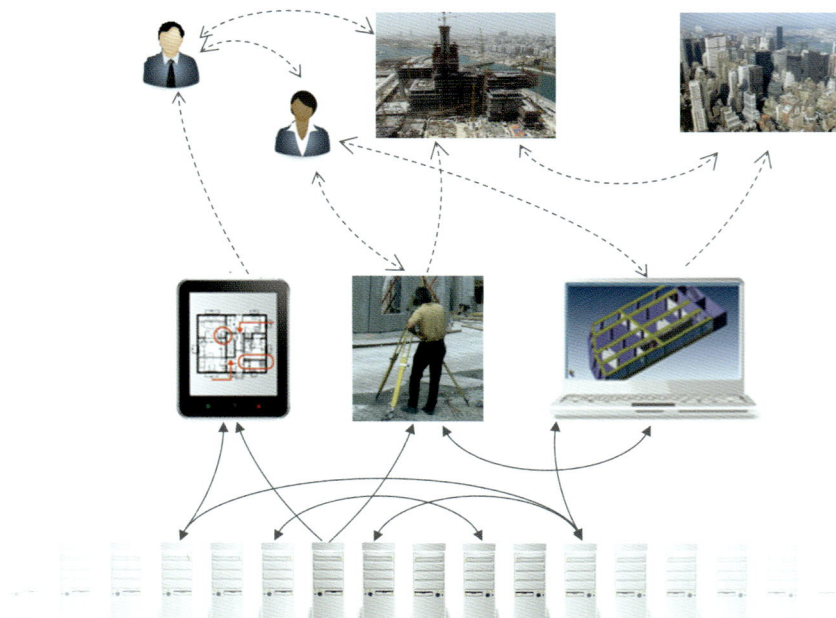

advances have eroded this distinction of encapsulated media objects. The XML specifications and extensions such as the Semantic Web[5] have eroded the walls of media objects and are diffusing this information into the structure of the Web itself, allowing it to process this information as part of global semantic structures and operations. Recent developments in HTML5 are increasing the capacity for the browser canvas to function as a 2-D/3-D spatial application environment, offering a framework that can potentially allow architectural intent to break out of the confines of CAD/BIM application data blobs and diffuse into the network.

Until now, the Net could connect information spaces to one another – at great distance – but not to physical space itself. Built on physical devices and connected over physical wiring, information space stopped at the monitor glass, requiring human intervention to translate digital intention into form. Capabilities are now coming online that transform information beyond representation directly into physical space through technology such as 3-D printing or stereolithography (SLA), or computer numerical control (CNC) machine tools that convert and process geometry into built objects. Most significant – beyond the seduction of autonomous robots making – is that the same manifold transformations between parametric and geometric space can now directly connect the digital to the physical, into a continuously connected cybernetic spatial network of information and physical space.

The future of architectural computing is this network: cloud-based information stores connected to people, places and artefacts through portals, devices and other digital–physical transponders. Gehry Technologies' recent research and technologies efforts are focused on developing the initial components of such a connected network of design information. While nascent, a networked spatial approach to design informatics is thus beginning to emerge, focused on the capacity of digital technologies to foster integration at distance in both location and content.

Gehry Technologies envisions a disparate network of centres of information that are specific to a particular team's set of interests, and maintained to serve that team's specific needs. The centres will include digital means for communicating and transmitting the information, as well as spatial (geometric) and computational structures for mapping between the different sets of interests. This connected network of information in the cloud will be tailored through portals and digital devices to directly connect the disparate spatial phenomena and the interested parties. The portals will collect and transform information, presenting it to a team member in a way that is specific to that person.

This technical architecture will profoundly impact the tools that design professionals use, but far more significantly will infuse the processes of design and delivery, our identities as professionals, our connection to our work, and work to society. This is true of any discipline. Architecture will, however, be uniquely impacted by spatial aspects – the ways that networked space and spatial structure weave their way through the Web and out into the world. Algorithmic geometry – the transformations, mappings and embeddings that connect the data stores and bridge the digital–physical divide – will structure the spatial connectedness of this network. ᴅ

Notes
1. Bernard Tschumi, *Architecture and Disjunction*, MIT Press (Cambridge, MA), 1994.
2. George Stiny, 'Introduction to Shape and Shape Grammars', *Environment and Planning* B 7, 1980, pp 343–51.
3. Ferdinand de Saussure, *Course in General Linguistics*, trans Roy Harris, Duckworth (London), [1916] 1983.
4. Bas C van Fraassen, *The Scientific Image*, Oxford University Press (Oxford), 1980.
5. Tim Berners-Lee, James Hendler and Ora Lassila, 'The Semantic Web', *Scientific American Magazine*, 17 May 2001.

Gehry Technologies, GTeam™ platform, 2012
Gehry's new GTeam platform integrates project-based social collaboration with interoperable geometry, metadata analytics and task-specific visualisation.

SPATIAL COMPUTING FOR THE NEW ORGANIC

CHRISTIAN DERIX AND ÅSMUND IZAKI

In the last few years, parametric design has predominated in architectural research and practice. **Christian Derix and Åsmund Izaki** of the Computational Design and Research (CDR) group at Aedas|R&D explain how the research and design unit, based at Aedas in London, has pursued an alternative course by shifting the focus to behavioural and perceptive occupant simulation of spatial configurations. A human-centric approach, it draws its inspiration from earlier British pioneers in spatial computation, as well as the designers of the Organic Architecture movement of the early 20th century.

Aedas|R&D and Tibbalds Planning and Urban Design, Dynamic Visibility Analysis, Guy's and St Thomas' hospital extension access study and Greenwich Millennium Village, London, 2010
Aedas developed a group of dynamic visibility analysis models for several projects that allow architects to inform building or urban masses during concept design stages or to evaluate designed spaces from an occupant's perspective.

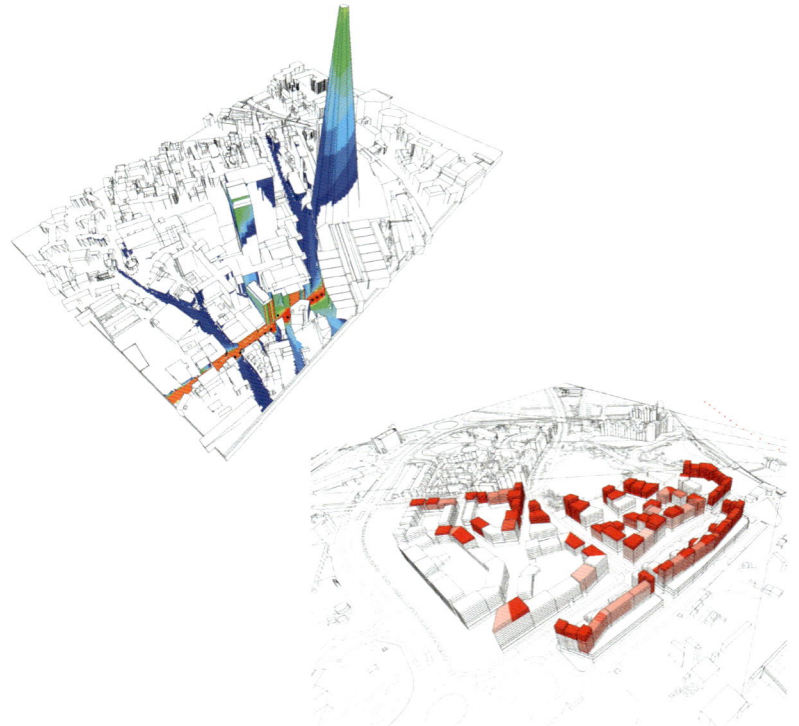

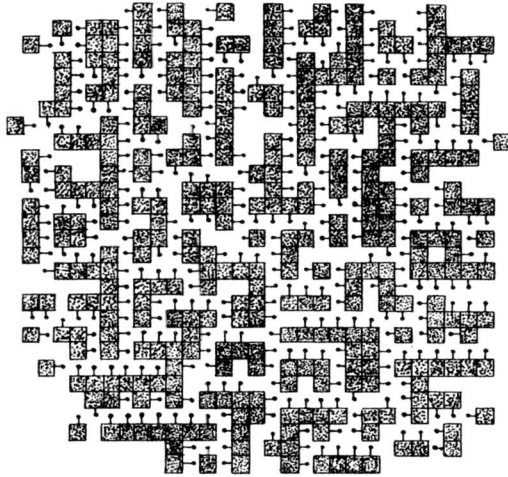

Paul Coates, A Large Computer-Generated 'Beady Ring' Surface, 1981
Coates transcoded the syntax from Bill Hillier and Julienne Hanson's original Space Syntax to generate permeability fields by using a type of cellular automaton, an artificial life technique. Drawing from Hillier and Hanson's *The Social Logic of Space*, Cambridge University Press, 1984, p 219.

The post-parametric computational design phase began long before now. When the Computational Design and Research (CDR) group at Aedas|R&D was set up in 2004, parametric modelling was just about to launch into its heyday, with the design community entranced by generating more efficient geometries of arbitrary shapes. Schools like the Architectural Association (AA) in London have since dedicated most of their innovation to 'parametricism'. The economy was booming and new iconic buildings were erected hastily. In such a climate, instead of another 'Advanced Geometry' or 'Modelling' group, Aedas decided to form a computational design group that would explore the application of artificial life and intelligence based on self-organisation, bottom-up processes and distributed representation to architectural design projects. Here, the organisation of space is understood mainly from an occupant's perspective, meaning the perception of spaces and the representation of their properties in relation to the user and his or her actions.

It is rather poignant that after 15 years of parametric form generation, an economic crisis provided a stimulus to the world of construction to focus less on iconic new-build surfaces than on the adaptation of existing spaces for different occupations and operations. As a result, behavioural and perceptive occupant simulation for design computation of spatial configurations, as proposed and conducted by the Aedas CDR group, continue to gain momentum. This article is an attempt to embed the developments of the CDR group, and the debate about self-organisation, in an architectural discourse rather than in popular science hyperbole.

PEOPLE IN SPACE

Clearly, we are standing on the shoulders of British giants: Paul Coates and John Frazer pioneered generative self-organisation for architectural spaces with design computation; Philip Steadman and Michael Batty researched mathematical representations of space; and Bill Hillier created what was originally a generative theory of architectural design spaces called 'Space Syntax'.[1] Hillier's syntax represents an abstraction of movement in a field (not space) and resolves the elementary unit of a system to the relationship between local affordance of action and contextual boundaries. Global spatial patterns result from mutual constraints between people and spaces, reflecting also social conventions. Coates understood that computation and techniques from artificial life could provide the transcoding platform to design with Hillier's theory, and subsequently encoded the original syntaxes for Hillier's *Social Logic of Space* publication.[2]

Hillier believed that to formulate a better syntax, a firm grip on spatial analysis based on occupant perception was required. This resulted in the common understanding of space syntax as movement analysis, based on models such as axial line analysis or, later, visual graph analysis. Coates and Frazer continued to develop many design heuristics based on bottom-up computing in the 1990s, introducing evolutionary computing, spatial cellular automata, Lindenmayer systems and many agent-based design models for architecture. But generative computing, mathematical representations and spatial analysis remained largely academic and isolated. In setting up the CDR group, Aedas's aim was to validate Coates and Frazer's research for computational design heuristics and synthesise them to design spatial configurations in practice.

THE SYNTHETIC ORGANIC

The notion of human-centric design in architecture can be traced back to the Organic Architecture movement of the early 20th century. While many see the form–function relation of Louis Sullivan and Frank Lloyd Wright as the key principle, it was the German architects such as Hugo Häring or Hans Scharoun who emphasised the user (here, the occupant) and perception of space as design drivers for their spatial compositions.

Scharoun's design approach originates from Häring's concept of *Wesenhafte Gestalt*, a form-generation process whereby spatial configurations emerge from the interaction between human behaviours and surrounding space.[3] *Wesenhafte* refers to the essence of being and also structural nature, indicating that spatial structures (*Gestalt*) emerge from a mapping of user behaviours. A building is seen as a place of human occurrences where geometric appearances play a subordinate role. A correlation between user and space is insinuated that Häring and Scharoun call 'concordance' (*Konkordanz*). To design space means to design the affordance of actions for the user between physical delimitations. Scharoun simulated user experiences as if moving through his buildings virtually, and formed them into spatial configurations. However, he was careful to point out that behaviours and occupancy patterns would be generic and not determined. A synthesis of local concordances between space and behaviour with the building function expresses the essence of the user.

Hillier developed this human-centric principle of concordance for a design theory of architectural space,[4] where

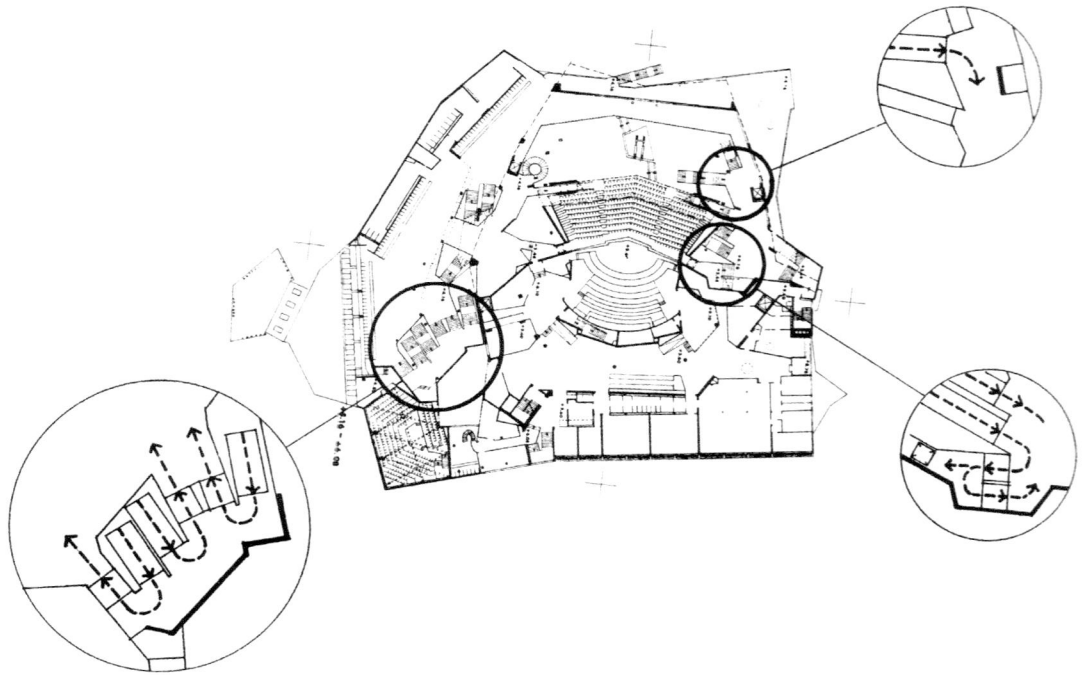

the notion of 'inverse law' represents the correlation between
occupation and spatial patterns. He thus arrived at the concept
of 'generic function', which states that the nature of a built
configuration is observable through its generic occupation, not by
its functionally determined areas with specified dimensions and
constraints. Having compiled and tested architectural, cognitive
and systemic models of computation, the Aedas CDR group set
out to develop a new synthetic organic design methodology that
would allow architects and designers to design human-centric
spatial configurations. The following sections outline some
principles for a methodical approach towards a new organic
architecture through interactive, computational design. Through
continued research at Aedas and at various universities, such
approaches are becoming more prominent within architectural
agendas.

ALGORITHMIC TRANSPARENCY

For a computational model to enable an understanding of
spatial structure and some of its affordances, a transparency
of algorithmic logic and process is required. By visualising the
processing of an algorithm step-by-step, its components and data
in a diagrammatic near-notational form, the logic and behaviour
of the system become transparent. Experience of developing
design simulations with stakeholders found that integrating
many project aspects in one model, or specifying a building or
masterplan in detail, only confuses the user. To resolve this,
the process represented in an algorithm needs to be reduced to
a limited set of behaviours and parameters that can be clearly
visualised. Seeing a model struggle to resolve a situation allows

the designer to identify with the algorithm,[5] and this empathetic
coupling provides the basis for a dialogue between model and
designer, and between designers and stakeholders. A narrative
is constructed through visible behaviours leading to a quasi-
conversation between the designer and the computational model.

AUTONOMY OF THE MODEL

The idea of the model as design conversation partner is also
reflected in Frei Otto's approach of searching design spaces
using material properties and physical laws.[6] Constructing and
manipulating experimental models meant he could discover
suitable architectural solutions methodically. Otto's models are
autonomous in the sense that their behaviour stems from internal
mechanisms that are independent from a designer's intentions. If
a local element is adjusted, the global change of state is difficult
to anticipate without observing the model. Resulting designs
have as much to do with the autonomous behaviour of the model
as with the adjustments made by the designer.

In the CDR group's computation-based models, autonomy
does not come from material and physical properties, but rather
from algorithmic behaviour; searching for consistent algorithmic
models that are easy to understand and interact with that can
be mapped to meaningful spaces for occupants. In this mode of
working, the idea of 'representational fidelity' means something
quite different from the way of using CAD: the aim here is
not to seek to reproduce a formal sketch or abstract idea of the
master architect, but rather to find concordance with the logics
of the algorithm and the architectural intentions for occupation
and use.

Aedas|R&D, Representational Fidelity, Khalifa bin Zayed Al Nahyan Foundation competition entry, 2008
below: A series of combinatorial algorithms were developed for this project, where the algorithmic logic correlates directly to the heuristics of a designer without imitating them. The models visualise the struggle to find good combinations that allow for better evaluation and promote participation.

Aedas|R&D and Davis Brody Bond, Algorithmic Concordance, National September 11 Memorial Museum, New York, 2007
bottom: Here, models of movement and volumetric visual perception visualise the correlation between geometry and occupation. The models were used to inform the ramp within the museum that takes visitors along an experiential path.

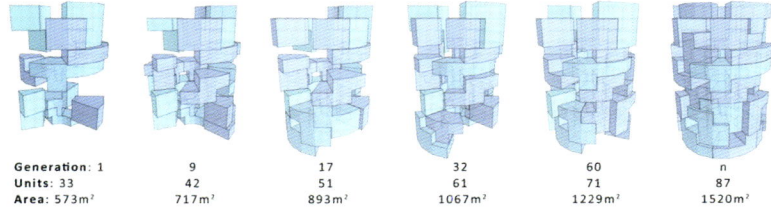

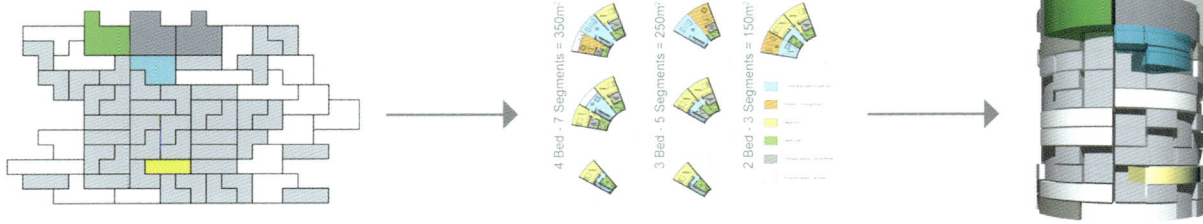

Generation: 1	9	17	32	60	n
Units: 33	42	51	61	71	87
Area: 573m²	717m²	893m²	1067m²	1229m²	1520m²

ELASTICITY OF ORGANISATION AND PROGRAMME

As digital animation tools inspired architects such as Greg Lynn to design architectural surfaces seemingly formed out of malleable elastic materials, the CDR group is considering how other parts of architectural design processes can be 'elastically' manipulated, either interactively by a designer or through self-organisation. On a building scale these could be organisational associations such as adjacencies and corresponding circulation strategies, or visual connections and land-use distributions on an urban scale. Just as the elasticity of shape was initiated by the digital modelling techniques of stretching and smoothing geometry, new spatial behaviour diagrams are enabled through programming in object-oriented languages where the bespoke construction of the dynamic data structures and algorithms controlling them are more easily accommodated than in parametric modelling software.

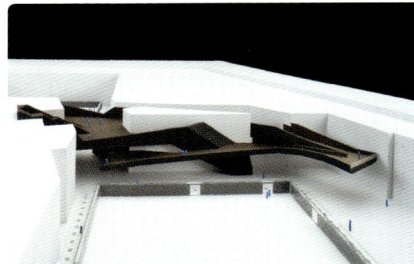

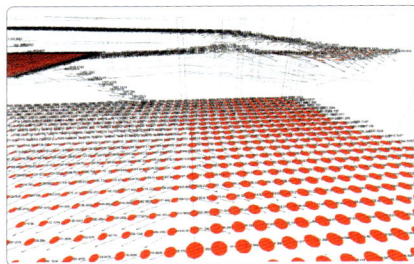

NEW WORKFLOWS BASED ON ASSEMBLIES

The computational models developed at Aedas generally focus on a minimum number of spatial and behavioural aspects at a time. This constitutes a counter-intuitive approach that opposes the alluring drive to create universally integrated systems. The modularisation of software allows a project team to tailor algorithmic processes to specific concepts. New workflows emerge when complementary models are assembled at different stages and scales. Models are collated into networks by linking and controlling their data exchange while the designer retains the role of mediator between conflicting or synergetic performances.

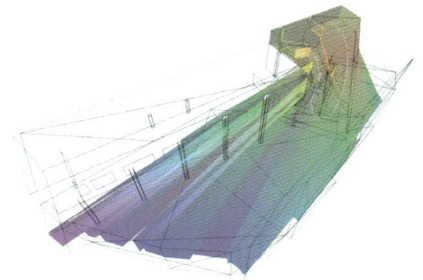

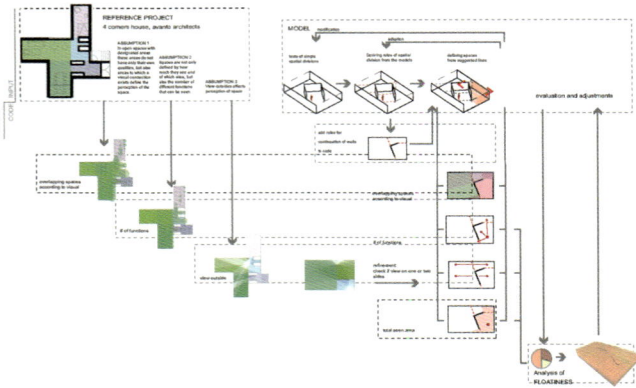

Katariina Knuuti, Jana Bäumker, Juan Carlos Venegas Del Valle and Anna Wojcieszek, Floating Room, Implicit Space design studio (Christian Derix), Technical University of Munich, Munich, 2012
This student project developed an algorithmic design system to define affordances of strongly programmed spaces through their co-presence with weak or generic spaces.

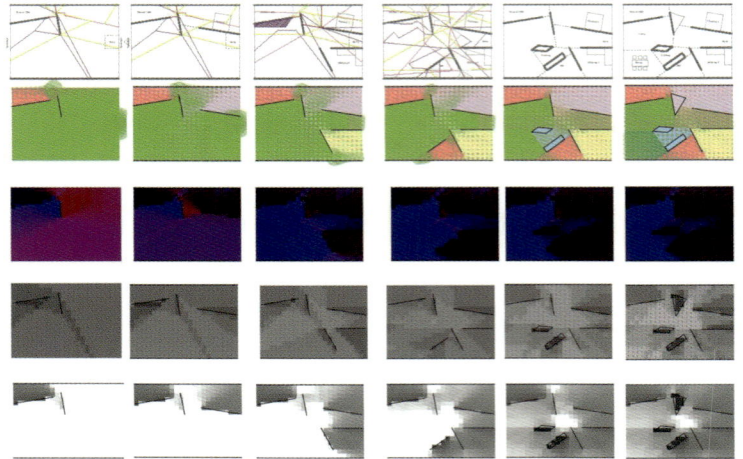

Aedas|R&D, Algorithmic Consistency, Fraunhofer Institute for Workplace Organization, 2011
below: Three behavioural models were developed for a laboratory building that exchange configurational data on different scales – site, building and interior – based on usage patterns implicit in the building programme.

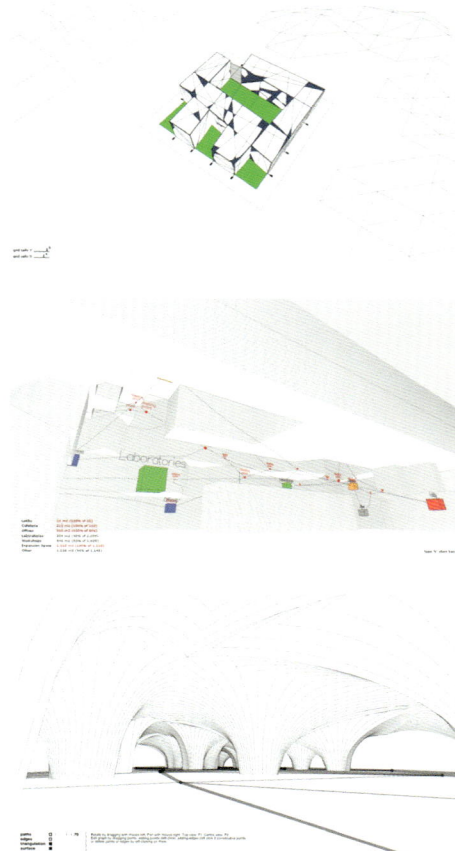

Aedas|R&D, Behavioural Mapping and Operational Occupancy Simulation, New consulate office of the Federal Republic of Poland, London, 2011
In order to balance occupation and operations in the new consulate office, a behavioural analysis was conducted and abstracted into a statistical simulation that visualises correlations between spatial configuration, occupation and operation.

Aedas|R&D, Elasticity of Programme, 2009–11
A series of interactive space planning models allows architects at Aedas to explore configurations with topological constraints. The topology simultaneously self-organises based on a physical-force simulation while the designer arranges the mass.

categories
Cores & Voids
1. School Building
2. Admin block
3. Student Accommodation
4. Staff Accommodation
5. Health & PE Center
6. Dinning & Food Service
7. Admin & Guidance at Entrance
8. Masjid
9. Car Parking
10. Play Areas
11. Other Open Areas
12. Hotel
12. Hotel FOH/BOH

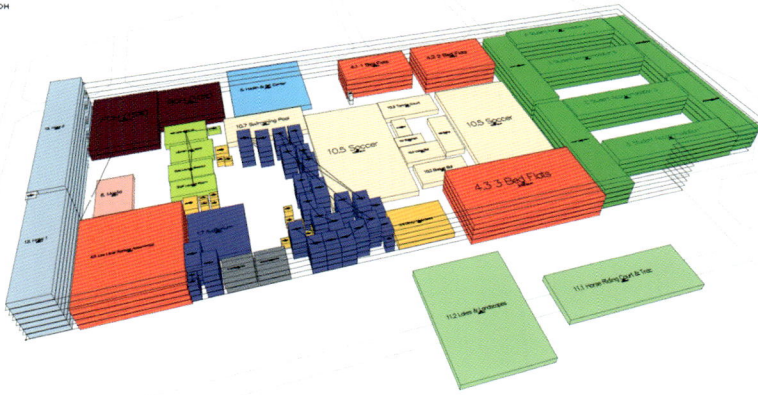

All floors
Number rooms: 106, Total area: 7,204.73 m2
Including cores/voids: 116, Total area: 7,508.92 m2
All floorplates: Perimeter length: 856.26 m, Total area: 11,498.42 m2

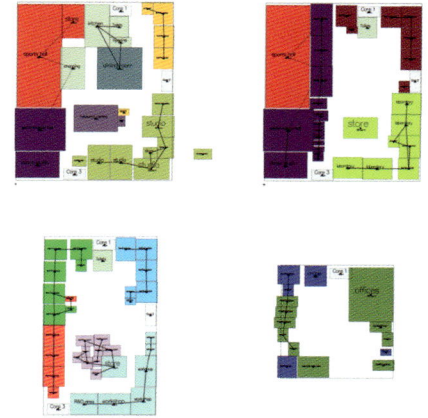

Despite the establishment of a loose-fit computational assembly for human-centric spatial design in practice, no example of a complete behavioural configuration exists.

APPROXIMATING SPATIAL PHENOMENA IN ALGORITHMIC PLANNING

As Steadman declared in his *Architectural Morphology*,[7] and Hillier discovered in 'generic functions', weakly programmed spaces constitute the essence and *Wesenhafte* of spatial typologies that can only be understood through occupant behaviours. Strongly programmed spaces have so far been the domain of rigid parametric models, ideal for linear problem-solving as an optimal solution is believed to come from solving a set of constraints.

This split still exists: Hillier's research and most of the Aedas CDR group's spatial behaviour models have been applied to weakly programmed spaces such as circulation or the organisation between functional areas, circulation and social spaces. Scharoun's approach, on the other hand, consisted of improvising local spatial concordances and then assembling them into global morphologies rather than simulating global building configurations. This allowed him to extend the notion of generic function to programmed spaces, as global phenomena would partially permeate functional spaces, an approach systematised by Herman Hertzberger in the 1970s.

In computation, we must recognise that spatial phenomena do not stop at some clearly defined geometric threshold,[8] a danger resulting from certain ontologies or model representations like graphs. In applying computation to space planning in practice, we must learn to understand and integrate weak with strongly programmed spaces through assemblies of simple algorithmic behaviours. Only then can hybrid operational spaces such as flexible teaching or collaborative workplaces be co-generated from a human-centric perspective that cognitively ties into spatial phenomena on the building scale. ∆

Notes

1. Bill Hillier, Adrian Leaman, Paul Stansall and Michael Bedford, 'Space Syntax', *Environment and Planning B*, Vol 3, 1976, pp 147–85.
2. Bill Hillier and Julienne Hanson, *The Social Logic of Space*, Cambridge University Press (Cambridge), 1984.
3. Eckehard Janofske, *Architektur-Raeume: Idee und Gestalt bei Hans Scharoun*, Vieweg & Sohn Verlagsgesellschaft (Wiesbaden), 1984.
4. Bill Hillier and Adrian Leaman, 'How is Design Possible?', *Journal of Architectural Research*, Vol 3, No 1, 1974, pp 4–11.
5. Christian Derix, 'Mediating Spatial Phenomena Through Computational Heuristics', *Proceedings of the 30th Annual Conference of the Association for Computer Aided Design in Architecture*, ACADIA, New York, 21–24 October 2010, pp 61–6.
6. Frei Otto and Bodo Rasch, *Finding Form: Towards an Architecture of the Minimal*, Edition Axel Menges (Stuttgart), 1996.
7. Philip Steadman, *Architectural Morphology: An Introduction to the Geometry of Building Plans*, Pion (London), 1983.
8. Christian Derix, 'Approximating Phenomenological Space', in IFC Smith (ed), *EGICE 2006*, *LNAI 4200*, Springer (Berlin Heidelberg), 2006, pp 136–46

Text © 2013 John Wiley & Sons Ltd. Images: pp 42, 45(t), 46(bl&br), 47 © Aedas; p 43 © Cambridge University Press. Drawing from Hillier and Hanson's *The Social Logic of Space*, Cambridge University Press, 1984, p 219; p 44 Drawing from Eckehard Janofske, *Architektur-Räume: Idee und Gestalt bei Hans Scharoun*, Vieweg & Sohn Verlagsgesellschaft (Wiesbaden), 1984; p 45(b) © Aedas + Davis Brody Bond Architects and Planners; p 46(tl&tr) © Christian Derix

47

STRUCTURAL EMERGENCE

ARCHITECTURAL AND STRUCTURAL DESIGN COLLABORATION AT SOM

KEITH BESSERUD, NEIL KATZ AND ALESSANDRO BEGHINI

At Skidmore, Owings & Merrill (SOM) there is a strong culture of collaboration between architects and engineers, and innovation in computational technologies – the firm fervently embraced the computer over 50 years ago. Here a cross-disciplinary team from SOM, architects **Keith Besserud and Neil Katz** and structural engineer **Alessandro Beghini**, describe their current work on FE algorithms and how this has informed recent projects.

SOM, Convention Center, Tanggu, China, 2009
The final shape of the roof was generated using a genetic algorithm (GA), providing a more efficient structural solution while accommodating specific programmatic requirements.

A unique tradition of multidisciplinary innovation has flourished at Skidmore, Owings & Merrill (SOM) since the firm's inception, perhaps most notably between the architects and structural engineers. The firm's aggressive adoption of computational technologies in the 1960s further reinforced this collaboration, facilitating the creative marriage of novel structural concepts and architectural expression on projects like the John Hancock Center (late 1960s) and the Sears Tower (1973) in Chicago by architect Bruce Graham and structural engineer Fazlur Khan. This spirit of architectural and engineering collaboration feeds the development of conceptual and technical invention to this day at SOM, leading to new structural and architectural paradigms.

Of course, computation continues to play a key role in these speculative collaborations. Compared to the 1960s, we now have the benefit of computers that are much more powerful, analytical algorithms that are much more sophisticated, and visualisation techniques that render the analytical data in ways that make it much more immediately understandable. The net result is that on a given project, with typical time constraints, it is now possible to evaluate many more design proposals and gain much deeper insights into theoretical concepts.

With visual mappings of the flows of the forces and coloured heat maps that depict the distribution of stresses and magnitudes of displacements, architects can immediately develop a powerful intuitive understanding of how the overall shape of a building affects its structural nature.

From a structural engineering perspective, the ability to explore these types of theoretical concepts is due in large measure to the emergence of finite element (FE) algorithms over the past several decades. Although the key FE concepts were originally developed in the 1940s and formalised into algorithms in the 1960s (for the aerospace and nautical industries), it is only more recently that they have become commercialised and more readily useable on architectural engineering projects.[1]

Like most firms, SOM frequently uses commercially developed finite element analysis (FEA) software programs to assess structural performance. However, in addition to developing expertise as users of these types of software programs, there is also deep interest in contributing at a more fundamental level to the ongoing evolution and advancements of FE algorithms.

For example, SOM engineers are actively collaborating with Professor Glaucio Paulino and his students at the University of Illinois at Urbana-Champaign, focusing specifically on the definition of FE mesh elements. Traditionally, 2-D FE meshes have been idealised as regular rectangular or triangular elements, delineated as close to identical as possible. However, the researchers at the University of Illinois have found that irregular (instead of regular) 2-D meshes offer interesting potential benefits. By utilising irregular hexagonal[2] and polygonal elements generated from Voronoi algorithms,[3] these meshes can improve the mathematical stability of the optimisation algorithms and eliminate the 'chequerboarding' effect often generated with regular quadrilateral and triangular meshes. In developing this research, the University of Illinois team has created custom meshing algorithms and FE solvers in MathWorks®' MATLAB® that have been used experimentally by both the university researchers and SOM engineers on various of the firm's projects as a means of validating the research. Most recently, research into this Voronoi approach to meshing is being extended from 2-D domains into 3-D domains.

In addition to the meshing and solving capabilities of commercial FE programs, the visualisation of data is another valuable capability, especially with regard to reinforcing transdisciplinary collaborations between architects and engineers. With visual mappings of the flows of the forces and coloured heat maps that depict the distribution of stresses and magnitudes of displacements, architects can immediately develop a powerful intuitive understanding of how the overall shape of a building affects its structural nature, even without a solid understanding of the mathematics or algorithms.

This ability to get a clear window into the structural performance of a given design scheme allows designers to speculate more intelligently and more immediately about possible modifications to improve the design. SOM designers and engineers have found that, like the graphic statics analytical methods conceived decades earlier, the visualisation of the structural forces in FEA can often lead designers to possible design solutions which can be directly inferred from the visualisations.

The efficiencies of FE algorithms and power of computers mean that it is possible to evaluate a very large number of designs in a relatively short amount of time. One way of navigating through this potentially vast solution space to find better-performing designs would be to intuitively attempt to determine each iteration after evaluating each round of structural analysis. However, such a process would likely be inefficient if the goal is to identify a set of globally best-performing designs.

Alternatively, automated search algorithms can be used to identify a set of optimal solutions, usually with much greater efficiency. In practice, these optimisation techniques are a valuable means of helping designers to not only identify best-performing designs, but also to develop an understanding of why the best solutions perform so well. Whether the optimal solutions are actually adopted by the design team is usually a matter of additional non-structural criteria, such as programmatic requirements or budgetary constraints, or aesthetic considerations; however, even if the optimal solutions are not adopted explicitly, the knowledge gained in the process is usually still of great value.

Two of the primary search techniques that SOM architects and engineers have been using are based on genetic algorithms (GAs) and gradient-based algorithms (for example, density methods). With both techniques, FE algorithms provide the means of establishing structural performance. Typically, GAs are used for shape-optimisation exercises and use FEA in the fitness function, while gradient-based methods are used for topology-optimisation exercises and use FEA to determine the most efficient distribution patterns for the structural material within a given design domain.

The GA used by SOM was developed in-house. Written as a stand-alone application in Visual Basic .NET (VB.NET), it can be connected to any type of simulation program that has an application programming interface (API) that can interface with VB.NET. The simulation software (for example, FEA, radiation analysis or cost analysis) determines the fitness of each design; the GA determines the parametric values for each design in a given population (taking the fitness of each design in the previous population); and a specially developed additional code automates processes of moving inputs and outputs between the GA, the simulation software and the geometry modeling software.

SOM's custom GA works very well for single-objective design problems, but for multiple-objective explorations the firm is also experimenting with commercial optimisation engines such as Red Cedar Technology's HEEDS® MDO and Esteco's modeFRONTIER®. It is also aligned with academic efforts to explore 'human in the loop' optimisation techniques which allow designers to intervene with the optimisation process during execution, and also with optimisation strategies that incorporate definitions of 'novelty' as a driver of the search process.[4]

SOM, John Hancock Center, Chicago, Illinois, late 1960s
Structural engineer Fazlur Khan (left) and architect Bruce Graham with a design model of the John Hancock Center, featuring the braced-frame structural system that was devised for the project.

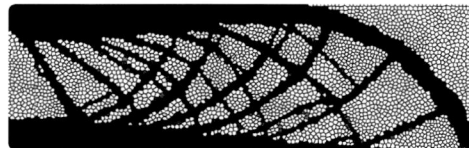

The efficiencies of FE algorithms and power of computers mean that it is possible to evaluate a very large number of designs in a relatively short amount of time.

Professor Glaucio Paulino, Cameron Talischi and Chau H Le, Centroidal Voronoi Tessellation (CVT) mesh, University of Illinois at Urbana-Champaign, Urbana, Illinois, 2009
Compared with quadrilateral meshes (upper mesh), the CVTs provide greater mathematical stability for finite element (FE) algorithms and lower compliance values in optimisation applications.

GAs have been used at SOM for shape-optimisation searches for both towers and long-span roof structures, such as that for a large convention centre in Tanggu, China (2009). Here, the designers had defined a series of undulations that correlated to the varying ceiling heights required for the performance spaces and circulation spaces beneath. Although it was generally understood that the undulating form had certain stiffness characteristics that would work well from a structural perspective, the designers were still interested to know what an optimal structural solution would look like, with deviations from the original surface constrained to specific upper and lower limits. The result presented by the GA was a shape that was a recognisable descendant of the original, but exhibited a much more efficient distribution of stresses across its surface.

The GA was also used for the Yongsan office tower competition in Seoul, South Korea (2009). In this case, the logic of the building form was parametrically predefined as a set of circular concentric floor-plate profiles whose radii were allowed to fluctuate in the optimisation process according to maximum and minimum thresholds that would allow for marketable lease spans. In other words, the economic criteria were managed as constraints that had upper and lower boundaries, while the structural performance criteria were configured as the fitness function (minimising deflection at the top of the tower). The GA ultimately presented a building form reminiscent of a teardrop with a profile that curved outwards as it went up from the ground, and then retreated inwards, tapering to a point at the very top.

The teardrop shape came as a surprise to the designers who were intuitively expecting a more conically tapered shape to emerge as the optimal form. The structural engineers, however, recognised the profile as having similarities with the Michell frame concept they had been actively researching. Michell frames are a family of minimum material solutions for a variety of load and support conditions composed of orthogonal fields of lines. In other words, they represent an optimal structural frame solution for a cantilever or, more relevantly, a tall tower.

On subsequent tower projects – the TransBay Transit Center in San Francisco and Shanghai Center in Shanghai (both 2010) – the knowledge developed in the Michell frame research work became even more directly manifested. Here, the architects and structural engineers chose to make a formal expression of the lateral bracing members on the exterior of the buildings by tracking the lines of principal stress, similar to the geometric arrangements exhibited in the Michell frame.

The teardrop shape came as a surprise to the designers who were intuitively expecting a more conically tapered shape to emerge as the optimal form.

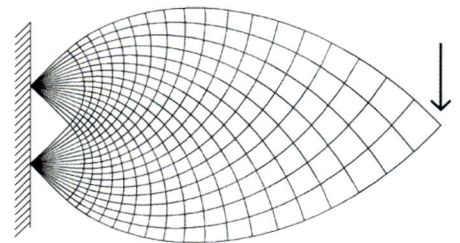

Michell frame
The Michell frame represents an optimal topology for a cantilever structure.

top: SOM, TransBay Transit Center competition, San Francisco, California, 2010
opposite: SOM, Shanghai Center, Shanghai, China, 2010
For these two tower proposals, the lines of principal stress as revealed in finite element analysis (FEA) models and echoed in Michell frame diagrams were expressed architecturally on the exteriors of the buildings.

SOM, Yongsan office tower competition, Seoul, Korea, 2009
The structurally efficient teardrop shape for the building was revealed through the use of a genetic algorithm.

SOM, White Magnolia office tower, Shanghai, China, 2010
A gradient-based optimisation algorithm was used to identify the most efficient arrangement for a structural system for a pre-established complex building shape.

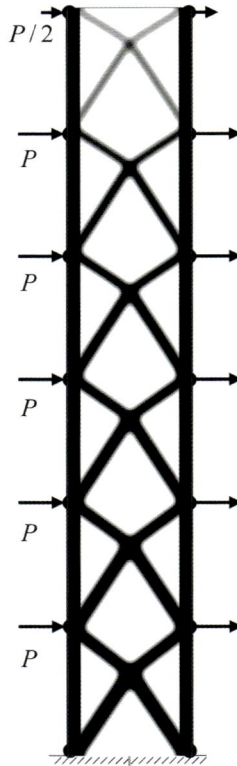

above left: Lauren L Stromberg, Analysis of cantilever cross-bracing, University of Illinois at Urbana-Champaign, Urbana, Illinois, 2012
above right: SOM, Office building, Sydney, Australia, 2012
In the diagram on the left, researchers at the University of Illinois, in collaboration with engineers at SOM, demonstrated that the optimal location for the intersection point of a cross-brace was not the midpoint, but instead a position somewhat above the midpoint, again confirming the relevance of the Michell frame. The rendering on the right shows the application of the optimal brace design on an office building.

The lateral bracing schemes for the San Francisco and Shanghai projects are also revealed in topology-optimisation exercises using gradient-based search algorithms. These types of algorithms operate on a design domain that contains a fixed amount of structural material that is initially distributed evenly across the domain, but then iteratively redistributed in order to realise the most efficient use of that material. For two additional projects in Shanghai, topology optimisation revealed very novel proposals for the expression of optimised structural systems; one for the White Magnolia office tower (2010) and another for a commercial development (2011) in which the multi-span bridge element connects three towers. The latter study was conducted in collaboration with Professor Paulino's research group at the University of Illinois.

Finally, to come full circle, the iconic cross-bracing of the John Hancock Center was revisited in a sense for an office building in Sydney, Australia (2010). For this project, a series of diagonal cross-braces are again expressed on the exterior of the building, but the optimal topology for a structural braced frame is one in which the diagonals intersect at locations higher than their midpoints.[5] The optimal solution for the shear bracing, as revealed in the gradient-based search algorithm, again shared some similarities with the Michell frame solution.

Architects and structural engineers at SOM work together in a long-established spirit of research-driven collaboration that has yielded many important designs in which the architectural and structural concepts evolve in synchronicity. Today, these collaborations are facilitated through the use of computational algorithms that draw the two groups even closer in processes that require them to jointly define performative goals and constraints, to define geometric forms in terms of their parametric relationships, and to speculate about the likely performative qualities of different formal strategies. Algorithmic tools such as FEA programs and GAs are critical to expediting processes of searching vast solution spaces for well-performing designs, and are facilitating the exploration of new, previously inaccessible theoretical paradigms and emergent formal typologies. ⌂

Notes
1. Kenneth H Huebner, Donald L Dewhirst, Douglas E Smith and Ted G Byrom, *The Finite Element Method for Engineers*, Wiley-Interscience (Chichester), 4th edn, 2001, p 12.
2. Cameron Talischi, Glaucio H Paulino and Chau H Le, 'Honeycomb Wachspress Finite Elements for Structural Topology Optimization', *Structural and Multidisciplinary Optimization*, Vol 37, No 6, 2009, pp 569–83.
3. Cameron Talischi, Glaucio H Paulino, Anderson Pereira and Ivan FM Menezes, 'Polygonal Finite Elements for Topology Optimization: A Unifying Paradigm', *International Journal for Numerical Methods in Engineering*, Vol 82, No 6, 2010, pp 671–98.
4. Joel Lehman and Kenneth O Stanley, 'Abandoning Objectives: Evolution through the Search for Novelty Alone', *Evolutionary Computation*, Vol 19, No 2, 2011, pp 189–223.
5. Lauren L Stromberg, Alessandro Beghini, William F Baker and Glaucio H Paulino, 'Topology Optimization for Braced Frames: Combining Continuum and Discrete Elements', *Engineering Structures*, Vol 37, 2012, pp 106–24.

Architects and structural engineers at SOM work together in a long–established spirit of research–driven collaboration that has yielded many important designs in which the architectural and structural concepts evolve in synchronicity.

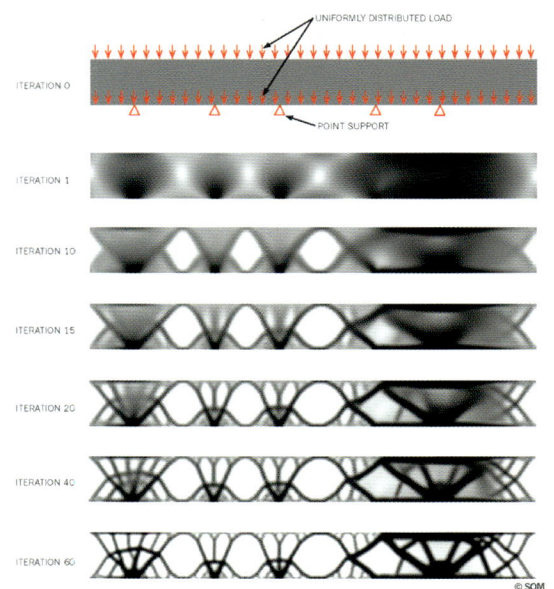

SOM, Commercial development project, Shanghai, China, 2011
A gradient-based optimisation algorithm revealed an irregular pattern for an optimal structural system for the bridge component of this project, which was incorporated as part of the architectural tectonics.

BRADY PETERS

REALISING THE ARCHI- TECTURAL IDEA

COMPUTATIONAL DESIGN AT HERZOG & DE MEURON

Kai Strehlke heads up the Digital Technology Group at Herzog & de Meuron, a team of 12 based in the firm's Basle office. Herzog & de Meuron is a practice that is all about the architecture. However, how does technology interact with design in a practice that is all about the architectural concept? Guest-editor **Brady Peters** puts this question to Strehlke, revealing an approach that is all about finding the right tool and some very artful scripting to make the concept work.

Herzog & de Meuron is an award-winning architecture practice based in Basle. Founded in 1978, it currently has five partners and an office of more than 370 designing projects that range from exhibitions to buildings and masterplans. Its projects evolve by way of a constant dialogue between the practice, its partners and colleagues. While the office's projects do not come from a single controlling author, they are also not fragmented – each contains clarity. The work is 'strongly conceptual'.[1] Kurt Forster writes: 'By narrowing the premises from which the idea of a project arises, the architects increase the power of that idea to the point of letting some projects ride on a single premise.'[2]

In architecture, this conceptual world of design is balanced by the pragmatic world of construction; however, it is also influenced by technology. One approach is to buy a particular technology and experiment with it. For example, many architecture schools are investing in robots and exploring the potentials of this technology. Similarly, 3-D animation software has been hijacked to generate architecture. Architect Kai Strehlke, Head of the Digital Technology Group at Herzog & de Meuron, explained that the approach of the office is fundamentally different: 'The focus is, first of all, only on the architecture. So when we use methods of computation, it is not a technology that we try to do something with it; the focus is more on design intent and the architectural idea and concept. We try to find the right tool, and develop the tool to make the concept work.'[3]

HERZOG & DE MEURON, SÜDPARK, BASLE, SWITZERLAND, 2012

previous spread: Interlocking shapes make it difficult to see where apartments begin and end. The facade appears to be designed from the outside, however the main consideration was actually the experience from within.

above right: Factory prefabrication of facade components.

The Digital Technology Group is a small team of 12 people working in the office in different fields: computer-aided design (CAD) management, building information modelling (BIM), parametric design and scripting, visualisation and video, and digital fabrication. The team can be consulted at any point in the design process, from concept design, to design development. As Strehlke explains: 'Very often a team approaches the Digital Technology Group for a small script that they usually want the same day. The group is very fast in programming the initial computational design tool for them. If our support for the design process is helpful, we continue to work closely with the design team to develop that tool in a more sophisticated manner.'

As these custom digital design tools are developed from the architectural idea, the Digital Technology Group is not restricted to any particular technique, and works on projects of all scales, from furniture to facades and urban design. As Herzog & de Meuron founder and Senior Partner Jacques Herzog has said: 'We see a huge potential for the computer in the very hybrid and eclectic design processes we have developed over the last 20 years which combine all techniques from primitive to technologically advanced with no personal preferences.'[4] Rather than being experts in free-form surfaces, the main driver

for the Digital Technology Group is to grasp the idea the office's designers are trying to develop and then write a specific tool for it. Strehlke says: 'Normally what we do is write one tool, one piece of software for one project. This reflects the architecture of the office, as we try not to copy ourselves. There is not a style of Herzog & de Meuron; each building conceptually stands by itself. Therefore, when we develop tools we also develop them in an extremely dedicated way.'

At Herzog & de Meuron, just as each building design is specific, so is the strategy behind each tool. The Digital Technology Group works with available software, but, trying to stay dynamic, is open to everything. While scripting is often used as a technique, the group will also use tools that designers are more easily able to understand. And while the office has expertise in several BIM software systems, these are not seen as necessarily adding to the architectural design, but as allowing the whole building to be seen as a complete data structure, or database system. When the group works with a design team, it is often only on one system or part of a building, for example the facade or a staircase. This part then becomes very special and is designed using computational tools. It is here that the two worlds of computation and the architectural idea are brought together.

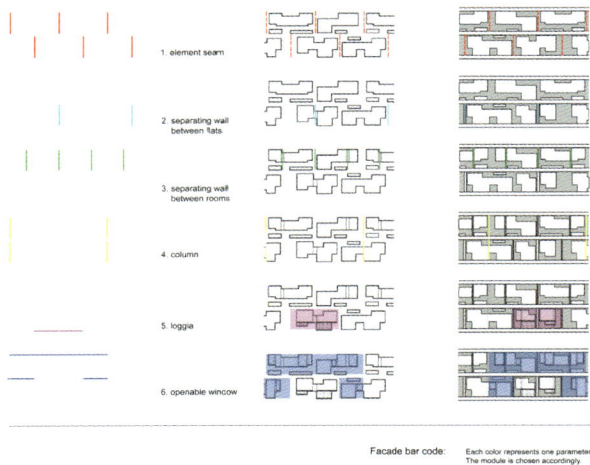

Facade bar code: Each color represents one parameter. The module is chosen accordingly.

214_Südpark_Baufeld_D: Generate Tender Documents

Tender documents:

In a final step the script generates an A3 plan for each of the 296 modules and generates an excel file with all relevant masses.

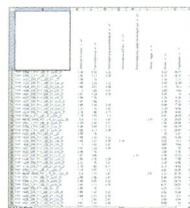

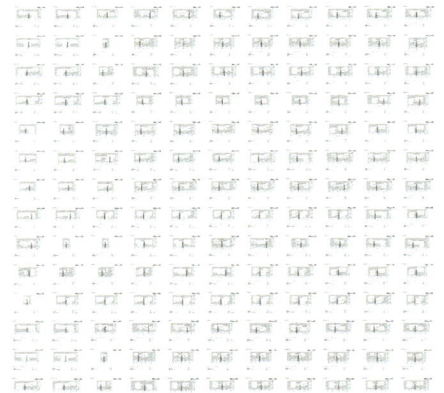

top: The generation of the facade was informed by a computer program developed in-house by the Digital Technology Group. Randomisation was used to generate the initial pattern, though later on in the process the design became fixed. Computational design techniques were used to control the data structure right up to the end.

bottom: Production drawings and data spreadsheets for facade elements were generated in RhinoScript. A new script was then developed in-house that re-generated a complete facade from the production information and spreadsheets as a way of checking the data.

Strehlke is adamant that, in the office's use of computational tools, 'performance is the only consideration'. He explains: 'Ornament as decoration is not what we try to achieve.' While he admits that there is often an ornamental aspect, the designs are not primarily visually driven. The generation of geometry and material configurations are performance driven.

When considering aspects of performance in the architectural design process, feedback from engineering consultants is sometimes slow, and there is a need for feedback that is quicker and simpler. 'For example,' says Strehlke, 'when looking at environmental performance we get a booklet of many pages from the consultant, and this is too much information to really trigger the design directly.' As a result, the office often develops such tools itself; for example, it has written its own solar design tools to determine the hours of sunlight a design will get. As the tools are developed in house, the architects are able to react much faster to design iterations. 'Ultimately, though, the team will communicate with the project consultants to see whether what we have done is correct,' says Strehlke. However, he cautions that: 'very often teams use these tools to prove that their building is located in a good way, that it is working, and this takes the focus away from the main design idea. In architecture, we always work at different levels of abstraction, and we always focus on certain points. However, these performance tools, though they can be very helpful for certain designs, can also distract.'

Here, the development of computational tools emerges from the architectural idea, and the building's performance is a primary consideration for the development of a form. Architectural design is always a balance of many contradicting constraints, and so it is important that issues of performance are not all considered equally, and that the primacy of the architectural idea remains.

HERZOG & DE MEURON, MESSE BASEL –
NEW HALL, BASLE, SWITZERLAND, DUE
FOR COMPLETION APRIL 2013

top: Visualisation of the project. The design concept comes from a simple idea – two boxes, one on top of the other, slightly twisted to produce a hyperbolic surface. The facade thus faces towards the street, or towards the sky.

right: 2-D CNC-milled components are assembled into a complex 3-D structure. This facade strategy has both double curvature and variably sized openings.

While the Digital Technology Group's scripts are an important part of the design process, the building of physical models and testing of design concepts at various scales play an equally important role. A digital workshop in the office thus complements the traditional workshop. Here, digital fabrication machines such as cardboard cutters, laser cutters and CNC milling are used because the office believes that the physical model is vital to understanding architecture, to anticipating the construction of a building or component. It is now possible to write computational tools to generate almost any kind of geometry. However, the office is not interested in arbitrary geometric possibilities. As Strehlke says, the goal is to anticipate fabrication 'so that the design is not only buildable, but meaningfully buildable, buildable in a way that does not explode costs.' A digital workshop in the office thus complements the traditional workshop. Thus, the office does not have any 3-D printers, as these are seen to be associated with the ability to produce any geometric configuration without the constraints of assembly.

It can be argued that computational design tools need to be more closely connected with the building process. Herzog & de Meuron's Digital Technology Group sees integration with fabricators as an important part of informing the computational design. Through approaching fabricators early in the design process, techniques and machine sizes can be incorporated as parameters in the custom digital tool, and then used to make the design more efficient, more buildable, and more integrated with the architectural idea. However, as Strehlke explains: 'Very often we are constrained by the regulations of the contract, and not allowed to contact fabricators before the bidding phase. This is a big problem in architecture today, and something that, in my opinion, has to change in the future. We have to try to find different ways of working between the architects and fabricators.'

Herzog & de Meuron's computational design team is thus very much a part of the practice's overall conceptual approach to design. As Jacques Herzog said in his acceptance speech for the Pritzker Prize: 'this conceptual approach is actually a device developed for each project by means of which we remain invisible as authors. ... It is a strategy that gives us the freedom to reinvent architecture with each new project rather than consolidating our style.'[5] ∆

Notes
1. Kurt W Forster, 'Pieces for Four and More Hands', in Philip Ursprung (ed), *Natural History*, Lars Müller Publishers (Baden), 2005, p 42.
2. Ibid, p 54.
3. Conversation between the author and Kai Strehlke, 5 September 2012.
4. William JR Curtis, 'The Nature of Artifice', *El Croquis* Vol 109/110, 2002, p 29.
5. Jacques Herzog and Pierre de Meuron, 'Acceptance Speech 2001 Pritzker Architecture Prize', *El Croquis*, op cit, p 12.

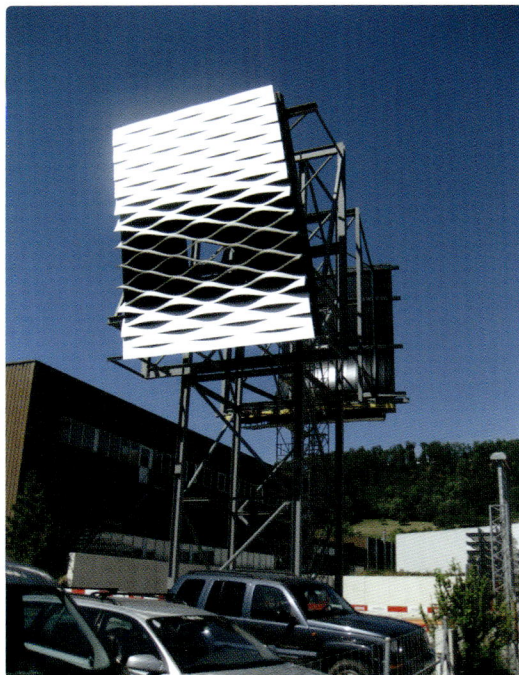

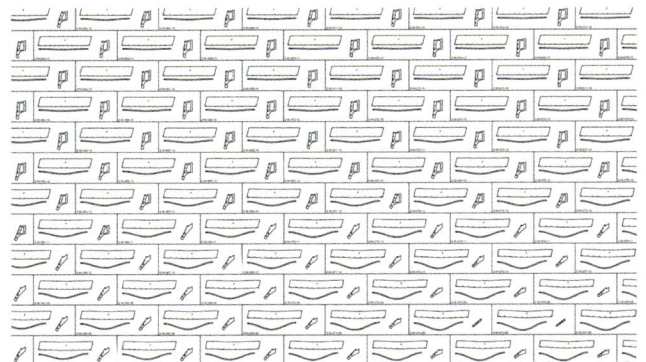

above left: Fabrication prototype. This double-layer cladding system has a rainscreen of wavy elements over a facade composed of standard components; where there are glazing panels in the facade, the wavy screen opens up to allow views out.

above right: Fabrication drawing for CNC milling. Computational design techniques created a system for communicating the fabrication information.

Much emphasis in computation has been put on the potential of building information modelling (BIM) and other software in the coordination of the design and construction process and on building performance. What, however, can modelling techniques offer to shift the focus to simulating the user experience? **Shrikant Sharma and Al Fisher** of Buro Happold SMART Solutions, which offers specialist computational innovation services to external clients, describe how their team has developed SMART Move, a crowd-modelling software that has been used in the development of the designs for Wilkinson Eyre's Exeter University Forum and Foster + Partners' Thomas Deacon Academy.

Computational analysis and building information modelling (BIM) technologies not only help in predicting the performance of buildings in terms of structural and energy efficiency, they also enable virtual prototyping before they are constructed. This helps tackle construction and design coordination issues early on, significantly reducing design, material and construction costs.

What remains a challenge, however, is virtualising the operation of a building, or predicting and optimising its performance from a 'user experience' perspective. This is a major limitation, given that the success or failure of a building largely depends on its operational efficiency and the comfort of its occupant and visitors.

But how are visitor comfort and user experience modelled? Visitor comfort may seem like a subjective measure, but it can be expressed in terms of simple parameters that define the levels of comfort, safety and general well-being; for example, inside a building[1] or airport,[2] or as a pedestrian.[3] Parameters such as journey times (in a rail or airport terminal), waiting times (in a hospital), and congestion densities (within sports stadia) are all a big part of visitor comfort and safety in movement. Similar comfort parameters, such as thermal and wind comfort, may also need to be defined.

SHRIKANT SHARMA AND AL FISHER

SIMULATING THE USER EXPERIENCE

DESIGN OPTIMISATION FOR VISITOR COMFORT

MODELLING VISITOR MOVEMENT

Modelling of visitor comfort in movement involves simulating human behaviour, which varies according to spatial layouts, context, environment and interaction with other users. A vast amount of research and development work is underway in the academic and commercial world to model, visualise and assess the impact of designs on visitor comfort and safety. Agent-based simulation of people movement, which uses microscopic behaviour of individuals and groups as they move through a space, is increasingly being used to test the effectiveness of building designs.[4]

Crowd modelling software such as the Buro Happold SMART Solutions team's SMART Move[5] utilises predictive models of crowd behaviour under various environments and scenarios, and their interaction with building geometry, signage, processes and events. This enables simulation of the complex interaction of hundreds of thousands of people in scenarios such as day-to-day circulation, mass arrival/ egress and emergency evacuations. The SMART Solutions team has been looking at ways to make such crowd modelling technology increasingly accessible, scalable, faster, and easy to use. Its approach involves a social force model[6] that has been extended for rapid, real-time assessment of building designs and operational planning. Real-time performance is achieved using a combination of optimised spatial representation, variable model resolution and dynamic time stepping. Emphasis is placed on real-time user interaction, achieved by fully embedding SMART Move within a 3-D BIM environment and linking the spatial model with the BIM model. These features have led to rapid performance improvement: complex modelling scenarios can now be set up with a few clicks and the simulation typically runs in a few minutes.

Rapid analysis and live interaction mean that designers can interactively tweak the design on the fly, enabling design decisions to be optimised within a workshop environment. This is especially useful for the early stages of design when high-level decisions can have a major impact on the costs and performance of the final design.

The examples covered below illustrate the application of the Buro Happold SMART Solutions team's people movement modelling to two recently completed educational projects in the UK.

EXETER UNIVERSITY FORUM

The design intent behind the newly opened Exeter University Forum and Reception Building, by Wilkinson Eyre Architects, was to integrate the variety of functions and movements within the entrance and foyer space, flexible mixed-use teaching areas for use by all departments, a new student services centre, refurbished library and food court. This was achieved by identifying and mapping the diverse movements of students, staff and visitors within the circulation spaces, followed by conceptual and detailed flow simulations to assess the performance of the circulation provisions within the design, including stairs, corridors and entrances. The study looked at issues such as safety and comfort during horizontal and vertical circulation as well as at assembly points adjacent to the lecture hall and auditorium entrances. Congestion issues were considered during critical scenarios such as meal break times or lecture theatre changeover. People movement modelling ensured that the comfort of the visitors was fully tied into the design development of the Forum in terms of the shaping as well as sizing of the circulation spaces.

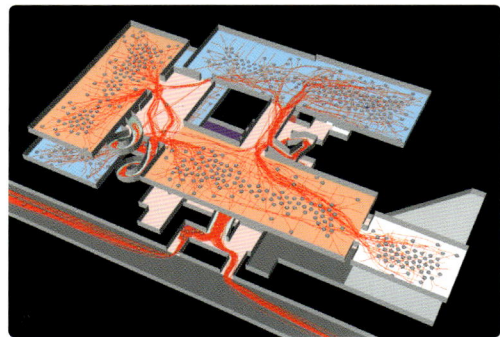

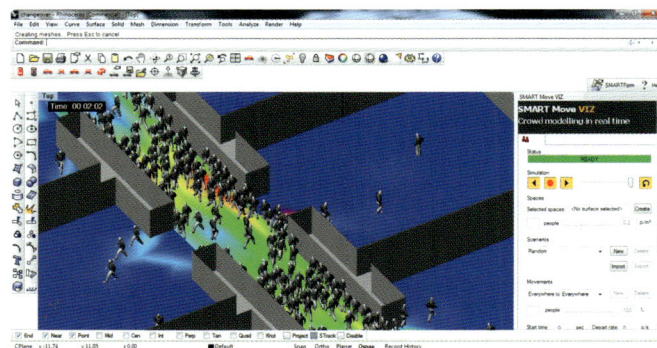

Buro Happold SMART Solutions, SMART Move software
top: Modelling of visitor movement pattern within a building showing over- and underused areas. Dots visualise individuals within the building and lines denote the trails left by individuals.

bottom: Real-time modelling of people flow and comfort. Fully integrated into Robert McNeel & Associates' Rhinoceros®, the simulation enables rapid evaluation of parameters such as comfort levels, congestion, journey times and queue lengths, and optioneering of multiple design parameters.

Foster + Partners and Buro Happold, Thomas Deacon Academy, Peterborough, Cambridgeshire, 2007
right: Density map during class changeover at Thomas Deacon Academy. Colours denote comfort levels (red = high density). Simulation allowed testing of different stair positions to save a potential 70 per cent of stair width and over 40 per cent of corridor space.

below: Modelling of student circulation was a key factor in optimising the locations and widths of stairs and corridors, minimising safety risks and saving substantial costs.

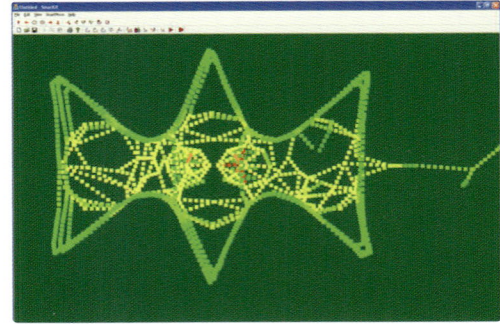

Novel simulation technologies are helping designers and planners to predict the ways in which people interact with their designs, as well as how to shape their designs to achieve maximum comfort and experience.

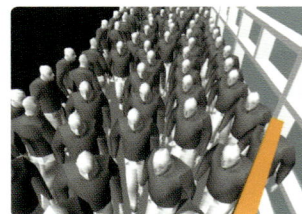

Simulation work on Thomas Deacon Academy involved capturing real-world data (for example, class discharge times with and without a central bell) for modelling input and verifications.

THOMAS DEACON ACADEMY

The largest of the schools within the UK Government's Academies Programme, the multi-award-winning Thomas Deacon Academy is a pioneering new learning environment that aims to reinvent the traditional school model. Designed by Foster + Partners, this state-of-the-art academy is a 2,200-pupil secondary school replacing three existing schools.

People movement modelling was key in the optimisation of the circulation design of the school. Dynamic people flow simulation was used to predict pupil and staff circulation patterns and congestion 'hotspots' within the proposed layout. The proposed solutions involved a combination of design solutions such as distributed placements of circulation stairs (to achieve their optimised usage), and management solutions such as removal of the school bell (to minimise the density of students during class changeover).

School bells have a direct impact on how quickly the various classes discharge, which in turn affects the number of students circulating in the corridors at the end of a class. Similarly, a centralised and integrated design attracts higher footfalls. Virtual simulation models in SMART Move allowed quantitative evaluation of various design and management options, predicting the efficiency of operations and student comfort in terms of densities in corridors, time to get to next class, queue levels at the top of stairs, time to access lockers, and so on. The Thomas Deacon Academy example shows how visitor comfort modelling can not only help to optimise the design of circulation spaces, but can also integrate and refine the management aspect of the circulation strategy to significantly reduce design and construction costs.

THE FUTURE: FULLY INTEGRATED BUILDING PERFORMANCE MODELLING

Novel simulation technologies are helping designers and planners to predict the ways in which people interact with their designs, as well as how to shape their designs to achieve maximum comfort and experience. The industry is now looking at prototyping not just the virtual 3-D model of a building, but also its holistic performance before it is put into operation. The more we are able to predict, optioneer and optimise building performance and operational efficiency during the early stages of design, the more costs will be saved and overall success ensured. ᴆ

Notes
1. Baruch Givoni, 'Comfort, Climate Analysis and Building Design Guidelines', *Energy and Buildings*, Vol 18, 1992, pp 11–23.
2. DJ Oborne, 'Passenger Comfort – An Overview', *Applied Ergonomics*, Vol 9, Issue 3, September 1978, pp 131–6.
3. John J Fruin, *Pedestrian Planning and Design*, Metropolitan Association of Urban Designers and Environmental Planners, University of Michigan (Ann Arbor, MI), 1971.
4. D Helbing, 'Self-Organized Pedestrian Crowd Dynamics: Experiments, Simulations, and Design Solutions', *Transportation Science*, Vol 39, No 1, February 2005, pp 1–24.
5. SB Sharma, 'A Static-Dynamic Network Model for Crowd Flow Simulation', *6th International Symposium on Space Syntax*, Istanbul, 12–15 June 2007.
6. D Helbing and P Molnár, 'Social Force Model for Pedestrian Dynamics', *Physics Review Letters*, E 51, 1995, pp 4282–6.

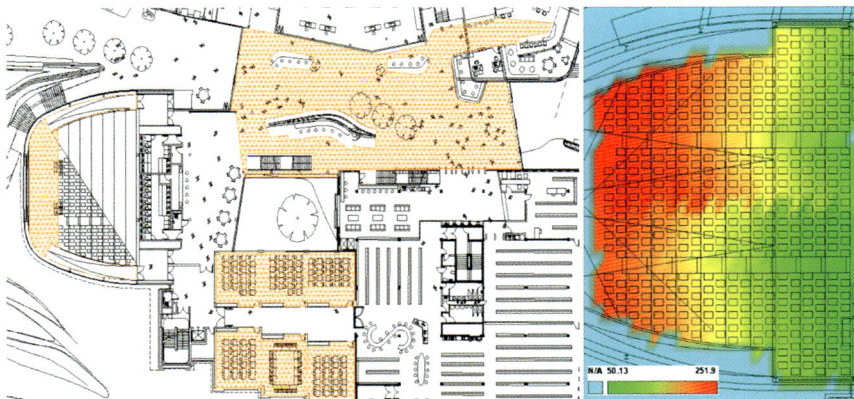

Wilkinson Eyre Architects and Buro Happold, Exeter University Forum, Exeter, Devon, 2012
Modelling of Exeter University Forum auditorium discharge. Colours denote the time for an individual at the origin to exit the auditorium.

above right: The project provided a perfect opportunity to incorporate user experience as a key parameter within the design.

Mexico has a great tradition of craft and its artisans have a deep understanding of space, light and material. Stone, wood and masonry have historically been the key material elements of this language, and skilled artisans are able to create almost anything from them. In addition to this, a sophisticated knowledge of structural engineering has developed as a result of Mexico's unique and difficult soil conditions. For Fernando Romero EnterprisE (FREE), the challenge lies not solely in the craft of building or the engineering of a project, but in the creation of a culture of collaboration. How can architects organise and communicate design information to allow for new possibilities of building form?

THE DESIGN PROCESS

The Museo Soumaya was conceived as an iconic structure with two missions: to host one of the largest private art collections in the world, and to reshape an old industrial area of Mexico City. A structure of this complexity had never been attempted in Mexico, which presented various risks for the client, design and construction teams. One of the challenges was how to realise this ambitious project without precedent or local expertise. The management and coordination of the various teams was critical to its success, as were the new techniques that were developed using laser scanning, parametric modelling and other algorithmic techniques to design and model the project in three dimensions.

The exterior form of the Museo Soumaya is a double-curved surface that represents the concept of the museum as a container for the work, with the size of each floor plate responding to the nature of the collection on that floor. The surface was refined early in the design process through the use of study models, and the final physical model was laser scanned to create a digital model and define the design surface. Structural engineers Arup used the digital model to ensure the 26 curving columns and horizontal steel rings lay on the design surface.

Between the surface of the interior finish and the exterior panels is a complex 3-D structure comprising not a single repeating strut, as every element is adapted to the local surface conditions. Here, the design team selected a free-form space-frame solution by the firm Geometrica for the facade structure and to provide support for the facade panels.

FERNANDO ROMERO AND ARMANDO RAMOS

BRIDGING
A CULTURE
THE DESIGN
OF MUSEO
SOUMAYA

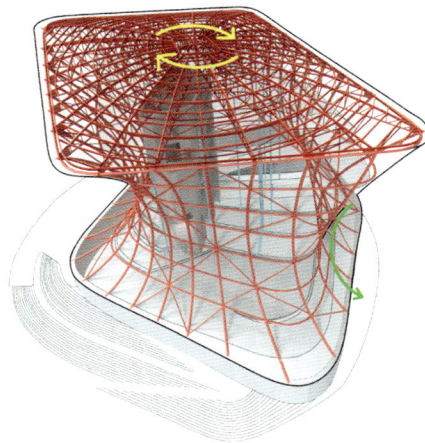

Fernando Romero and Armando Ramos of Fernando Romero EnterprisE (FREE) describe how the firm's design for an iconic museum in Mexico City, which adopted complex computational techniques, required them to develop an integrated and highly collaborative approach to design; with a central digital 3-D model being applied throughout the construction phase.

FREE, Museo Soumaya, Mexico City, Mexico, 2011
opposite: View of the museum entrance on the south facade.

above: Structural diagram showing the inner columns of the parking grid, the 28 steel columns, concrete belt, seven steel bracings that take the lateral forces, and the concrete core that takes the gravity force.

PANEL DESIGN AND FABRICATION

The aim was for the building's facade to be composed of hexagonal aluminium panels. The challenge here was that as the facade structure was already decided upon and being assembled, there was very little room for modifications or rationalisation. Each node in the facade structure holds the centre of gravity of a single hexagonal panel and three incoming struts.

A Gaussian analysis of the design surface identified areas with most curvature. The design intent was to have a consistent gap between all of the surface panels. The geometric solution was to stretch each hexagonal panel to maintain the spacing, with each panel responding in size and angles to the local geometry of the surface. This initial study resulted in over 16,000 unique hexagonal panels which presented both cost and fabrication issues.

Using the Gaussian analysis, the surface was divided into two zones: the most curved and the most regular. For the most regular zone, similar-sized hexagons were grouped into 'families'. These accounted for 80 per cent of the surface. For the most curved zone, the unique hexagonal panels accounted for the remaining 20 per cent of the surface. Parametric modelling techniques developed by Gehry Technologies were used to create the families.[1] Here, the panels were compared for similarities and grouped. Following this process all of the geometric data for the panels was extracted and reapplied to the surface, allowing for the verification of the panel sizes and adjustments to be made to the gaps between them. This adjustment and comparison was carried out until the desired result was achieved.

For the hexagonal panels, Gehry Technologies created shop drawings using the firm's Digital Project™ 3-D modelling tool. Custom computer programs were then used to extract every panel from the 3-D model and to create more than 14,000 2-D shop drawings. The entire mechanical system, ducts, structure and piping were aligned, detailed and coordinated using a central 3-D model, which enabled quick decisions to be made in real time by the whole team at crucial moments of the project.

bottom: Diagram exposing the panelling process: upper left indicates that the sphere packing is the dual of a hexagonal mesh; bottom left indicates the result of executing the sphere packing over the entire surface; the middle section shows the process of stretching the pattern to remove panels with abnormal proportions; upper right shows the process of selecting custom panels versus standard panels; and lower right shows the clustering process for sorting the panels by a K-number of clusters.

top: Exploded axonometric showing a detail of the facade with a double-layer secondary triodesic structure (green and red) as the support structure for the hexagonal panels.

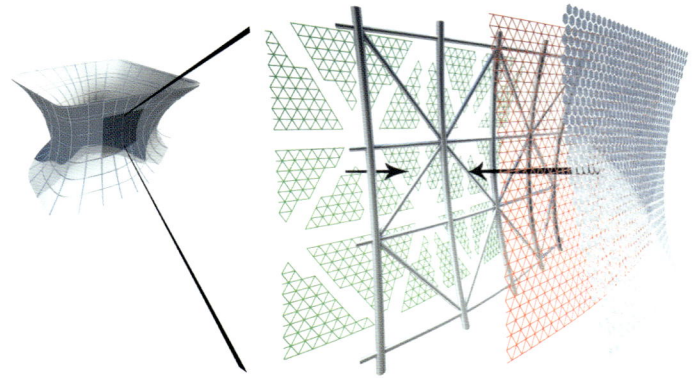

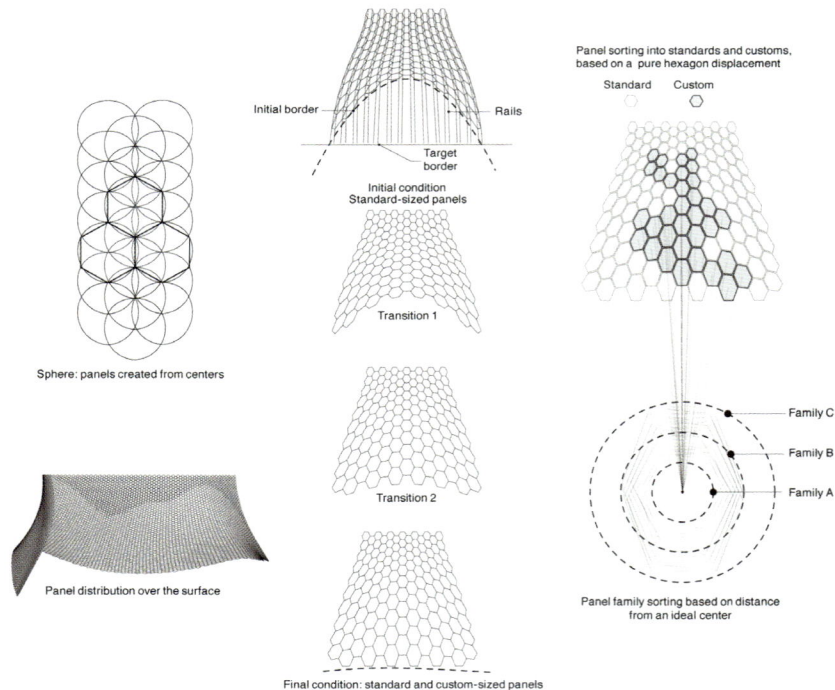

Sphere: panels created from centers

Panel distribution over the surface

Initial border · Rails

Target border

Initial condition
Standard-sized panels

Transition 1

Transition 2

Final condition: standard and custom-sized panels

Panel sorting into standards and customs, based on a pure hexagon displacement

Standard   Custom

Family C
Family B
Family A

Panel family sorting based on distance from an ideal center

COLLABORATION AND INTEGRATION

The whole project team continued to work on the central digital 3-D model throughout the construction phase, thus the design team was able to access and communicate precise information about the building at all times, which was delivered in such a way that everyone had what they needed in a way they understood it; different aspects of the building could be designed simultaneously; countless iterations of the design could be quickly studied; and, the graphic definition of the variables drivers gave a very clear understanding of the design intent. Due to the complex form of the building, the design of interior elements such as ramps, structure and roof would not have been possible using a traditional 2-D drawing and design process that leaves a lot of room for interpretation. Looking at the project in an integrated, holistic way, where all the elements and how they interact with each other are visible, was fundamental to both comprehending the complexity and documenting it.

As architecture becomes more complex, what is required is a simple, integrated process to understand and communicate this complexity. In architecture, unlike in other design disciplines, the process is unique to every project and so constant recalibration is necessary. How do we learn from other industries where there is greater investment in planning due to scalable production quantities? We cannot continue to use traditional linear design processes. A concurrent, integrated process is required in which all the different stakeholders come together – and the only way to achieve this is through technology. ⌂

Note

1. Alexander Pena de Leon, 'Rationalisation of Freeform Facades', in T Fischer, K De Biswas, JJ Ham, R Naka and WX Huang (eds), *Beyond Codes and Pixels: Proceedings of the 17th International Conference on Computer-Aided Architectural Design Research in Asia*, CAADRIA (Hong Kong), 2012, pp 243–52.

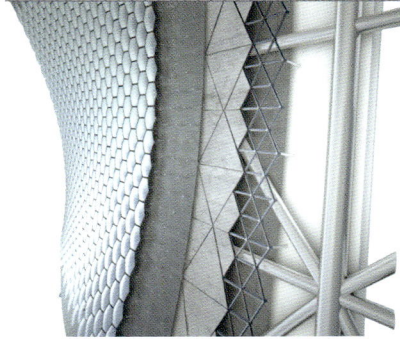

top: Facade layers from the interior: insulating durock, primary structure composed of bent oil-rigging structural tubes, triodesic secondary structure, waterproofing panels supported by the secondary structure, and the hexagonal panels supported by purlins mounted on the secondary structure.

centre: View of the south facade showing detail of aluminium hexagon cladding panels.

bottom: View of the completed structure with shimmering aluminium hexagon cladding.

INTEROPERABILITY IN SPORTS DESIGN

David Hines leads the parametric and advanced geometry group at Populous, the global design practice renowned for its expertise in sports facility design. Here he describes how Populous and Buro Happold created a shared model environment for the Aviva Stadium in Dublin (2010), enabling a smooth parametric-to-BIM-to fabrication process. A watershed initiative, it provided the prerequisite stepping stone for developing a parametric bowl tool for designing stadia.

ARCHITECTURAL BUILDING
INFORMATION MODEL

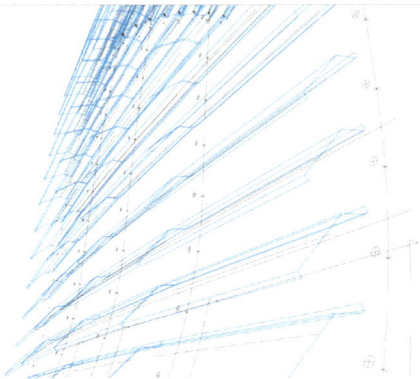

CONTRACTORS CONSTRUCTION
BUILDING INFORMATION MODEL

Populous Architects, Aviva Stadium, Dublin, Ireland, 2010
BIM models from architect to contractor to construction. The models established critical building element set-out data that subsequently coordinated subcontractors' information models through to fabrication and site construction.

From early on in the design process of Dublin's Aviva Stadium (2010), a reference for the detailing, execution and overall design of the building was a Swiss watch. The beauty lies in the detail of individual parts, the relationships between the parts, and the functionality and elegance of the watch as a whole. A Swiss watch is appreciated from both near and afar, and thus its admiration is scale-less. It was these traits and design appreciation that Populous tried to capture in the design of the stadium. Each part had its own function and beauty, yet through the relationships established by the computational design process each part also maintained an association with all other parts of the building, allowing the architecture to be more than a collection of singular building elements and become a beautiful functioning whole.

The Aviva Stadium was developed and executed using a combination of Robert McNeel & Associates' Rhinoceros® and Bentley Systems' GenerativeComponents™ (GC). Together with engineers Buro Happold, Populous undertook the process of coordinating the design through a shared model environment. The shared model was established by a single script file, a structural grid and a spreadsheet of numeric data, producing a single design surface that was used as a set-out aid to drive the positioning of the steel frame (engineers) and all cladding and roofing elements (architects). The ability for both firms to work from the starting point of one shared surface allowed design development of engineering and architectural detailing to evolve independently yet governed by the same starting surface, hence ensuring inter-office design coordination.

This was a unique way of ensuring coordination, with the structural design taking place within the surface shape, and architectural detail of the cladding and finish outside of it. During the detailed design process, the global design surface underwent several changes. These form changes were picked up in the spreadsheet of numeric data and fed back through subsequently developed setting-out scripts of the engineers' and architects' work so that all previously determined relationships upon a new design surface were maintained. This allowed global design alterations to be carried out simultaneously with detailed design development, eliminating any abortive work.[1]

The design surface was used to set out over 3,500 tons of primary steel, 62,000 roof-panel anchor points, and 4,114 differently positioned facade panels each with its own support casting brackets aligned to four rotation and alignment set-out points on the curved aluminium mullions. In total, 36,000 square metres (387,501 square feet) of building structure and surface was parametrically defined and manufactured off site. Both Populous and Buro Happold delivered the final 3-D centreline model and spreadsheet-based data sets as part of the construction documentation handover.[2]

The use of parametric platforms in the Aviva project enabled the design to be tested and driven to a high level of detail from which each subcontractor could work independently. The focus of this parametric-to-BIM-to-fabrication process was to remain sufficiently adaptable without losing sight of the design vision or the realities of construction and fabrication sequencing. Parametric design means we are now able to design more parts, more accurately, at an earlier stage, and therefore create new methods of delivering construction information. While parametric modelling has allowed us to design variations, building information modelling (BIM) is the process through which we can coordinate design execution.

In the wake of the success of the Aviva project, Populous has further developed and implemented BIM within its stadium bowl design process, which has resulted in the development of a fully adaptable parametric bowl designer tool. This computational design tool generates a fully resolved 3-D bowl geometry using a variety of tiers, capacities and geometric set-out parameters. Once compiled into a model, the nature of a bowl design can be pushed within the established model parameters, driving new undiscovered configurations while at the same time maintaining standard principle relationships.

Workflow

Structural design

Envelope geometry

Cladding design

Structure analysis

Construction documentation

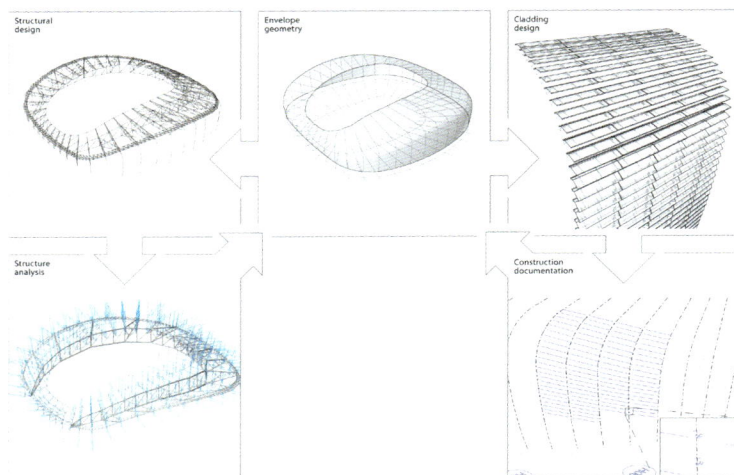

The Aviva Stadium (previously called the New Stadium at Lansdowne Road) is the first truly site-responsive stadium of its kind in the world. Its form, mass, materials and aspect are defined by the site and its surrounds.

Diagram of the design surface and workflow between Populous and Buro Happold. The design surface allowed a smooth BIM collaboration between the architect and the engineer throughout the design development stages.

The use of parametric techniques and BIM processes allows architects to incorporate as many aspects into the design process as can be quantified or simulated.

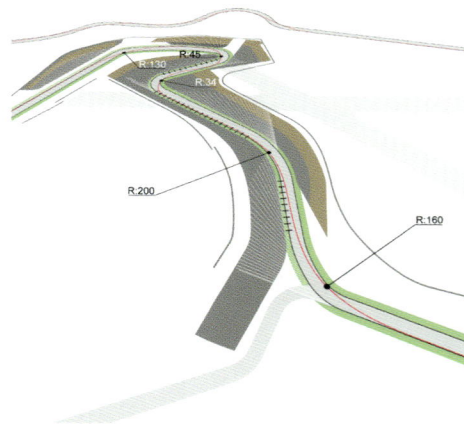

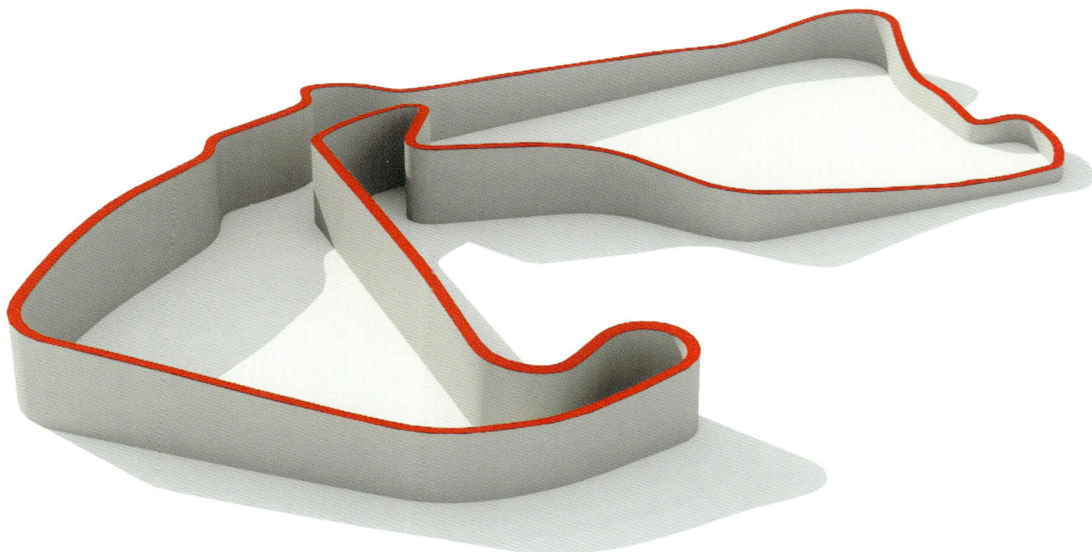

Still from the 2012 London Grand Prix video by Santander
top: Populous worked closely with Santander's Formula 1 drivers to design and simulate the possibilities of a London Grand Prix street circuit.

Populous Architects, Silverstone Circuit, Silverstone, Northamptonshire, 2011
centre and above: Typology and circuit design. The interoperability of trajectory, speed and racetrack profile allows the designer to define safe and dynamic race circuits.

For the commission to design a new pit lane building and redesign a portion of the Silverstone Formula 1 track (2011), the architects returned to the core of what parametric design can offer. The challenge here was to design a track, associated safety barriers and safe spectator positions while also optimising the driving experience and spectator viewing. Populous's solution was the combination of a parametrically driven track and safety-barrier design tool, a computer-game simulation to define an optimum racing line/speed, and a simulator machine to market test-track options with professional drivers, which resulted in a dynamic spectator/driver experience. Together, the driver, simulator and track design input created a more desirable circuit for drivers as well as entertaining and competitive racing for spectators.

Building on previous work in spectator experience, the parametric workflow for Silverstone was expanded to include time and trajectory.[3] This process has also been further adapted in the design of other race circuits including a proposal for the design of a Formula 1 night circuit through the streets of London (2012) that included input from Santander's drivers Jenson Button and Lewis Hamilton. Using specially developed parametric tools, the existing road conditions could be modelled and analysed in order to deploy the required safety barriers and spectator positions, as well as simulating the track experience for the drivers to test in a simulation machine environment. The development of these computational tools and methods has enabled the design of a racing environment to be fully tested and further enhanced prior to implementation.

Experience has shown that the use of BIM as a process for delivering coordinated construction information works. But while it is both necessary and useful that standard BIM elements and libraries are becoming readily available, Populous's goal is to support the evolution and professional abilities of sportsmen and sportswomen and enhance spectator experience. The use of parametric techniques and BIM processes allows architects to incorporate as many aspects into the design process as can be quantified or simulated. However, while the speed and abilities of the designer have been accelerated, there is also a need for new expertise and for the maintenance and coordination of complex 3-D construction information that allows the architect to maintain a central role throughout the whole design and building process. ⌀

Notes
1. Roly Hudson, Paul Shepherd, David Hines, "Aviva Stadium: A Case Study in Integrated Parametric Design', *International Journal of Architectural Computing*, Vol 9, No 2, 2011, pp 187–203.
2. Roly Hudson, Paul Shepherd and David Hines, 'Aviva Stadium: A Parametric Success', *International Journal of Architectural Computing*, Vol 9, No 2, 2011, pp 167–85.
3. Roly Hudson, Drew MacDonald and Mark Humphreys, 'Race Track Modeller: Developing an Iterative Design Workflow Combining a Game Engine and Parametric Design', *Parametricism (SPC) ACADIA Regional 2011 Conference Proceedings*, 2011.

Populous Architects, Aviva Stadium, Dublin, Ireland, 2010
The interior view of the Aviva Stadium visually ties together the seating bowl, steelwork and roof surface as one.

FROM M
THINK
TO   PR
DE

soma Architecture and Knippers Helbig
Advanced Engineering, Thematic
Pavilion, Yeosu World Expo, Yeosu,
South Korea, 2012
During the day, the louvres are used to
control light conditions within the building.
After sunset, the analogue visual effect of
the moving lamellas is intensified by LEDs.

MODELLING

PROCESSING

DESIGN

The introduction of computational design processes and particularly of computer-aided fabrication methods recast roles across the design team. As **Jan Knippers**, founding partner of Knippers Helbig Advanced Engineering and Head of the Institute of Building Structures and Structural Design (ITKE) at the University of Stuttgart explains, it offers structural engineers a unique opportunity: the potential to break through the barriers of conventional model thinking (thinking in discrete typologies) and to embrace process design and new forms of interaction.

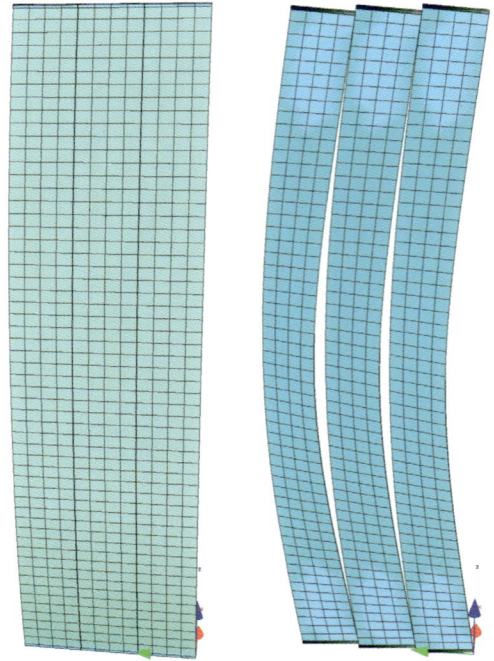

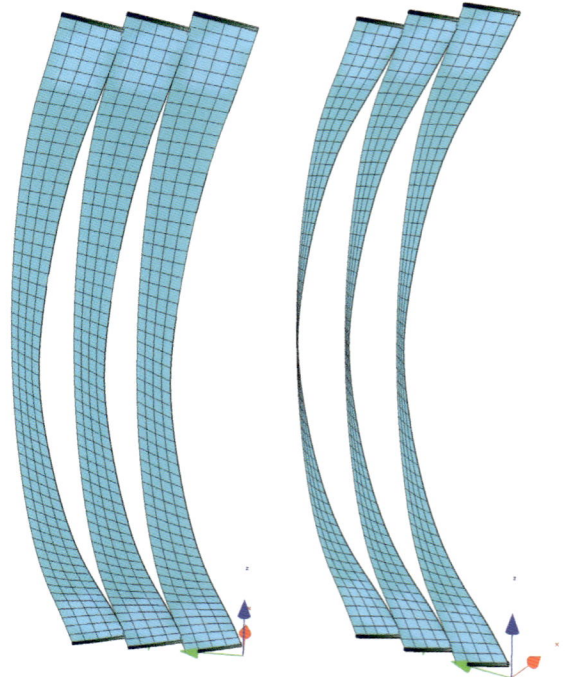

Hand lay-up process of the glass-fibre reinforced polymer louvres.

Finite element (FE) simulation of the large elastic and reversible deformations of the anisotropic glass-fibre reinforced polymer louvres.

The introduction of automated fabrication technologies requires a new interpretation of the entire design process. The introduction of computer-aided fabrication methods means more than just the use of new tools: it is the breakup of traditional role models that bears the potential for innovation. The implementation of digital design strategies in practice requires the development of specific tools for meshing, geometry development and for data exchange between different parties. Off-the-shelf programs are not available or not satisfactory, thus specific solutions adapted to meet the project's specific requirements are necessary.

While architecture explores the specific conditions of location and function, and searches for a unique identity and aesthetic expression for each building, engineering is different. Calculability, predictability and controllability are necessary to achieve structural integrity. Mechanical theories and construction principles are constantly evaluated and approved. Development in this field is therefore slow and leads inevitably to a set of well-defined structural typologies that are used repeatedly in building construction practice. Engineers are trained in 'model thinking', in knowing all these typologies and then choosing and applying the most appropriate one for a given design task.

Structural analysis was introduced in building construction during the second half of the 19th century, and since then all structures were based on the paradigm of calculability. An example of this is the development of the typology of the hinged arch. These systems were not more efficient than older arch structures such as the cable-stiffened arch of Victoria Station in London from 1862, but enabled an exact and reliable calculation of internal forces. At the end of the century, the typology of a three-hinged arch was used for nearly all large exhibition halls or railway stations such as the Galerie des Machines, Paris (1889). Even though the limitations of calculability no longer existed, these typologies, encouraged by model thinking, ruled the design of structural systems for many decades; for example, the three-hinged arch of Waterloo Station, London (1990). Each model is based on a set of well-defined rules for the development of its geometry and the calculation of internal forces. It has its own boundary conditions and limitations that allow for solutions only within a specific framework.

The introduction of computational design offers the potential to break through these barriers of model thinking (thinking in discrete typologies) in structural engineering. The article here looks at three areas that highlight the impact of computational design strategies on the development of load-bearing systems.

GENERATING FORM THROUGH COMPUTING STRUCTURAL PERFORMANCE

Firstly, computational design provides a technical means to develop new structural forms. This has been a focal point for nearly 20 years, addressed by all major architecture schools and many large design firms around the world. However, architects usually focus on the design of complex geometries and not on the performance of structures. 3-D modelling allows for innovation not only in architecture. Progress in the field of computational mechanics and simulation technologies also offer new opportunities, though are seldom recognised.

The facade for soma Architecture's Thematic Pavilion at the Yeosu World Expo in South Korea (2012) is a particularly successful example of this. The project has 114 louvres of up to 14 metres (45 feet) in length made of glass-fibre reinforced polymers with a maximum thickness of 8 millimetres (0.3 inches). The stiffness of the louvres is locally adjusted by the concentration and orientation of the glass fibres. A compression force is applied to the top and bottom that results in an elastic deformation. In engineering, this type of large nonlinear deformation is usually considered as a buckling failure and therefore avoided, but here this function is utilised for opening and closing the louvres. The Yeosu facade is a completely new interpretation of deployable structures, even though the geometry is simple and the manufacturing processes has been well known for many years. All lamellas are laminated with common glass-fibres and thermoset resins in a simple hand lay-up process on one identical mould with one constant radius.

It is the change of perspective, the allowance of a controlled buckling and of large elastic deformations that are in complete contradiction to any traditional engineering design goals that leads to this new kinetic system far beyond existing typologies. In this specific case, technical prerequisites are not 3-D modelling software or digital fabrication, but advanced computational mechanics that enable the simulation of anisotropic material and therefore the differentiation of its elastic properties.

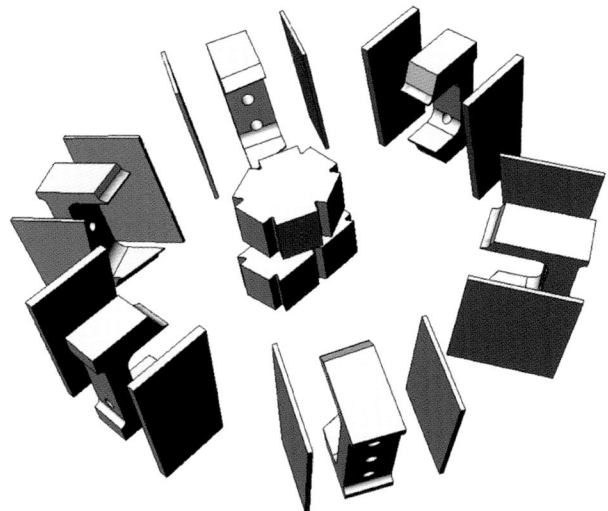

Benoy and Knippers Helbig Advanced Engineering, Westfield London shopping centre, White City, London, 2008
Exploded view of nodal connector. Each of the 3,000 connectors consists of 20 different steel plates.

THE INFLUENCE OF DIGITAL MANUFACTURING

Secondly, computational manufacturing provides a new approach to the construction of structures. Particularly impressive in the early 1990s was the ingenious creativity of Jörg Schlaich and Hans Schober of Schlaich Bergermann & Partner in the development of a new system for single-layer lattice shells. Their goal was to form a triangular grid by using as few different elements as possible. This led to the specific arrangement of steel members, diagonal cables and bolted connectors that gave this type of structure its specific appearance, emphasising the beautiful, elegant and intelligent detail of the nodal connector.

Today, such considerations are of less relevance. Structures such as the roof for Benoy's Westfield London shopping centre (2008) are made of thousands of plates of different geometry and different thicknesses, each one exactly adjusted to the specific loading at the specific point of the structure. This leads to a very different appearance of the lattice shell, characterised not by any visible details, but by the high precision made possible by computational design and manufacturing. The intelligence and creativity of engineering does not go into the construction of the detail or rationalisation of geometry, but into the parametric generation and control of data.

Practice has shown us that even for quite simple tasks such as the mesh generation of a single-layer lattice shell, off-the-shelf computational solutions are useful only to a very limited extent. New computational solutions need to be developed and adjusted to meet the requirements of the specific project.

For Westfield London, a planar grid was mapped on the 3-D surface. However, for SBA International's Expo Axis at Shanghai World Expo (2010), a more complex strategy was necessary. Here, the concept of grid generation followed the strategies of Richard Buckminster Fuller. Larger mega-triangles were mapped in a more or less manual process on the 3-D surface of the glass cones. These were subdivided into smaller triangles of identical geometry with vertices connecting six members. Special vertices connecting five to seven members were assembled at the corners of these mega-triangles as they are unavoidable for non-developable surfaces. Buckminster Fuller used this approach in the 1950s to generate his famous geodesic domes based on the dodecahedron or icosahedron to achieve spatial structures with as many identical members and vertices as possible. In Shanghai, this concept served as the starting point for computational optimisation. A tool based on dynamic relaxation was developed to even the member length and the vertex angles. Force density was increased in the areas where very high loading of the membrane force is applied and results in a higher density of the grid. This approach led to a smooth and stable grid, adapted to the loading of the structure.

The line model of the grid served as a basis for the entire process and was developed and controlled by the structural engineers. This makes sense, as the structural engineers get involved at the interface between the development of form by the architect and manufacture by the contractor, even though many engineers are not at all prepared for this task.

The challenge for engineering is not the construction of the detail or the rationalisation of geometry, but the development of the meshing tools and the precise transfer and control of data. An interaction between global shape and meshing has to exist first to achieve a smooth grid before analysis and manufacture can begin. The structural analysis results are then forwarded to the contractor, who usually proposes a concept for nodal connectors based on his or her manufacturing capabilities and then provides the shop drawings. The latter are transferred back for a detailed structural check of nodal plates and bolts and, after their final adjustment, the actual process of manufacture and installation can begin. This intertwined interaction between global form, generation of mesh, structural analysis and fabrication has little or nothing in common with the classical linear sequence of design: form by the architect, structure by the engineer and, finally, fabrication and installation by the contractor.

The shopping centre roof consists of two parts and has a total surface of 18,000 square metres (193,750 square feet). The bolted connectors do not allow for any adjustment of the geometry during assembly.

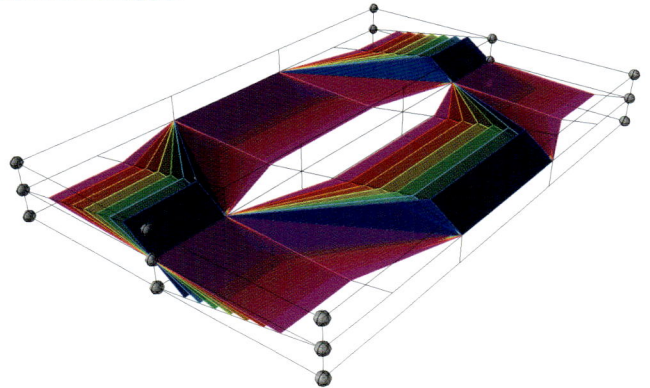

The challenge for engineering is not the
construction of the detail or the rationalisation
of geometry, but the development of the
meshing tools and the precise transfer and
control of data.

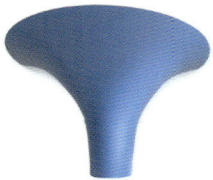

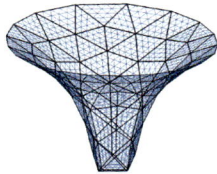

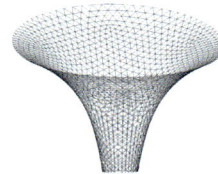

SBA International, Expo Axis, Shanghai World Expo,
Shanghai, China, 2010
above: Meshing process for lattice shells. The six glass cones have
a height of 45 metres (148 feet), and direct natural light to the lower
levels of the building. Their diameter at the foot is approximately 16
metres (52 feet), and 80 metres (262 feet) at the upper edge.

left: The 1,000-metre (3,280-foot) long Expo Boulevard is covered
by a PTFE-glass membrane with a total surface of 65,000 square
metres (699,654 square feet) and a free span of almost 100 metres
(328 feet). The roof is carried by masts and six cone-shaped lattice
shells.

It requires a new interpretation of the entire process and the involvement of the different players and the communication between them.

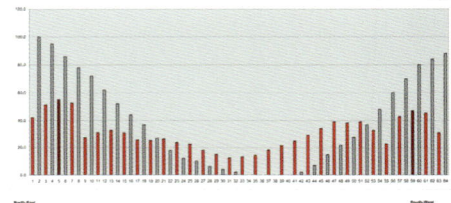

COMPUTATIONAL DESIGN AND THE DESIGN OF PROCESS

The third point is that the use of computational design linked to computationally driven manufacturing breaks down traditional linear and hierarchical design strategies. Though this often goes unrecognised, it is as important for innovation in architecture as the introduction of new computational tools. It requires a new interpretation of the entire process and the involvement of the different players and the communication between them. With computational design and manufacture, who is doing what and how the data is transferred is not defined at the beginning and has to be discussed and agreed upon each time. There are several models currently in practice: larger design offices set up their own groups to handle free-form geometries, and specialised geometry experts with little connection to the actual process of design and construction are involved. The allocation of responsibilities depends not only on the specific task of the project or the competences of the involved players, but also on the contractual situations or tender processes, which differ in various parts of the world. It is this breakup of traditional design strategies that has significant potential for innovation.

The new Terminal 3 for Bao'an International Airport in Shenzhen (2012) offered the opportunity to extend and redefine the role of structural engineers. The concept, by Massimiliano Fuksas, showed a space structure covered on both sides by a perforated cladding in the form of a stretched metal sheet consisting of 60,000 different facade elements and 400,000 individual steel members. While the structural system is quite simple, the geometry of the cladding is very complex. A stretched metal sheet can easily be mapped on a developable surface, but for a double-curved shape additional modifications are necessary regarding the evenness of the glass panes as a restricting boundary condition.

The size and slope of the glass openings are the two design parameters that were adapted to meet the local requirements of daylight, solar gain, viewing from the inside towards the airfield, as well as the aesthetic intentions of the architect. A parametric data model was set up, organised in four layers: two for the neutral axis of the double-layered grid structure, and one each for the inner and outer facade. The parametric model was generated using relatively simple computational tools, mainly in Robert McNeel & Associates' Rhinoceros® and Microsoft's

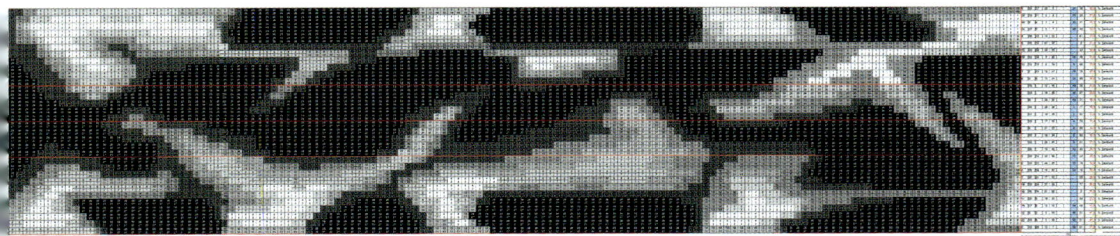

Excel. This allowed for a simple communication on global form and on the parameters of tessellation between architect and engineer that did not require any knowledge of highly specialised software. Global form and tessellation were adjusted constantly during the entire design process. After generating and evaluating approximately 50 different models for the terminal roof, a very simple linear sequence of panels was chosen as can now be seen on the completed building. In this project, the main challenge for engineering was the generation of the parametric data model, which allowed a new form of communication and collaboration between architects and engineers to develop.

Computational design and manufacture offer the means to design new structures beyond existing typologies. However, the potential of these technologies is not perceived by the architecture and construction industry today. It can be seen from the examples illustrated here that today nearly all free-formed load-bearing structures are lattice systems covered by a cladding of glass or metal, because only these systems can be adapted to meet complex geometries at reasonable construction cost. A next step could be the integration of various functions such as load transfer or thermal insulation in performance-oriented multifunctional systems. This requires new tools for design and manufacture, but more than that, new forms of interaction between the various designers, architects and engineers involved, made possible through computational design and manufacture strategies. ⌁

Massimiliano Fuksas and Knippers Helbig Advanced Engineering, Bao'an International Airport Terminal 3, Shenzhen, China, 2012
top: Panoramic view of the steel construction in March 2012.

centre: Excel sheet for allocation of the various panel types.

Text © 2013 John Wiley & Sons Ltd. Images: pp 74-5, 76(r) © soma Architecture; pp 76(l), 77, 78, 79(t,ct&b), 80, 81 © Knippers Helbig Advanced Engineering; p 79(cb) © Milos Dimcic

UNStudio, Knowledge Platforms interchange diagram, 2012
The organisation of the UNStudio Knowledge Platforms emphasises
the interchange between the platforms themselves and with building
and research projects.

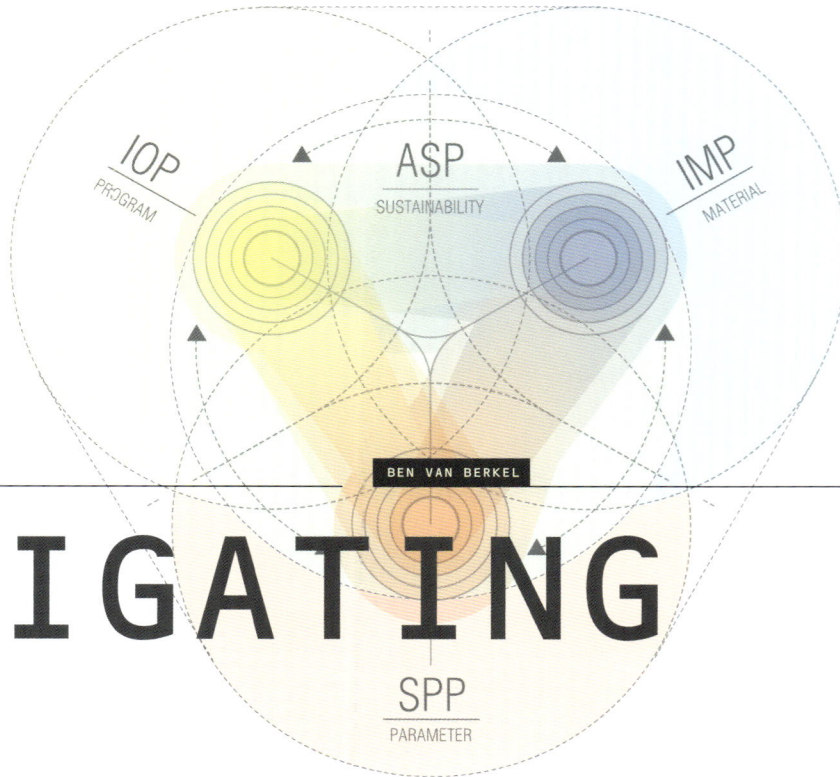

BEN VAN BERKEL

NAVIGATING THE COMPUTATIONAL TURN

UNStudio has developed its own practice model for connecting colleagues and collaborators and sharing accumulated knowledge and techniques: the 'Knowledge Platform'. **Ben van Berkel** with members from the UNStudio Smart Parameter Platform describe three projects at very different scales – the Burnham Pavilion in Chicago (2009), Raffles City in Hangzhou, China (2011) and Arnhem Central (2012) – that encapsulate UNStudio's working methods and approach to computational processes.

UNStudio, The Rubber Mat, Rotterdam, The Netherlands, 1997
bottom: Incorporating property value, rent, density, business growth and
green space growth, the Rubber Mat was a model of change instead
of an urban plan. Within the four mats (dwelling, work, fun and green
space) one can find the areas suitable for building and moving in time.

UNStudio, Diagrams, programmatic activity pattern and midtown cross-section,
IFCCA (Design of Cities) competition entry, Manhattan, New York, 1999
top: The concept of the parametric is deeply rooted in UNStudio's work and thought.
The early use of diagrams organised complex relations (time, flow, structure,
economics) between the various programmes of a project.

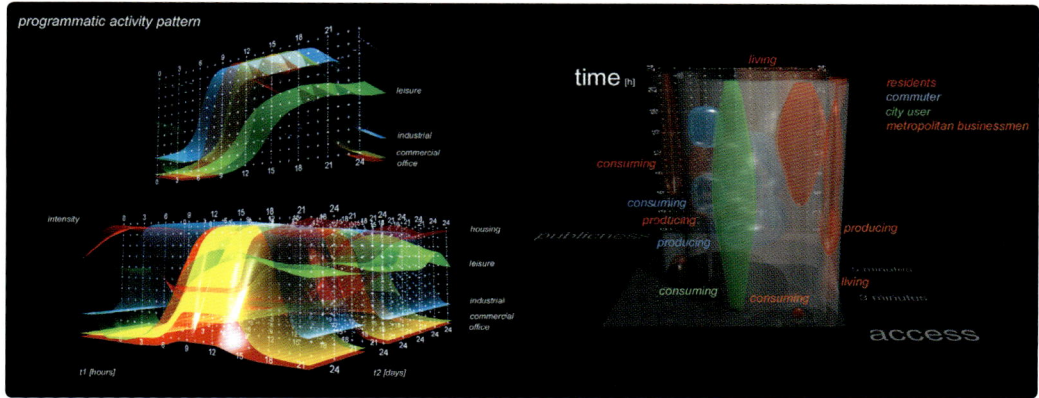

As a united network of multidisciplinary producers and actors, UNStudio has had computational thinking at the heart of its practice since its inception. Early uses of algorithms and diagrams, such as the Rubber Mat or the 'deep planning principle', organised and instrumentalised abstract geometries and concepts to assimilate the complexity of contemporary architecture. Before the ubiquity of computation in architectural design and construction, these uses of both geometric and non-geometric data presaged the multi-platform way the practice works today. The underlying thinking of this design process is now enabled by advancements in software, as the parametric thought process has evolved into a computational work process.

Along the way, the accumulation of techniques and strategies of design models, computation and other non-standard domains has compelled the practice to organise and share knowledge as a network connecting colleagues and project teams. This cataloguing of techniques, materials and principles bridging UNStudio's daily practice and its commitment to ongoing exploration and research, has evolved into 'Knowledge Platforms'.[1]

Similar to the role of a design model in the process from concept to building, the key function of the Knowledge Platforms is to act as a dynamic hinge between practice and research. This interactive and nonlinear nature of the platform–project relationship allows the effective cross-fertilisation of research innovations with new design approaches. Acting as laboratories for UNStudio's accumulated knowledge, the platforms evaluate new concepts, techniques and methods in individual phases and inevitably develop them over the lifetime of a project. The Smart Parameters Platform (SPP) is pivotal in its interactive role with the other platforms and with active projects. Through computation in its most specific and broadest senses (tools, software, thinking, design models), the SPP leads the initiative to bring together the various parameters that define a project.

In addition to formal and geometric parameters, the Knowledge Platforms operate on a number of non-geometric parameters: social, economic, political and material, among others. Due to the inability of computational tools to individually translate or quantify these parameters, it is essential to understand how this external information is brought into the design process through various platforms and at multiple levels of intensity and specificity. Because of this, computational investigation introduces a new level of responsibility for the architect; one that requires a discerning approach to the design process, during which computation does not replace inspiration or an idea, nor the operation of a design model.[2] As it spans the design process, providing control of increasingly actual parameters, computation moreover fosters an augmentation that a design model is not able to achieve.

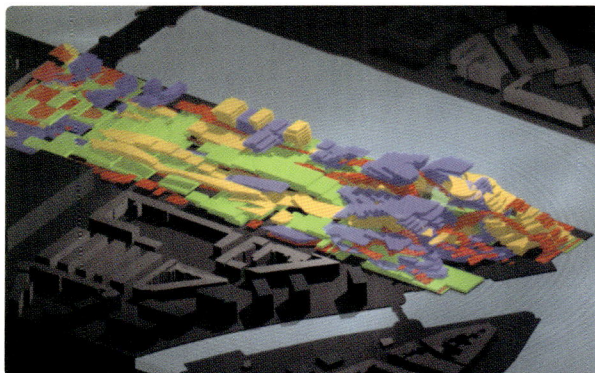

UNStudio, Structural Diagram, Burnham Pavilion, Millennium Park, Chicago, Illinois, 2009
top: The temporary pavilion is composed of three identical openings that support an otherwise straightforward horizontal structure and surface.

bottom: The Burnham Pavilion reframes Chicago's skyline through a reorientation of the diagonal vistas of Daniel Burnham's 1909 Plan of Chicago into the vertical.

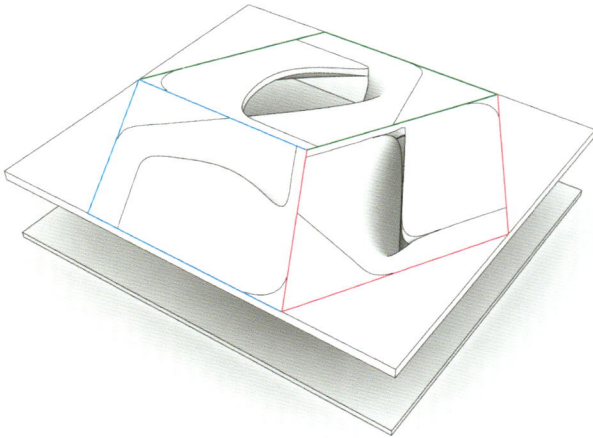

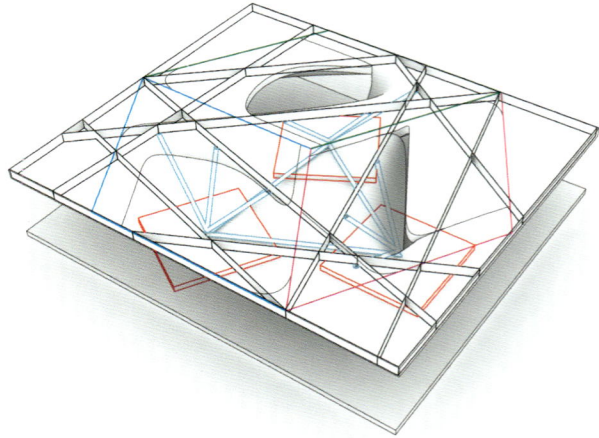

INTUITION AND COMPUTATION

Small projects, such as the Burnham Pavilion in Chicago (2009), are key testing grounds for computational strategies. The pavilion is composed of a horizontal surface with openings that indulge the desire for a formal and visual relation to downtown Chicago. It is influenced by two economic and material constraints: a structural system that is required to be essentially post and beam, and the repetition of the form of the openings in the surfaces. Grasshopper® visual programming is used to instrumentalise these parameters intuitively within the site's specificity. The solution is to create the holes within simple, parallelogram frames connecting directly to the main structure that can be duplicated and rotated to direct vistas diagonally upwards. The resulting design augments the experience of the city through the mutual exchange of Daniel Burnham's 1909 Plan of Chicago and the meta-data in the horizontal surface.

UNStudio, Raffles City, Hangzhou, China, 2011
below: Facade screenshot. A fully integrated Digital Project facade model was created for the Raffles City project. The process for this project is a leading example of UNStudio's multi-platform workflows.

right: Facade mock-up. Even after rigorous computational design and testing, understanding the relationships and meaning of form and material at the scale of the building remains essential.

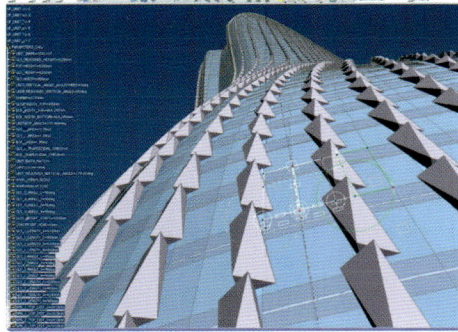

The 400,000-square-metre (4.3-million-square-foot) Raffles City mixed-use development in Hangzhou, China (2011) demanded an integrated design solution that incorporates programmatic complexity, scale, sustainability goals, social and economic constraints, and fabrication methods in Asia. Consequently, the roles of parametric systems and tools must be equally malleable and diverse. By customising and merging the functions of tools such as Robert McNeel & Associates' Grasshopper® and RhinoScript, and Gehry Technologies' Digital Project, this complex interweaving has not only allowed the design model to remain the driver of the project, but has also led to the processing and assimilation of a greater amount of parameters to achieve a simpler, more efficient design solution.

Such integrated, nonlinear workflows have generated both the building's driving envelopes and arrangement of component families that define the facade's six disparate, evolving systems. For each of these systems, which follow the project's twisting geometry and embed environmental and economic constraints, Grasshopper and/or RhinoScript serve as both form generators and envelope optimisers, incorporating floor areas and heights to create driver geometry and systemised data sheets. Together, the geometry and data sheets act as the skeletal system of the building information model (BIM). Component-driven curtain-wall panel optimisation occurs within Digital Project, which analyses sustainability, fabrication and installation parameters (vertical tilt, horizontal angling, and glass panel geometry and type efficiency) to self-optimise during automated instantiation, thus simplifying fabrication demands and cost.

As design processes are constantly looping, algorithms of optimisation and design intersect as frequently as software platforms, with demands continuously outpacing tools, requiring constant redevelopment and consolidation of the capabilities of existing parametric systems to perform to even higher expectations. The result is an embedded series of streamlined parametric tools integrating increasingly numerous parameters into a focused, synthesised design end-product.

MULTIUSE AND FLEXIBILITY

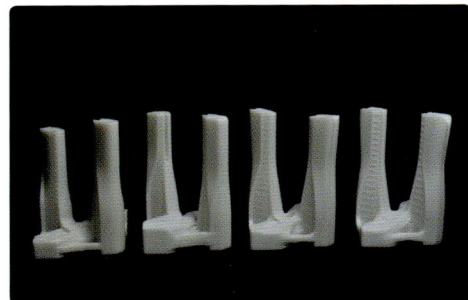

Massing study models were an indispensable tool for the design of this large-scale mixed-use project. These models were 3-D printed throughout the iterative process of optimising the exterior geometry of the project while considering different ways of allocating programme within. During this process, critical rotation and tilt angles of sample facade areas were tested to anticipate further envelope development and to ensure both the continuity of the overall form and a high degree of modular repetition.

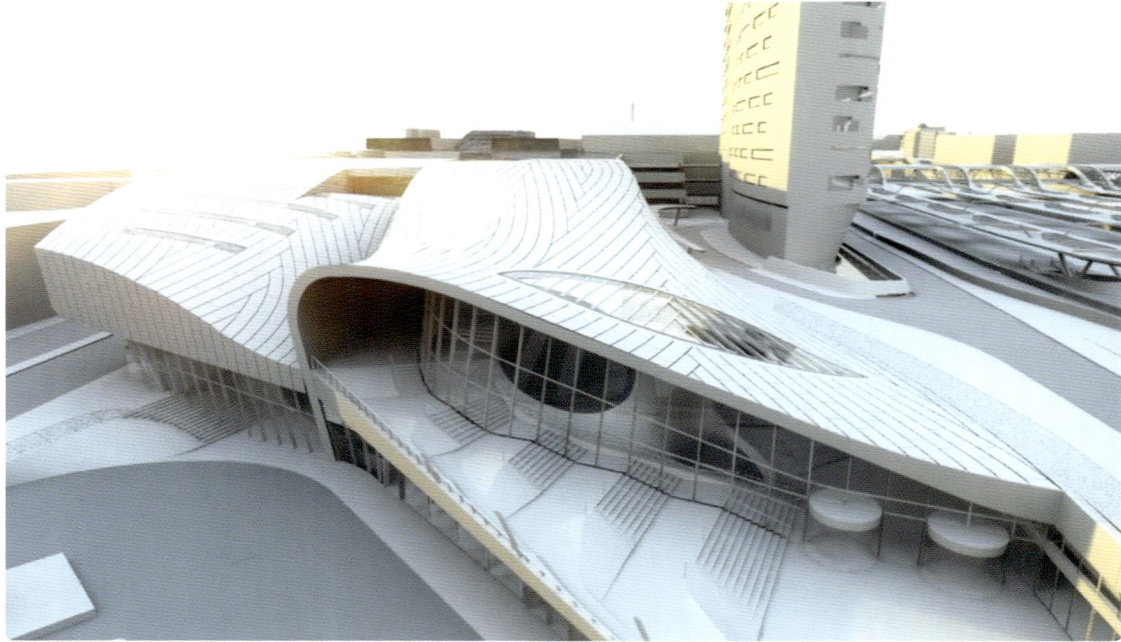

UNStudio, Arnhem Central station, Arnhem, The Netherlands, 1996–2014
The project has been a driver of innovation since its beginning more than 10 years ago. Many of UNStudio's working methods were used here first, and new techniques are still being developed today.

FULL SPECTRUM

It is clear now that computation is ubiquitous, and form-making and form-controlling are no longer its most expedient uses. Whether it is through proprietary and customised software or a single piece of code, computation's primary potential lies in its flexibility to communicate design across multiple disciplines via associative data.

The Arnhem Central station and masterplan project (1996–2014) has spanned more than a decade, and therefore encompasses many of UNStudio's working methods. It was the genesis of early concepts such as the V-model and the Deep Planning Principle, and continues to drive innovation in the practice. One of the key innovative systems is the roof panelling, where the complexity of the woven pattern represents a balance of structural, material and economic parameters.

The tool for this – based on the Visual Basic .NET (VB. NET) programming language within Rhinoceros© – focuses on the relationship of the panels to develop a pattern that is informed by fabrication constraints (maximum mould size, anchor locations and geometric efficiencies) and the result of a dialogue between these parameters and desired effects. To achieve this, a bottom-up approach, more closely related to the panel itself, is favoured over a top-down approach that would work down a list of functions or subroutines. Programmed objects acting as abstractions of the panels contain methods that autonomously create boundaries, check for geometric optimisation (ruled, cylindrical, flat), create anchor points, annotate and extract data. Instead of an exhaustive list of individual tasks, this system allows for disparate objects to actively inform each other's properties, creating the data necessary to build the panels. This panel geometry is then augmented with this metadata making it usable during the fabrication process directly from the 3-D model. This splitting of data and the methods creating it has proved successful and has therefore been developed into a general working method used in computation that we called SoftBIM.[3]

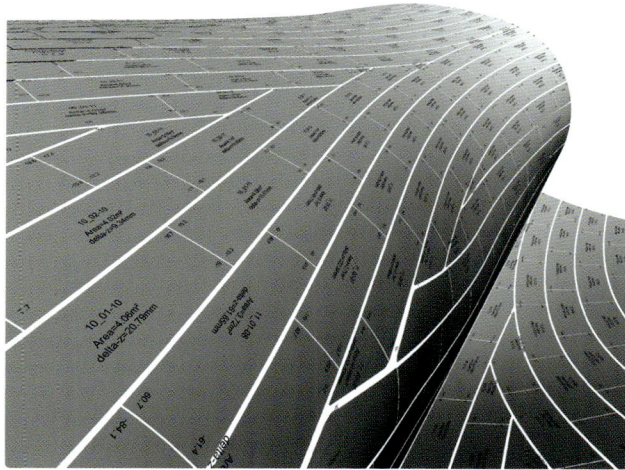

One-to-one mock-ups of the roof panelling of the Arnhem Central transfer hall. Derived from a computational process that generates all the panel boundaries while optimising the form for buildability, the glass-fibre reinforced concrete panels are tested for various moulding techniques.

PROJECTION

As a generation of UNStudio's computationally designed and coordinated projects are completing construction, the arc of the practice's developmental trajectory is being revealed, from the instrumentalisation of intuitive devices to the production space and dissemination of information through computation in the contemporary inventive economy.[4] It is clear now that computation is ubiquitous, and form-making and form-controlling are no longer its most expedient uses. Whether it is through proprietary and customised software or a single piece of code, computation's primary potential lies in its flexibility to communicate design across multiple disciplines via associative data. It is a uniquely demonstrative tool when manoeuvring actors and making specific knowledge available where it is desired. In this case, the continuous interchange of UNStudio's Knowledge Platforms is invaluable where computation speaks most clearly, celebrating the collaborative and augmentative. The innovative instrumentalisation and reciprocation of geometric and non-geometric metadata is the location of meaning in contemporary architecture. ⌀

Text by Ben van Berkel and the Smart Parameter Platform 2012: Rob Henderson, Marc Hoppermann, Garett Hwang, Filippo Lodi with input from Nuno Almeida, Arjan Dingste, Hannes Pfau, Astrid Piber, Christian Veddeler and the project teams of Burnham Pavilion, Arnhem Transfer Hall and Raffles City Hangzhou.

Notes
1. See www.unstudio.com/research.
2. UNStudio (Ben van Berkel and Caroline Bos), *Design Models*, Thames & Hudson (London), 2006.
3. Gustav Fagerström, Marc Hoppermann, Nuno Almeida, Martin Zangerl, Stefano Rocchetti and Ben Van Berkel (UNStudio), 'softBIM: An Open Ended Building Information Model in Design Practice', in Mark Cabrinha, Jason Kelly Johnson and Kyle Steinfeld (eds), *Synthetic Digital Ecologies: Proceedings of the 32nd Annual Conference of the Association for Computer Aided Design in Architecture (ACADIA)*, San Francisco, 2012, pp 37–46.
4. Ben van Berkel, 'Designing for the Inventive Economy', *SPACE*, No 532, 2012.

DOMESTICATING PARAMETRIC DESIGN

BRUCE BELL AND SARAH SIMPKIN

Small-scale domestic design has largely escaped the attention of the proponents of parametric design. **Bruce Bell** of Facit Homes and writer **Sarah Simpkin** describe how, with the aid of digital production methods, Facit is rethinking the sustainable house as a bespoke product produced by a single design–manufacturing team.

Facit Homes, House for Celia and Diana, Hertfordshire, 2011
The BIM model harnesses all of the information needed to build the house, breaking the entire building down into a series of small-scale individual components that can be simply joined together.

Facit's innovative construction system makes the translation of information from the BIM model into a 'chassis' a seamless process, as the digital image corresponds exactly to the building in every detail – even down to the exact placement of sockets and ducts.

Exploiting the algorithmic power of computers has been standard practice in manufacturing for more than 15 years, helping to make everything from small plastic toys to aircraft. In architecture, the possibilities of computer-aided design (CAD) have inspired the complex geometry of free-flowing glass canopies and ever more elaborate forms. But the home has rarely been seen as a set of components in the same way as a product or a complex megastructure. Design company Facit Homes is unusual in that it applies parametric and digital production methods to the creation of sustainable, 21st- century houses, an everyday challenge often overlooked by exponents of these technologies.

In its focus on strategies for assembly, Facit adopts a similar approach to the manufacturing industry. Instead of the traditional model of the architect and consultant team, the design, engineering, research and development, prototyping, production and assembly processes are all undertaken by a single entity. In this way, the house is conceived as a product and the client benefits from the simplicity of a single point of contact.

D–PROCESS

The idea that one day high-quality houses will be mass-produced like cars in a factory is still largely fantasy. This is due to high overheads, the logistics of transporting building-sized components, and the unwelcome degree of standardisation that industrial-scale production brings. But unlike existing prefabricated housing models, Facit's system enables every project to be entirely bespoke, and its highly insulated, precision-cut timber components do not need to be built in a factory.

Describing its methodology, the Facit team draws on the language of the automotive industry, with the house as a 'chassis' and the finishes selected by the end user, retaining a more traditional client/architect relationship. Every design is driven by the constraints of the site, brief, environmental conditions and local planning requirements, rather than based on standard 'typologies' or customisable templates. Parametric design – as part of a working methodology that Facit calls the 'D-Process' – is one of the tools that have made this tailored approach possible.

In recent years there has been increasingly widespread adoption of building information modelling (BIM) for large architectural projects. In parallel to this, Facit has developed proprietary systems that link BIM to small-scale digital manufacturing tools. At detailed design – the equivalent of RIBA Work Stage E – the team produces a 3-D computer model that harnesses information for every aspect of the building, from the angle of the walls and quantities of materials, to the position of every plug socket. The 3-D digital elements are then translated directly into physical components, an efficient system that cuts waste and provides an exemplar of lean manufacturing.

In recent years there has been increasingly widespread adoption of building information modelling (BIM) for large architectural projects. In parallel to this, Facit has developed proprietary systems that link BIM to small–scale digital manufacturing tools.

Rather than assessing the relative merits of on-site and off-site production, Facit is now exploring the benefits of digitally manufactured components over traditional hand-built housing. To bypass the complex logistics, expense and standardisation of factory mass production, the company deploys on-site mobile production facilities. These compact units contain all the equipment needed to manufacture the components for each house, eliminating the need to transport large-scale prefabricated structures – and the associated carbon emissions. The direct relationship between designing and making cuts lead times and overheads, placing Facit within the reach of individual self-builders. The company also appeals to developers, as its method is scalable for multiple houses through the deployment of more than one mobile facility.

HERTFORDSHIRE HOUSE

One of the company's largest projects to date is a five-bedroom family home on a rural site in Hertfordshire, which was completed in November 2011. The process began in the same way as any other bespoke house. The design evolved through discussions with the client and site visits, and sketches were then produced, refined and worked into the eventual plan for the building. Prototypes were created and tested in the studio and detail design agreed. Assembly had been a consideration from the outset, so at the point of producing construction drawings, Facit generated machine code for the production of the components; in this way, there is no interpretation by the contractor, but a direct relationship between the design information and construction components. The brief placed a high priority on achieving advanced environmental performance, to 2016 targets; Facit's building components are highly insulated timber units and the company works closely with the sustainable timber industry to ensure that the raw materials are responsibly sourced.

The Facit system combines on- and off-site production: while the chassis of the house was constructed on site, sculptural elements such as the digitally fabricated stair and balustrade were finished to the highest quality in the Facit workshop in London.

While the forms created by this domestication of parametric design might seem deceptively, deliberately simple, the complexity lies in the details and in making the process work. More time was spent developing the company structure and workflow to successfully deliver projects than on the basic technology.

The timber chassis, which includes the roof, internal and external walls, was fabricated and erected in just eight weeks. The second construction phase used local labour for plastering, finishes and electrical work, which was a straightforward process as the channels for the wiring were already in place. The final stage in the build was the digital production of smaller furniture elements and stairs in the Facit workshop, where they were pre-finished and later installed on site. Remarkably, the total build time for the Hertfordshire house, from breaking ground to moving in, was just seven months.

While the forms created by this domestication of parametric design might seem deceptively, deliberately simple, the complexity lies in the details and in making the process work. More time was spent developing the company structure and workflow to successfully deliver projects than on the basic technology. Facit's projects show how BIM and digital tools can be applied to meet challenging environmental targets with high-quality, bespoke homes. But perhaps the most exciting aspect is the new business model and new way of working that the technology is starting to define. ᴆ

PLANN
PARAM

With increasing pressure on available land for development, planning parameters continue to intensify. Since the early 1990s, such constraints on urban sites have provided a significant focus for MRVDV's design and research. The practice has worked on the creation of interactive software that enables designers to interact with the limits and opportunities highlighted by the visualisation and evaluation of these parameters. **Jeroen Zuidgeest and Sanne van der Burgh** of MVRDV and **Bas Kalmeyer** of think tank The Why Factory describe how parametric models are now being applied, leading the way to a whole new generation of open-source planning tools.

How can we respond to today's most pressing spatial challenges, those driven by socioeconomic factors and massive worldwide urbanisation, where everyone, everywhere, demands more resources and more space? By filling parcels of land with established solutions, those limited by economic, technical and zoning constraints, the development of answers to these spatial challenges is neglected, and critical social and ecological issues are ignored. How can we contribute to the rich, but increasingly complex, situation of the contemporary city? And how can we maintain an overview of possible design solutions in the face of this ever-increasing complexity?

Every project, whether a strategy for regional development, a masterplan or a building, is facing constraints and opportunities ranging from contextual influence to regulatory statutes, environmental conditions to circulation requirements. As design parameters, these constraints and opportunities give depth and identity to the proposal. Parametric design allows us to gain insight into the influences, limitations and possibilities of these parameters, providing a way to deal with the complexity that influences our built environment today.

MVRDV, Bastide Niel, Bordeaux, 2010
left: Gereration of plot volumes by extrusion.

right: Reduction of volumes in order to respect a 45-degree daylight angle from adjacent blocks.

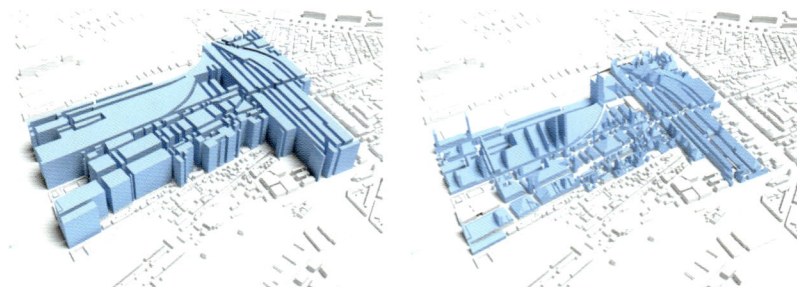

ING BY
ETERS

DESIGN BY RESEARCH, IMPROVEMENT BY UNDERSTANDING

MVRDV has been developing its research-driven methodology following data-based parametric studies since the early 1990s. This analytic approach was deepened by the development of several design tools and interactive software packages, for example the Functionmixer, the Regionmaker, the Climatizer and, more recently, the Villagemaker and The (Green) City Calculator still under development by The Why Factory and MVRDV, with the Netherlands Organisation for Applied Scientific Research (TNO) and engineers Arup, DGMR and others.

These self-built computer programs are tools for development and visualisation, evaluation and comparison, testing and optimisation. All aim to avoid static analytical models and enable the designer to interact with the constraints and opportunities exposed through the design parameters. They enable discussion of otherwise abstract and subjective issues on neutral and authorless ground, and are constructed on the basis of objective argumentation, bridging the gap with other disciplines and the wider public. The development of these computational tools has strongly influenced MVRDV's design process and vice versa; technological evolution allows for this development, while the need for insight forms the driver for the development of new tools.

Parametric models, driven by Robert McNeel & Associates' Grasshopper®, are the next step in this evolution which originated in writing personal tools in RhinoScript. The graphical algorithm editor has made possible the integration of MVRDV's parametric approach with the generation of design output without the necessity of having software programmers on board. Grasshopper has become a true design tool within the office.

Parametric design enables the generation of an endless stream of configurations and combinations emerging from data and rules, and provides insights in previously unseen problems and potentials. It helps to define a new vocabulary, and at the same time reveals the subjectivity of input – the selection of parameters as the conditions, the hierarchy of input and the weight factor of the different parameters together determining the outcome.

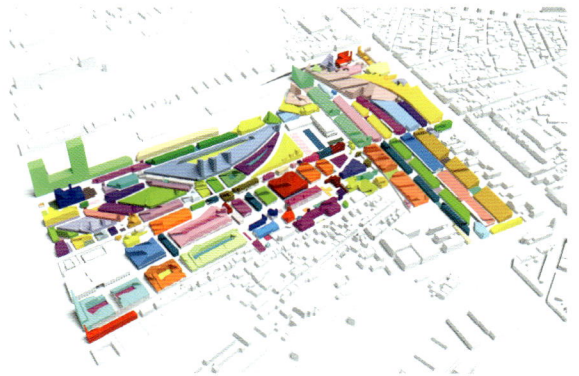

Final volumetrics of the masterplan are defined by environmental aspects such as physics and climate, as well as typological requirements.

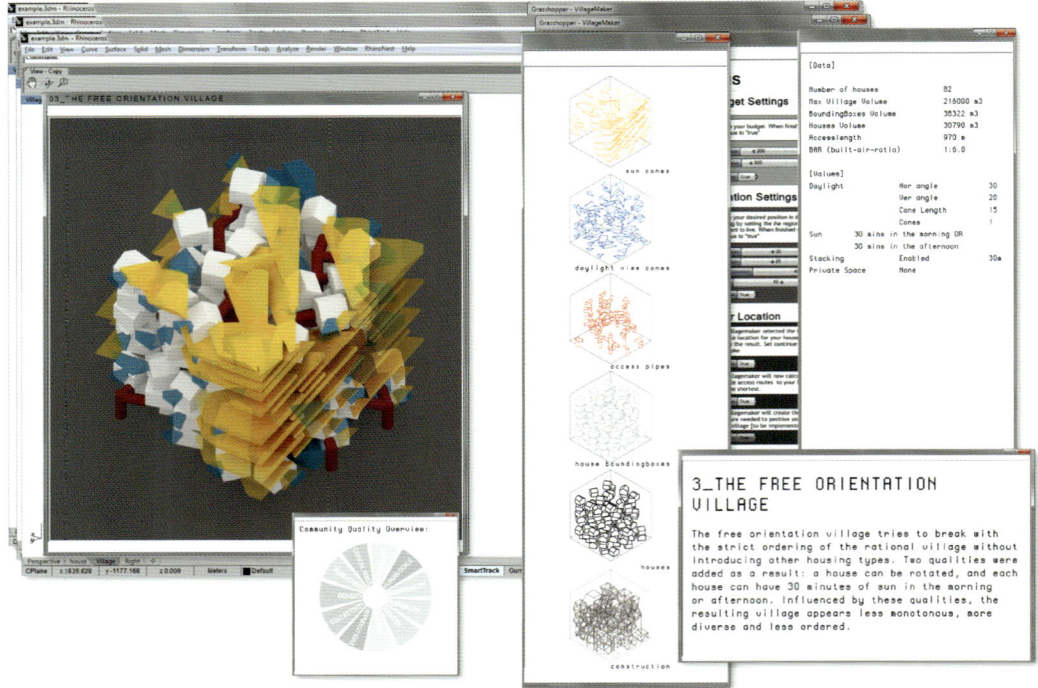

MVRDV/The Why Factory, Vertical
Village, 2012
Analysis of spatial configurations can be
made using the parametric model, providing
insight into complex interdependencies
between the different parameters.

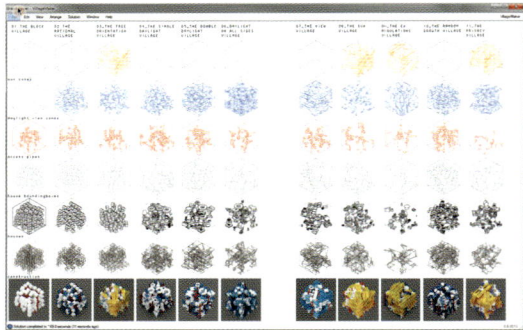

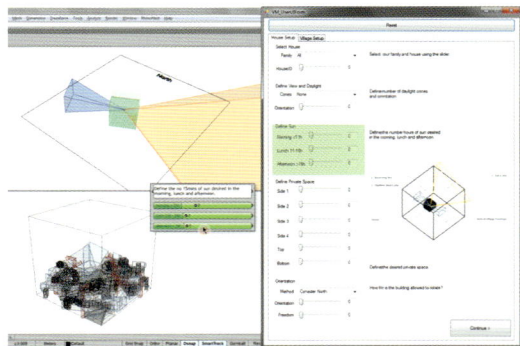

PLANNING BY PARAMETERS

An example of the use of scripting in a design project is
the Bastide Niel masterplan. This involves the conversion
of a former industrial and military site in Bordeaux into a
maximum social and sustainable area as a dense, mixed,
intimate neighbourhood, minimising energy consumption and
producing all needed energy on site. All existing buildings
are reused, surrounded with narrow streets defining the
plot division. Natural daylight and sunlight is maximised by
45-degree daylight angles and 22-degree sunlight angles
for all new volumes, ensuring every home has optimal
daylight and a minimum of two hours of sunlight a day. By
reducing the depth of volumes to a maximum 15 metres
(49 feet), 80 per cent of homes can be naturally ventilated.
Parameterising this energy strategy and its geometric
relationships defined the volumes and masterplan while
keeping the outcome flexible and adaptable.

centre: Overview of a range of different
spatial configurations: different setups of
parameters provide different outcomes,
now measurable in a comparative setup.

bottom: Specific coordinates for sun
positions can be implemented within a
virtual setup, as well as a built-in cost
gradient to make economic decisions.

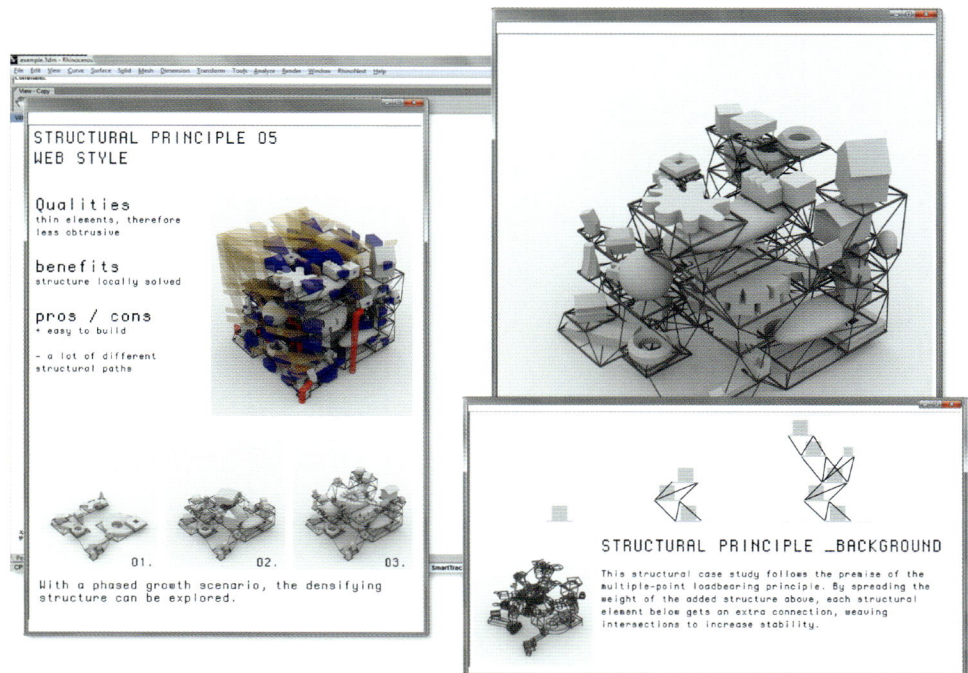

STRUCTURAL PRINCIPLE 05
WEB STYLE

Qualities
thin elements, therefore
less obtrusive

benefits
structure locally solved

pros / cons
+ easy to build

- a lot of different
structural paths

01.   02.   03.

With a phased growth scenario, the densifying
structure can be explored.

STRUCTURAL PRINCIPLE _BACKGROUND

This structural case study follows the premise of the
multiple-point loadbearing principle. By spreading the
weight of the added structure above, each structural
element below gets an extra connection, weaving
intersections to increase stability.

The visionary Vertical Village project is another example of the use of parametric design. The basic framework in the Grasshopper definition establishes safety and quality requirements, such as daylight and egress, for the village, and within this framework inhabitants act as they please. Not only does the VillageMaker define the physical structure of the village, it is also intended to be a Web-based, open-source software package, a platform for the further evolutionary development of a community where people meet, negotiate and share thoughts. This is will also be applied in the development of the Oosterwolde area in Almere, the Netherlands, which will begin in 2013.

THE CITY MAKER

Planning by parameters enables architecture and urbanism to become 'open source', allowing inhabitants to influence the outcome while maintaining quality control. Following the principles of the VillageMaker, the development of the CityMaker would enable a fully participatory urbanism, offering maximum involvement for citizens based on individual and collective creativity and intelligence. The CityMaker brings a complete bottom-up approach to the design process, allowing new urban districts to be fully generated by its inhabitants, and ultimately developing a city that answers to their behaviour, needs and desires. Taking the Vertical Village to the next step, the CityMaker could be the ultimate tool for planning by parameters.

The parametric, data-driven methodologies that MVRDV is using in its design practice are merely the tip of the iceberg. 3-D printers already enable us to represent a datascape as a physical model, however a next step could be the introduction of a connection to the physical world by linking microcontrollers to the inputs and outputs; parametric models being steered in a virtual reality environment. Future inhabitants could directly experience how their wishes and constraints influence the urban scheme. And taking this to an even further level, a real-time parametric material might generate a direct output that is continuously being updated. For MVRDV, parametric design is more than generating endless streams of possible outcomes; it is a way of thinking. ⌀

Based on a limited number of options, the plug-in for engineering calculates different setups of the location of the house, making an evolutionary growing structure feasible.

AFTER
AFTER
GEOMETRY

In the mathematics of quantum mechanics describing creation and annihilation of elementary particles, as observed at accelerators, particles at particular points arise from 'fields' spread over space and time. Higgs found that parameters in the equations for the field associated with the particle H can be chosen in such a way that the lowest energy state of that field (empty space) is one with the field not zero. It is surprising that the field is not zero in empty space, but the result, not an obvious one, is: all particles that can interact with H gain mass from the interaction.

— Mary and Ian Butterworth, 'The Higgs Boson Demystified: How Particles Acquire Mass', *Physics World*, Vol 6, No 9, 1993, p 26.

MOS, SAND software, 2009
Software that simulates particles (primarily dumb geometry cubes) – poured into containers, around objects, with holes added, magnets, surface friction, and strange gravities in order to produce aggregate structures.

Michael Meredith of MOS Architects examines his own practice's preoccupation with physics and the particle-oriented world, and the persistent problem of meaning and meaninglessness against the backdrop of the architecture of a previous era: a period that spanned the Deconstruction movement of the late 1980s and closed with Greg Lynn's seminal 1997 *Architecture After Geometry* edition of △.

01

BEFORE AND AFTER GEOMETRY

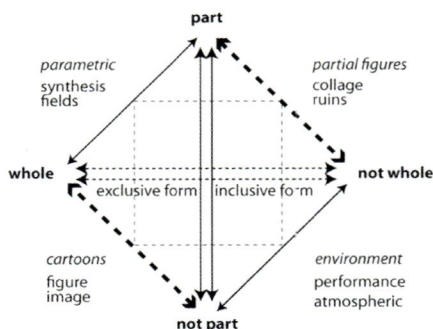

Diagram of architectural composition
This is the contemporary logic of architectural composition. Each category can be further dismantled into smaller and smaller parts. General strategies are parts without wholes, synthetic part/whole relationships, wholes without parts, neither parts nor wholes.

The point to be made here will be both minor and provincial. It will not be for everyone. It might not even be a single point: it begins with two half-points in the hope of making a point. The first starts with the 1997 issue of △ entitled *Architecture After Geometry*, edited by Greg Lynn.[1] *After Geometry* forms a sort of bookend for a decade that began with 'Deconstructivist Architecture', the Museum of Modern Art (MoMA), New York, show curated by Philip Johnson and Mark Wigley in 1988, and Wigley's catalogue text of the same title.[2] In part a reaction to 'Deconstructivist Architecture' and its catalogue, and also an important series of documents in its own right, *After Geometry* provided a basis for the disciplinary reactions of the subsequent decade, and is a point of departure for the other half-point here – some things we have been working on (see Part 2).

'Deconstructivist Architecture' was all about architectural objects. Johnson and Wigley project architectural agency onto objects and describe the unconsciousness of these objects as full of neurosis, desires, dysfunctions and contradictions that are normally 'repressed' in the construction of purer forms. The architect (repurposed as a therapist, ventriloquist or spirit medium) coaxes these 'latent' and 'intrinsic' distortions out of objects and makes it evident to the world that 'Perfection is secretly monstrous'.[3] As the term 'Deconstructivist' implies, the architectural forms identified in the exhibition are undergoing an internal-to-external 'twist' in which flaws invade, contaminate and disrupt forms and language. Wigley argues that the uncanniness of these monstrosities stems from the fact that they are actually more robust and structured as compromised, imperfect forms than they could ever be as opaque and perfect objects.

Yet, despite all the insistence to the contrary, Deconstructivist architecture seems to possess the same fragile veneer that Johnson and Wigley assigned to 'untroubled' and 'pure' form. The projects in the exhibition remain within the formal/linguistic/semiotic regimes that Johnson and Wigley claimed they had undermined. For instance, although we are told that 'deconstruction is not demolition', today the projects they championed appear to possess the unmistakable, picturesque quality of architectural debris. It is this litter of architectural ruins, affected through the delamination of meaning, which has proven most enduring. If 'Deconstructivist Architecture' inaugurated a ruined landscape of particulates, today the simultaneous desires of architectural autonomy and a historical avant-garde seem to co-exist among many other desires without much anxiety (in either objects or architects).

More than two decades after Decon happened, there is a strange pleasure in rereading *Architecture After Geometry*. Although it is still a relatively recent document, its images seem incredibly faded – prematurely, perhaps. What was once the state of the art has become awkward and dated in a really interesting way, like the once state-of-the-art special effects of *Terminator 2*. Even the language feels out of place. Who cannot look back and appreciate the almost comically overwrought sentences of academic architectural jargon from that time? Yet despite its own convolutions and self-obsolescing tendencies, the *After Geometry* issue helped define the disciplinary terrain of the 1990s and provided a context within which various reactionary alternatives could develop. For example, academics such as RE Somol reacted against the kind of Eisenmanian 'form' that Johnson and Wigley had promoted in 'Deconstructivist

Architecture'.[4] Moreover, two different futures were proposed in *After Geometry* that have both been subsequently realised to some degree. First, in Greg Lynn's own piece, 'An Advanced Form of Movement',[5] the destabilisation of form in Deconstructivist objects is transposed to the process of making form itself. Second, in Stan Allen's text 'From Object to Field',[6] these objects are recast and scattered into the materiality and complexity of the city.

Lynn's 'motion-form' was his proposal for an architectural avant-garde (without having employing that loaded/historical term). 'Architecture is the last refuge for members of the flat-earth club, whose simple ideas of a uniform gravity emanating from the earth translate without critical analysis into simple static models of verticality and orthogonal space,' he wrote. 'This is to say that, literally and intellectually, there is virtually no movement in architecture.'[7] The important thing, Lynn tells us, is to participate in the flows and forces that are constantly shaping and reshaping the built environment, and the only way to do this is by making the practice of architecture move. Architectural interactions can be set in motion, as it were, by adopting the tactics inherent in the 'medium' of animation software: motion, parameters and topology. In other words, animation software can mobilise the practice of architecture by liquefying Cartesian architectural form into something that is more 'baroque in spirit'.[8] This requires new architectural and compositional sensibilities for particle clouds, flows, deformations and, above all, liquid metal.

In the midst of all of this seemingly unfettered movement, however, Lynn is careful to state that he is not trying to dissolve architecture's autonomy. This is the awkward part of an otherwise smooth argument about the new tools and models available to architectural practice: the forms this practice produces remain uncontaminated and discrete from the swarms and eddies of space, defined in Baroque, Leibnizian terms. This insistence that form, thinned down and set in runny, soft motion, remains pristine, ties Lynn's position back into representation. If we include the notes Jeffrey Kipnis contributed to the same issue of Δ,[9] outlining a desire for architecture outside of formal analysis and driven by affect, the result is a projection of a kind of digital Rococo, possibly fuelled by parametric/computational techniques.

On the other end of things in *After Geometry*, Stan Allen suggested a different paradigm of particularity in 'From Object to Field'. If the authors of *Deconstructivist Architecture* were concerned with what they hoped would prove to be an autonomous object, and Lynn's motion-form was concerned with designing a design technique, Allen's 'field condition' was first and foremost concerned with repositioning architectural technique as something that participates within a site. (Lynn's site was simply architecture's repertoire of techniques.) Architects, Allen argued, ought to recognise that both they and their work interact with and are also shaped by the real. 'Working with and not against the site,' he writes, 'something new is produced by registering the complexity of the given.'[10] Through an art historical lens, Allen argues for a diffuse architecture that participates within a larger urban situation. Again, where Johnson and Wigley assign agency to the architectural object and Lynn to the architectural process, Allen assigns agency to the urban (including architectural typology) and its own organisational logics. Using the Cordoba Mosque as one of his examples, he proposes an embedded, contingent architecture of 'one thing after another', a collection of architectural particles that operate together as a field or a swarm such that there is no part-to-whole compositional hierarchy, just local deviations within a fog of parts.[11]

Yet, for all of Allen's insistence on his argument's materialist credentials and his recognition that urban vectors are not entirely, or even mostly, composed of physical objects, he is unable to break out of a pictorial-based compositional framework for his field-architecture proposals. The tactics he advances remain tethered to formal logics. The control that had been ceded to Decon objects in 1988, or procedures in Lynn's contemporary work, comes back to the architect under Allen's regime, only to be cast out again into the buffeting currents of urban aggregation and disaggregation. In the end, Allen's rejection of part-to-whole organisation remains semantic. His whole has become the aggregating cloud of the city or the repetitive patterns of

What was once the state of the art has become awkward and dated in a really interesting way, like the once state-of-the-art special effects of Terminator 2.

landscape, and his part is any piece of that same architectural object optimistically thrown out into the world 10 years earlier.

Lynn's proposed future was somewhat executed by architects like Zaha Hadid and Patrik Schumacher, Foreign Office Architects (FOA), Hernan Diaz Alonso and PATTERNS. Allen's vision was perhaps partially realised by the array of post-OMA offices – BIG, JDS, WORK Architects – who share a typology + shape + diagram + the 'real' data-driven diagrammatic/narrative approach. In both futures, representation is paramount. In the architecture identified as Deconstructivist by Johnson and Wigley, drawings resemble thickets of methodological narratives collapsed into two-dimensional lines, superimposed and nearly illegible. (James Joyce was a popular reference for students at that time.) Lynn's work, and that of his motion-form colleagues, has tried to erase Peter Eisenman's stop-motion methodology and replace it with the production of something more fluid or 'post-indexical'. The work engaged in the quote-unquote urban, on the other hand, might feature a hyper-realistic rendering accompanied by arrows explaining topological relationships. At the time, the discipline was shifting away from Eisenman and towards Rem Koolhaas, or away from a value system that privileged representation towards one that posited engagement with the 'real' – from art to life. (The real was represented through photography, photorealistic renderings, construction documents, maps and data-driven diagrams with large arrows.) Today, by contrast, both motion-form and field conditions seem to complement each other in a shared task of dismantling the forlorn Deconstructivist object into finer and finer grains of parts: the former by atomising the techniques of practice, the latter by atomising architectural objects into ever smaller motes of urbanity.

02

AFTER *AFTER GEOMETRY*: PARTICLES, RUINS AND DEBRIS

More than a decade after *After Geometry*, it seems we have given up on a unifying discipline (as either a singular narrative of form or the urban) and moved towards a more particulate and particle-oriented world. We play with multiple narratives simultaneously. We collect dead ends. This is due in part to the shared inadequacy of the singular techniques outlined above: after the Deconstructivist object, after the digital Rococo, and after the resultant bodies had hardened up again and were distributed piecemeal in the field of the urban, there remains the work of physically engaging with all this strewn-about and disaggregated matter. At some rudimentary level, architecture remains about matter, and thus about the matter that remains after semiotics and geometry, and even after *After Geometry*. And to remind ourselves that this matter is subject to basic laws of physics is not the collapse into a humanist tradition of craft or banal meaninglessness it might have previously seemed. This is where the Higgs Bosun discovery comes into play: given a particle – let us say, in our case, a particle of architecture, and keeping in mind that there is no such thing as inert and empty space, that particle will inevitably interact with the other random stuff of the world according to physical forces like gravity, electromagnetism, and strong and weak attraction.

MOS with Tobias Putrih, *On the Verge of Collapse (Overhang)*, 2008
Installation that utilised STACK software for a collaborative exhibition with the artist Tobias Putrih.

MOS, Rainbow Vomit, 2010
The first implementation of the SAND software, through a wall made of hundreds of blocks coated in glitter.

In this light, MOS plays with physics and the persistent problems of meaning/meaninglessness simultaneously. This falls roughly within the most prevalent contemporary modes of art and architectural production that investigate ambiguity, contradictory aesthetics, unfinished forms, fogs, ruins, landscapes, environments, distortions, geologies, temporalities and media. Understanding architectural particulates in a physical way opens the door for a more situational, relativistic approach to architecture as a contingent matter that can be orchestrated by architects in the contexts of chance, self-organisation and entropy.

...after the Deconstructivist object, after the digital Rococo, and after the resultant bodies had hardened up again and were distributed piecemeal in the field of the urban, there remains the work of physically engaging with all this strewn-about and disaggregated matter.

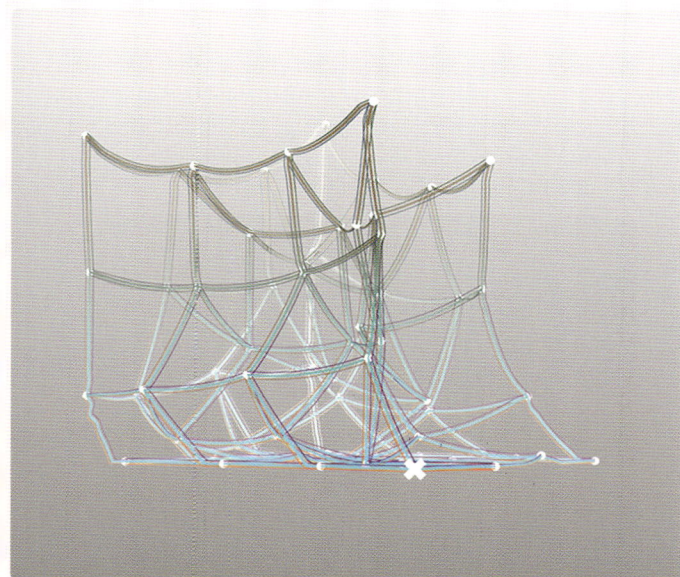

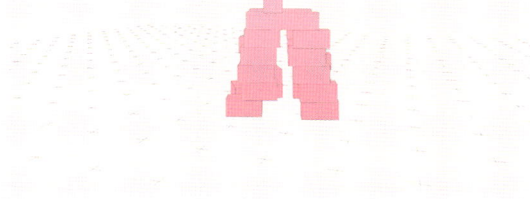

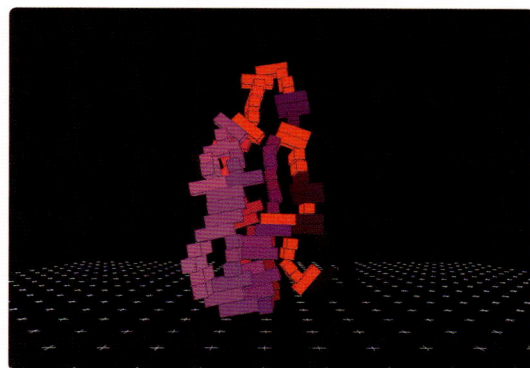

MOS, GRID software, 2010
Deformed matrices, lattices and Voronois, similar to Robert Le Ricolais's (1894–1977) studies of truss and column failures produced through real-time physics engine software, artificially weighted down and compressed to produce the sag and the flaccid droop.

MOS, STACK software, 2007
Stacking occurs within a specific range of overhang. Each unit simultaneously calculates its own self-weight and balance in real-time harmonic equilibrium as it grows, ultimately producing an upside-down tree-like structure that is always on the verge of collapse.

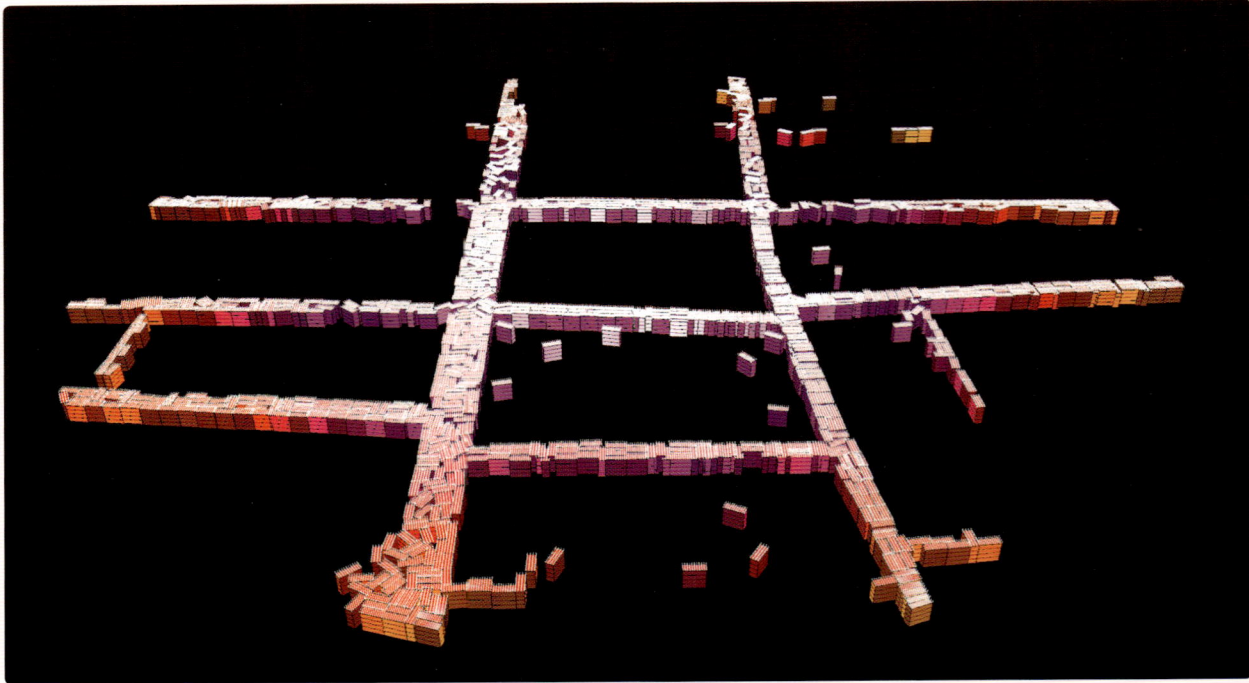

Within this context, the work of MOS seeks to play out both arguments of After Geometry *concurrently, both using and undermining autonomous, ineffectual and brittle spatio-physical concepts by misusing existing behavioural forces, tectonics and semantic relationships.*

MOS, Captured Output, software developed for the exhibit *MoMA Foreclosed: Thoughts On A Walking City, The Oranges, NJ*, 2012
top: Still from software written to model the flow of particles into an urban condition, creating an architectural log jam or lava flow of connected parts with variable gaps and spaces.

MOS, DRIFT software, 2009
Software designed for another scale and different matter, imagining an urbanism without infrastructure or streets, where building types cluster and aggregate based upon attraction and repulsion.

Within the ontology of particles, the specific relationship of part-to-whole is different, because there is no compositional or pictorial whole. The tradition of 'unity' that architectural discourse and practice had previously adopted from Heinrich Wölfflin's *Principles of Art History*[12] is no longer prevalent. (Compositional and formal unity transformed into an ideological unity through Decon, which has now evolved into a sort of multivalency.) Computational analytical tools ignore compositional legibility and focus on measuring use, activity and performance. The instrumentality of force, mass and materiality have become conceptual devices engaged with the 'real' as opposed to both the pristine ideality of representation through geometry and the privileging of urban physical conditions as though they were the sole shapers of social interactions. Within this context, the work of MOS seeks to play out both arguments of *After Geometry* concurrently, both using and undermining autonomous, ineffectual and brittle spatio-physical concepts by misusing existing behavioural forces, tectonics and semantic relationships. To do this, the simulated physics of video-game software is used alongside the 'real' physics of material experiments. Imagine Robert Smithson's *Peat Bog Sprawl* (1971) or Chris Burden's *Beam Drop* (1984) within a video-game environment where it is possible to tweak the realities of mass and/or gravity, constructing novel methodologies through the situational contingencies of physics to produce entropic structures. Representational space and real space are misused and indistinguishable within the process. Within the disciplinary and compositional vagueness of after *After Geometry* and the ontology of particles, dark matter and the multitude of simultaneous forces, the question remains: How do you operate as an architect, how do you organise formal, material and social relationships? ⚏

Notes

1. Greg Lynn, ⚏ *Architecture After Geometry*, Vol 67, No 5–6, 1997.
2. Mark Wigley, 'Deconstructivist Architecture', in Philip Johnson and Mark Wigley (eds), *Deconstructivist Architecture*, Museum of Modern Art (New York) 1988.
3. Ibid.
4. Robert Somol and Sarah Whiting, 'Notes Around the Doppler Effect and Other Moods of Modernism', *Perspecta*, Vol 33, Mining Autonomy, 2002, pp 72–7.
5. Greg Lynn, 'An Advanced Form of Movement', ⚏ *Architecture After Geometry*, Vol 67, No 5–6, 1997, pp 54–7.
6. Stan Allen, 'From Object to Field', ⚏ *Architecture After Geometry*, Vol 67, No 5–6, 1997, pp 24–31.
7. Lynn, 'An Advanced Form of Movement', p 54.
8. Ibid.
9. Jeffrey Kipnis, '(Architecture) After Geometry – An Anthology of Mysteries: Case Notes to the Mystery of the School of Fish', ⚏ *Architecture After Geometry*, Vol 67, No 5–6, 1997, p 43.
10. Allen, op cit, p 24.
11. Allen, op cit, p 25. Allen reuses Donald Judd's infamous description, 'one thing after another'. See Donald Judd, 'Specific Objects', in *Donald Judd: Complete Writings 1959–1975*, Press of the Nova Scotia College of Art and Design and New York University Press (Halifax, Nova Scotia, and New York), 1975, pp 181–9.
12. Heinrich Wölfflin, *Principles of Art History: The Problem of the Development of Style in Later Art*, trans MD Hottinger, G Bell and Sons (London), 1932; reprinted by Dover (New York), 1950, pp 184–95.

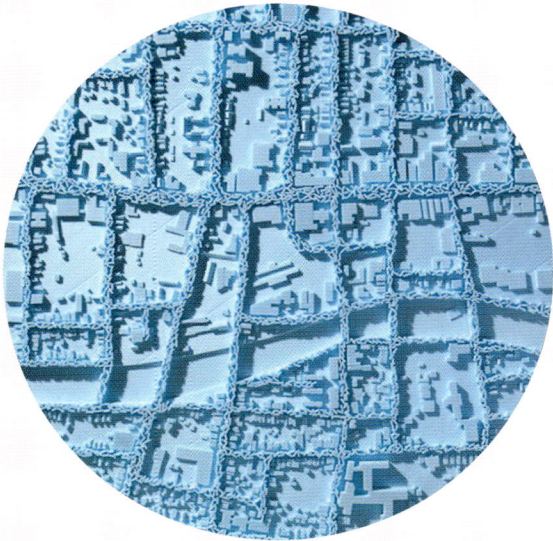

Model of low-rise four-storey buildings with a zoning-free mixture of commercial, office and residential spaces, including a variety of live-work spaces. Using the street as a site of development allows for a new model of zoning and development. Unlike typical urban renewal models that propose the wholesale reworking of a site, here new and old structures coexist: streets of traditional single-family houses are juxtaposed with the new urban development.

MOS, *MoMA Foreclosed: Thoughts On A Walking City, The Oranges, NJ*, 2012
Reclaiming the streets from a half-mile radius from the train station, creating a new urban site where the car is replaced by the pedestrian and the street reclaimed as public space for building.

ARTICLE 15

EMBED
INTEL

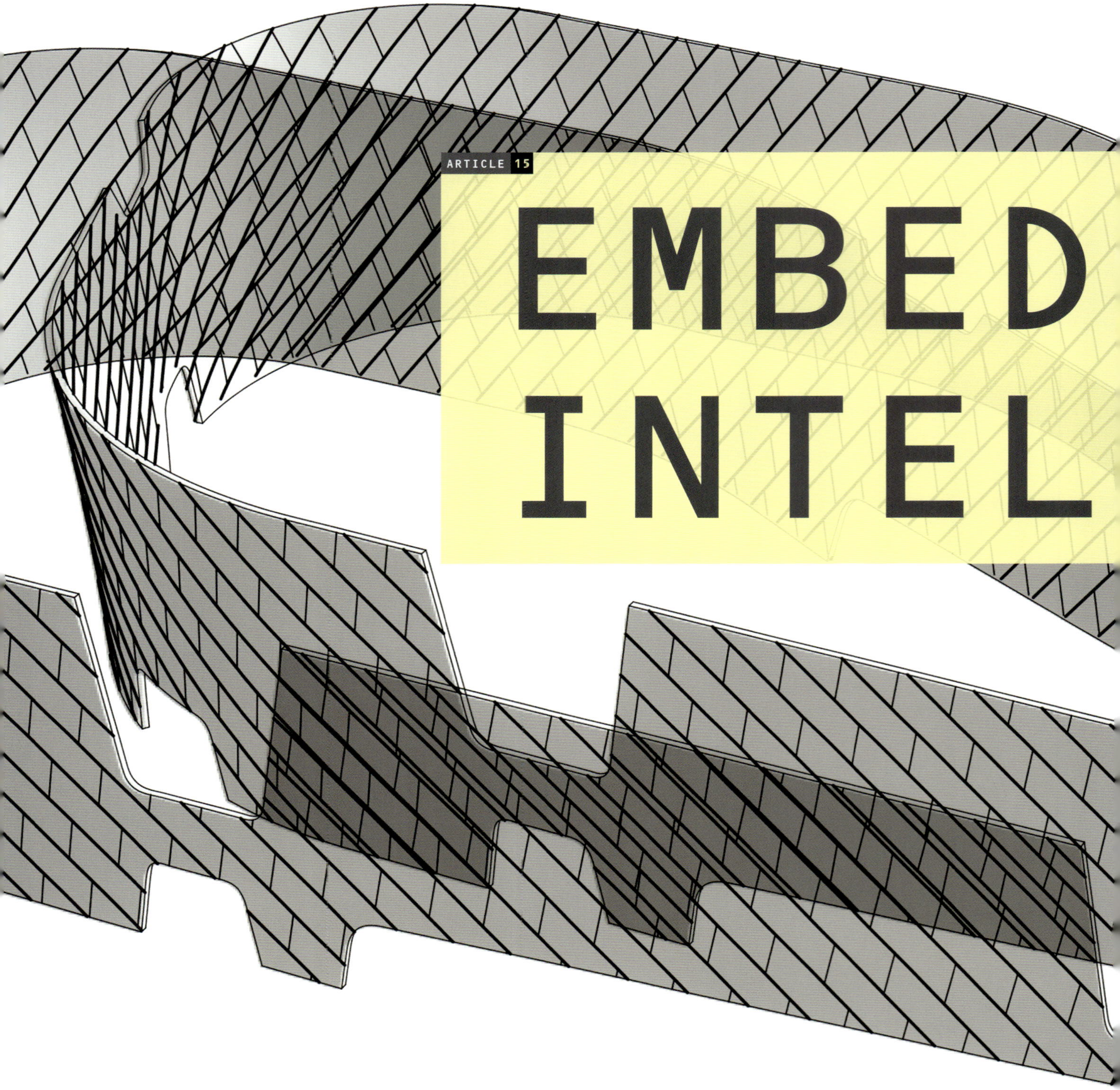

DING
LIGENCE

SETH EDWARDS

Architecture and Computation at Grimshaw, NY

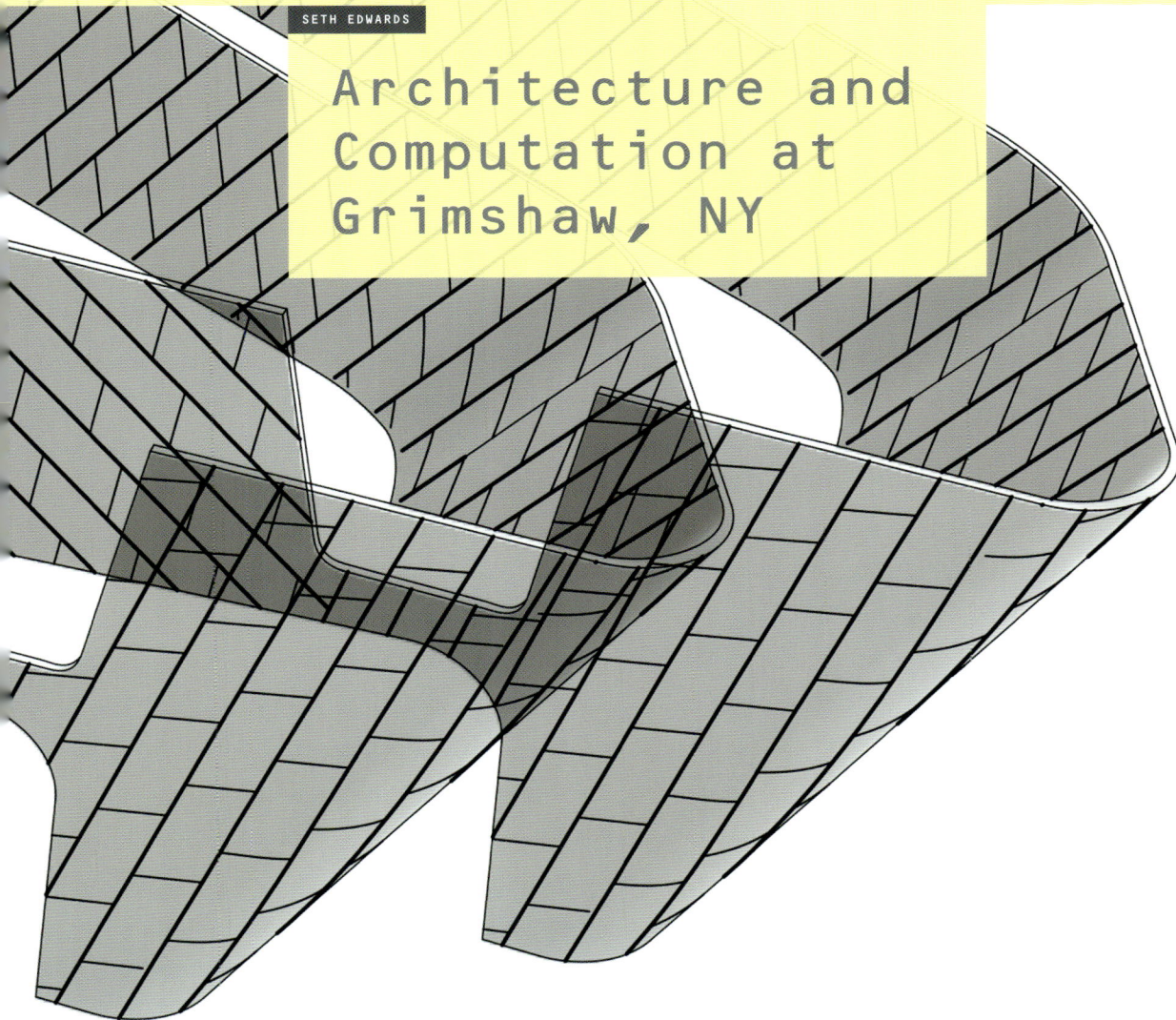

Research and development at Grimshaw is concentrated in two groups: Design Technology (DT) and Industrial Design (ID). **Seth Edwards** from Grimshaw's DT group explains how these dual hubs provide an essential resource for the practice, offering expertise in complex geometry, rapid prototyping and construction. He illustrates three projects, originating in the New York office, that exemplify this approach.

Grimshaw has a long history of developing logical systems to create space. The design and construction of the International Terminal at Waterloo (1993) is a testament to a methodology based upon explicit rules and relationships before a digital tool was fully realised to accommodate such an idea. Designing iteratively within the constraints of an eccentric site in this manner was a painstaking process that can now be streamlined through associative modelling and other computational techniques. At Grimshaw, in-house research and development of these tools is managed by the Design Technology (DT) and Industrial Design (ID) groups. ID is stationed within the New York office while DT is a global department with members in each of the firm's offices. Both groups comprise designers and architects with expertise in complex geometry, rapid prototyping and constructability.

The collective knowledge of Grimshaw DT and ID is a resource for the practice, aiming to assist all architectural project teams, and thereby ultimately facilitating informed and sensible design decisions based on the latest modelling, analysis and visualisation tools. Through this engagement, Grimshaw creates a forward-thinking, dynamic design environment for staff to deliver exemplary architecture. Computational design, as part of this workflow, is a fully integrated tool of the firm's design process rather than a discrete behaviour that drives project development: there is little interest in our tools designing for us. The following are examples of complete and ongoing projects within the New York office that demonstrate this continuing implementation.

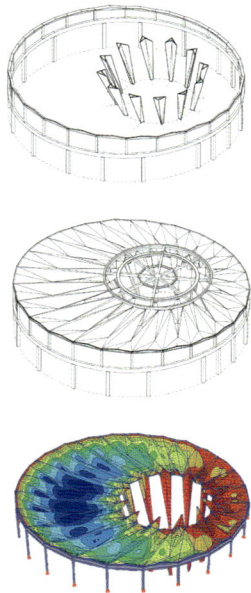

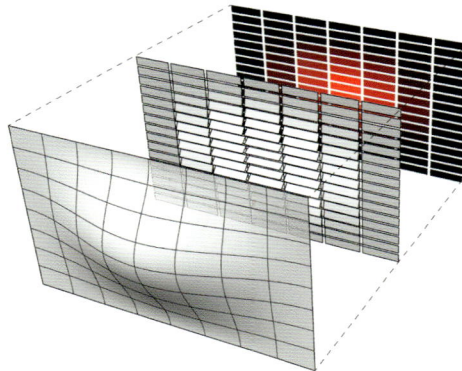

Grimshaw, Horno³: Museo del Acero, Monterrey, Mexico, 2007
The final iteration of the tessellated structure and FEA. The resultant form pushes the limits of steel fabrication by demonstrating how sheet metal can be transformed into structurally rigid forms by complex faceting.

The louvre variation was developed with a control non-uniform rational basis spline (NURBS) surface that was analysed with RhinoScript and converted to angles of rotation along a horizontal axis along the centroid of each individual louvre. This information was easily translated to 2-D Excel data.

Exterior view of louvre cladding.

HORNO³: MUSEO DEL ACERO

Horno³: Museo del Acero in Monterrey, Mexico, is the restoration of a derelict 1960s blast furnace complex and a new addition providing gallery space and museum facilities. The intervention needed to balance the preservation of a historic site with the creation of a dynamic symbol that showcased innovative uses of steel. Associative modelling systems were used to develop two elements of the design: a steel folded plate roof structure and an exterior louvre cladding system. The folded plate roof, developed by Grimshaw DT in Bentley Systems' GenerativeComponents™ (GC), was based on a simple set of geometric rules established on circular arrays of points with variable-based controls. The digital model was sent to engineer Werner Sobek for finite element analysis (FEA) and a feedback loop was created when the analysis information was returned. Through this dialogue, additional perimeter folds were developed to deal with local plate buckling, and the flattened model was sent directly to the steel fabricator. The subtle angle fluctuations of the exterior louvre cladding system were programmed with Robert McNeel & Associates' RhinoScript to permit views from certain interior areas of the cast hall gallery, and at other areas dissolve the monolithic shape of the furnace complex. The script outputs data directly to a Microsoft® Excel document that acts as an abstract elevation of the building. A printed version of the spreadsheet was used by the subcontractors to rotate the louvres into place.

GLASS STAIR FOR AMG DESIGN

Embedding material and assembly constraints into the design model is becoming a standard practice in the office when a direct connection to the fabricator is possible. Grimshaw ID has developed a feature glass stair with engineers Thornton Tomasetti using Autodesk® Inventor®, a 3-D mechanical design and CAD software, that will be located within the new office of architectural metal and glass fabricator AMG Design in New York. AMG wanted to both showcase their fabrication capabilities as well as create maximum transparency within the work environment. The concept became a glass staircase suspended by series of heavily pre-tensioned cables at the floor and ceiling. Initial attempts to understand the clashing of cable locations in relation to treads reinforced the limitations of non-parametric CAD software. The Inventor model was built with a series of variables including height of stair and cables, and number of cables and their corresponding fixing points, so that different types of assemblies could be tested iteratively as structural and mechanical information became available. As structural member sizes changed and the forces in the cables under load were more properly understood, this information was brought back into Inventor and the model was quickly modified to accommodate the changes. This shared, associative model will see the project through from design to construction.

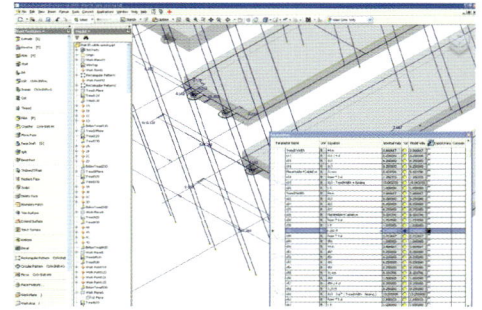

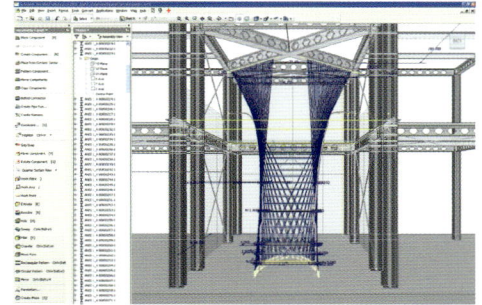

Computational design, as part of this workflow, is a fully integrated tool of the firm's design process rather than a discrete behaviour that drives project development: there is little interest in our tools designing for us.

Grimshaw Industrial Design, Staircase for AMG Design, Long Island, New York, due for completion in 2013
Glass treads and the compactness of the threading fixtures further emphasise the transparent, lightweight feel of the assembly.

Autodesk Inventor screenshots of the cable and tread parameters, as well as the full assembly within the steel space frame.

Resembling the hull of a ship, the form of the Living Core was developed over time ... through several iterations taking into account the structure necessary to contain these living support systems as well as the flexibility required of the museum programming.

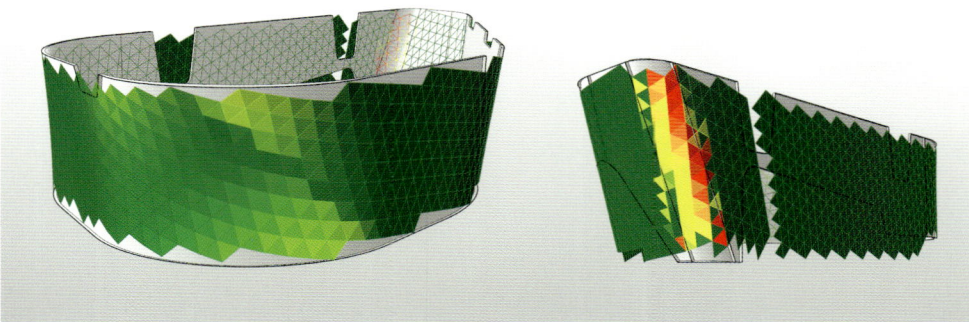

Grimshaw, Living Core, Patricia & Philip Frost Museum of Science, Miami, Florida, due for completion in 2014
above: Exterior rendering of the Living Core.

top: Grasshopper screenshot illustrating the initial pattern-generation progress. Meshing methods were used for panel optimisation and to understand areas of complex curvature.

THE LIVING CORE

The Patricia & Phillip Frost Museum of Science in Miami, a partly open-air structure, will be home to science exhibits, a planetarium, and the Living Core – a standalone aquarium and wildlife centre that contains a microcosm of South Florida's animal, fish and plant species. The Living Core will provide a visual framework for visitors to begin their museum journey, as well as a structural framework for a 2.3-million-litre (500,000-gallon) Gulf Stream tank and a back-of-house with living support systems that are integral to the health, comfort and care of a variety of species.

Resembling the hull of a ship, the form of the Living Core was developed over time using McNeel's Rhinoceros® and Grasshopper®, and Autodesk® Revit® through several iterations taking into account the structure necessary to contain these living support systems as well as the flexibility required of the museum programming. The resultant geometry consists of curved, vertical and inclined walls in seamless transition. This type of surface complexity will be facilitated with a bent steel grid developed with curved framing experts at Radius Track® that will span between structural floor elements and have tile cladding. The size of tiling remains constant throughout, reinforcing the monolithic nature of the Living Core, while varying in concavity and convexity to create areas of dappled reflection that will change throughout the day. Because the tile facade is exposed to the elements and must handle considerable heat differential, large expansion joints to accommodate the Miami climate are necessary. Special attention was paid to the design of these joints into a pattern that will strengthen the dynamic nature of the envelope while satisfying the dimensions of the netting rolls that the tiles will be supplied on. Grimshaw DT developed a patterning process that accommodates the form's double curvature and tests for maximum areas of deviation of a standardised pattern through a meshing sequence. The script simplifies the control joint pattern to a series of duplicate parallelograms that can be cut from the rolls of tile and applied with ease.

Computational design is neither a rote skill nor an obscure art, but an exceptional way of thinking that gives rise to new creative opportunities in space making, optimisation and constructability. With each project, Grimshaw DT and ID are committed to building a greater understanding of how the practice can precisely adjust its ideas to meet client requirements, regardless of project scale or software. This understanding is translated into form and detail, and the results are functional, economic and elegant. ◛

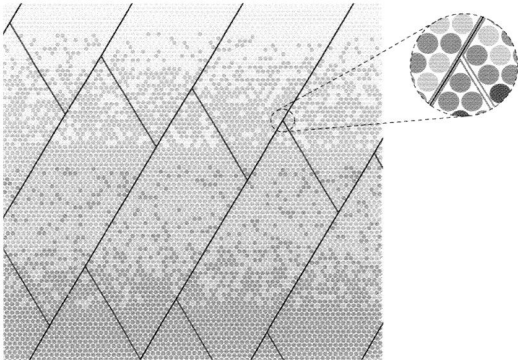

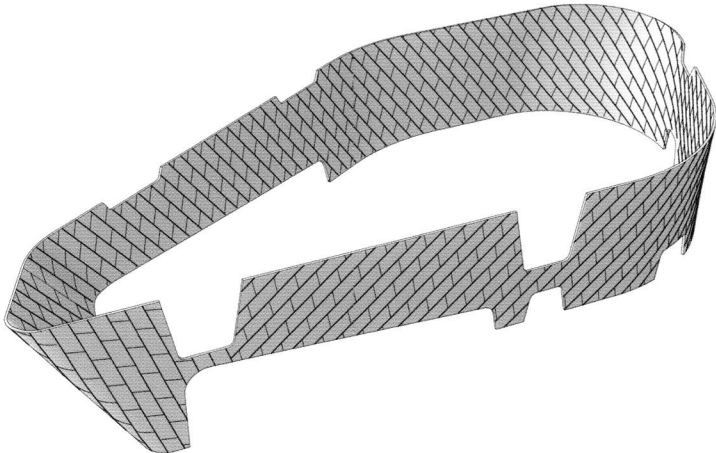

above and pages 104–5: The optimised Living Core envelope form and tiling pattern. Detail view of tiling pattern and control joints.

The Karamba plug-in developed by **Clemens Preisinger** in collaboration with Bollinger + Grohmann Engineers has been developed to predict the behaviour of structures under external loads. Intended to be used by architects rather than being solely confined to an engineering setting, it enables a seamless flow of data between structural and geometric models. Preisinger here describes the program's evolution and application.

Lengfeld & Wilisch Architekten, Skylink, Frankfurt Airport, Germany, 2011
Free parameters define the locations along the bridge where sets of diagonals attach to the main girders. This parametric arrangement allows specific geometry to be treated as series of numerical vectors that can be fed into any optimisation algorithm.

LINKING STRUCTURE AND PARA— METRIC GEOMETRY

soma Architecture, White Noise, Salzburg, Austria, 2010
below: Straight aluminium rods of uniform length, arranged in a seemingly random fashion, form the load-bearing structure of the Salzburg Biennale music pavilion.

top right The irregular layout of truss diagonals emerged from a genetic algorithm that optimised for structural performance and efficiency of material.

bottom right: Parameterisation strategy for the White Noise music pavilion. Member connectivity and thus structural performance depend only on the angles of the members with respect to a given reference surface.

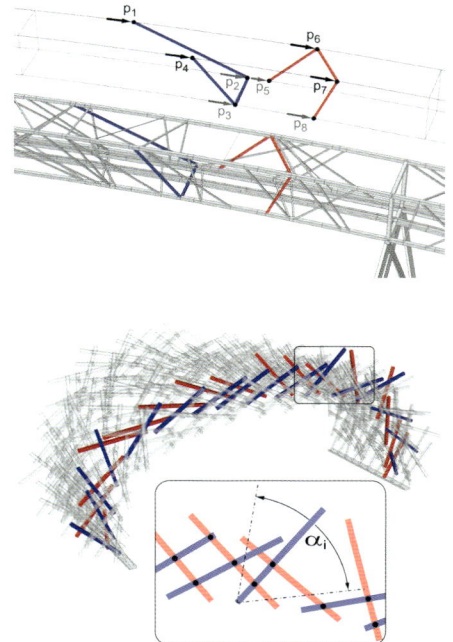

SKYLINK

Karamba is a finite element (FE) program for predicting the behaviour of structures under external loads. Though developed in a structural engineering firm, its main focus does not lie in this field. It is geared towards use within an interactive, parametric architectural design environment. One of the goals was to create a fast, lightweight tool that facilitates a seamless flow of data between structural and geometric models. The origins of the Karamba plug-in for Robert McNeel & Associates' Grasshopper® date back to a research project entitled Algorithmic Generation of Complex Space Frames,[1] carried out at the University of Applied Arts Vienna in collaboration with Bollinger + Grohmann Engineers. The project focused on the viability of applying genetic algorithms (GAs) to the structural optimisation of real-world structures.[2] GAs rely on a large number of evaluations of the function to be optimised – in the case of structural assessment these are FE calculations. It was found that the main impediment for scaling up the optimisation tasks was the time spent on the recurrent computation of the statical models, which amounted to days in some instances. This motivated the implementation of a custom FE code which now forms a large part of the calculation core of Karamba. The parallelisation of time-consuming calculation steps, a fast and extensive interface to scripting languages, and results calculation on demand, have led to a reduction of computation time of two to three orders of magnitude compared with using off-the-shelf FE programs.

The Skylink bridge links Frankfurt Airport with a 300-metre (984-feet) distant car park. The work of Lengfeld & Wilisch with Bollinger + Grohmann Engineers, it is a trussed bridge with the diagonal elements placed by the Karamba design tool.[3] The four longitudinal girders at the corners of the bridge are fixed. Two sets of connecting elements join the main girders: one set encloses the top, and the other encloses the bottom, resulting in the box-like truss. Along the sides of the bridge, the diagonal elements run in different planes so that complex, costly connections are avoided. The parameterisation used consisted of joining predefined poly-lines with sets of diagonals whose position was subject to optimisation.

Maximum displacement and mass of steel served as measures for ranking the solutions in the GA optimisation procedure. The number of variables to be optimised amounted to about 400, which made it a very large-scale problem for a GA approach. Roughly 200,000 variants of truss layouts were tested before arriving at the final result. The solution performs similar to a regular truss with respect to total mass and maximum deflection. Although the truss layout arrived at is probably not the global optimum, it certainly provides a useful alternative to conventional, regular geometries.

soma Architecture, White Noise, Salzburg, Austria, 2010
bottom: A close inspection of the music pavilion reveals its underlying
structural principle: beams in parallel planes connect to each other via
circular studs depending on their relative position.

Grasshopper definition of a structural model
Karamba components add physical meaning to a parametric geometry setup.

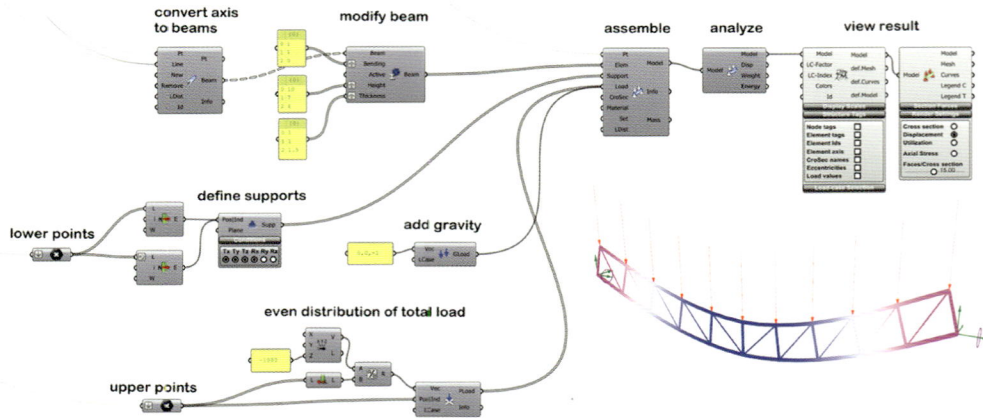

WHITE NOISE

Karamba has been used at Bollinger + Grohmann Engineers
for a number of projects, either for checking statical feasibility
in the early stages of design, or for performing structural
optimisation. A recent example of the latter is the design of
White Noise by the Austrian firm soma Architecture.[4] A mobile
pavilion for cultural events, it consists of a large number of
aluminium rods that interact in a seemingly chaotic manner.

The static system of the pavilion is made up of a number
of arches that span a distance of 12 metres (39 feet). Each of
the arches is made of multiple layers of rods. The members
of one layer connect to elements on the neighbouring layers
via short, circular studs. The number of connections between
neighbouring elements thus depends on their inclination with
respect to each other. The optimisation task here involved
selecting the elements orientation for minimum displacement
under given loads at minimum total structural weight. The
parameterisation of the geometry was done entirely in
Grasshopper, and the solution process handled by its built-in
probabilistic optimisation engine.

Shells under horizontal load
Left to right: principal stress lines; colour plot of material utilisation; force flow lines; displaced structure with colour plot of principal stresses.

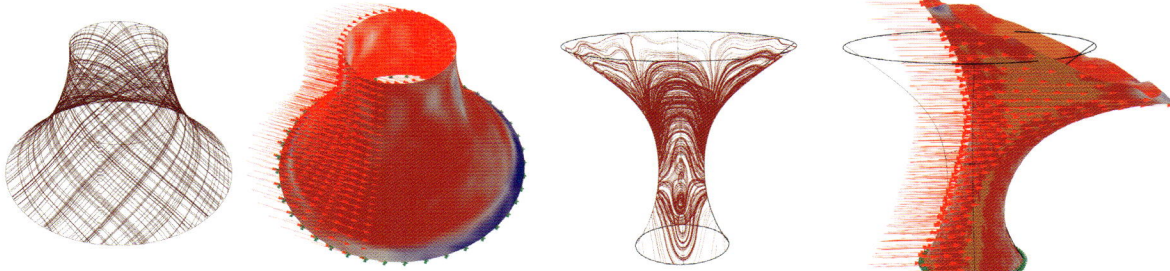

Grasshopper allows the integration of custom plug-ins that can then make use of the program's graphical user interface elements and thus interact with other plug-ins in a well-defined way.

INTEGRATION OF KARAMBA WITHIN AN INTERACTIVE MODELLING ENVIRONMENT

During the research project at the University of Applied Arts Vienna, the design of a user interface for the program package played a very minor role. However, in the day-to-day work of the design office at Bollinger + Grohmann Engineers, the necessary coding of geometric parameterisations as scripts proved cumbersome and reduced the range of possible users to a small circle of scripting experts. To solve this problem, the program was ported into existing software that offered an interactive, generative modelling environment. Grasshopper allows the integration of custom plug-ins that can then make use of the program's graphical user interface elements and thus interact with other plug-ins in a well-defined way. This led to the first public version of the Karamba plug-in.

Most aspects of a Karamba model can be made dependent on parametric input. Such a model consists of an assemblage of visual components which look and feel like the native software's building blocks. The fact that Karamba reacts immediately to any change of input parameters helps to understand structural mechanisms in the design. Using Karamba is like watching a film compared to a fixed image; one can easily create a series of images in real time by manipulating the corresponding user interface widget instead of the more traditional approach of having a systems response only at one particular state.

Although its development has been rooted in the context of Bollinger + Grohmann Engineers, Karamba has always been a stand-alone project. As development proceeds, the range of its applications constantly widens; for example, shell elements can now be included in calculations. But what is perhaps most interesting is how the structural properties that are normally hidden from view – deflections, natural vibrations, force flow lines – can be used creatively in an architectural context. With the advent of new digital tools that combine architecture and engineering, demand has grown for professionals who have knowledge in both areas. Karamba is the instrument for this new generation of architectural engineers and engineering architects to play their new tunes on. ⊿

Notes
1. Klaus Bollinger, Arne Hofmann and Clemens Preisinger, Algorithmic Generation of Complex Space Frames, Institute for Architecture, Structural Design, University of Applied Arts Vienna, 2010. Research project funded by the Austrian Research Fund FWF under the translational research programme, grant L538.
2. See David E Goldberg, *Genetic Algorithms in Search, Optimization, and Machine Learning*, Addison-Wesley (Reading, MA), 1998, and JL Coenders and LAG Wagemans, 'Engineered by Evolution, Two-Dimensional Frototype Application of openStrategy Form Finding', in *Proceedings of the IASS 2004 International Symposium Shell and Spatial Structures from Models to Realization*, 20–24 September, 2004, pp 66–7.
3. Mark Fahlbusch, Arne Hofmann, Alexander Heise, Klaus Bollinger, Manfred Grohmann and Jochen Mahlknecht, 'Skylink am Flughafen Frankfurt', *Stahlbau*, Vol 81, No 8, 2012, pp 638–42.
4. Stefan Rutzinger, Kristina Schinegger, Arne Hofmann and Moritz Heimrath, 'Adaptive Design of a Music Pavilion', Adaptive Architecture Conference, 3–5 March, 2011.

UNDRAWABLE ARCHITECTURE

HERITAGE BUILDINGS AND DIGITAL TECTONIC

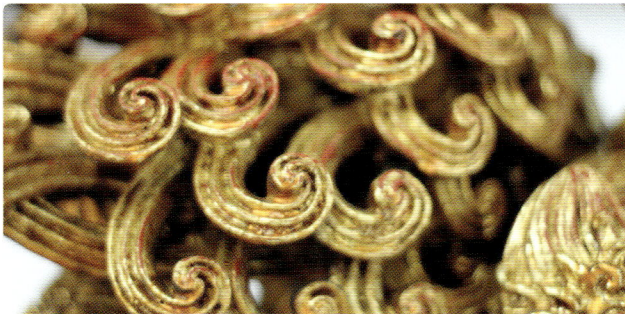

STYLIANOS DRITSAS AND KANG SHUA YEO

Traditionally architecture in Asia was not graphically represented or formalised, and relied on received knowledge being passed down from generation to generation. **Stylianos Dritsas and Kang Shua Yeo** describe the Heritage Buildings and Digital Tectonic research project they have been undertaking at Singapore University of Technology and Design (SUTD), exploring the potential of a start-to-end digital design process for historical building conservation.

Yueh Hai Ching Temple, Heritage Buildings and Digital Tectonic research project, **Singapore University of Technology and Design (SUTD), 2011–12**
top and bottom: Digitising ornamental details with 3-D scanning technology. The gilded wood bracket of a Chinese lion illustrating the complex interplay between form, material and the formation process in this traditional craftwork technique. Geometry and texture information is extracted from the object using hand-held structured-light 3-D scanning technology as seen in the background.

What if the cost of 3-D production from data acquisition to digital processing and printing was a mere fraction of what it is today? What if advancements in 3-D printing composite material reached parity or exceeded the performance of current building materials? How would that affect the design-build process; and what kinds of problems can we provision and research for? Extrapolating on the trends of the past decade,[1] we may foresee how design and construction will become even more information-centric than they are today. But the effects will be quantitative: complex large-scale projects are already stressing the limits of our computer modelling systems.[2]

What if we were in a situation where we could design below the part/assembly level, drilling down to material composition? How would we fair with design information of one order of magnitude larger? Here, the effects would be qualitative: we currently design under a reductionist paradigm; we use models as coarse but agile abstractions of reality; we work analytically using lines and planes. What if we were to enter a domain where the number of abstraction layers reached the limit of our cognitive tolerance: a domain of super-realism, to paraphrase Jorge Luis Borges,[3] where there are no planes, just as there are no planes in reality? Perhaps we are at the cusp of an imminent shift from a 'model and state' paradigm of work to a 'data and flow' digital design regime.

Every one or two decades, historical buildings require some form of conservation or restoration work. Unlike practices employed in the West,[4] where material preservation is paramount, it is common for large parts of buildings in Asia to periodically be disassembled and reconstructed. Perhaps the most famous example of this tradition is the Ise Shrine in Japan (circa AD 685), which is rebuilt every 20 years, and the Temple of Heaven in Beijing (circa 1420), which underwent disassembly, restoration and reassembly in 1971 and 1991. This has both technical as well as cultural significance: the dominant use of organic material, for example timber instead of masonry, paired with particular climatic conditions, means that structures require periodic maintenance and/or replacement of building components. By coincidence or necessity, the process is aligned with a very different philosophical understanding of historical value[5] that does not primarily interface with material and form, but rather with time and place.

Here lies the very interesting challenge of bringing digital design methodology within a domain of 'undrawable' architecture; undrawable, as a process of tacit knowledge passed along generations but never formalised, and as a product of artisan craftwork that was manually (re)produced and never rationalised. While not impossible, it would be impractical to attempt modelling such forms, and the end results would be dubious: specifying building works via drawings of an artefact that contains not a single straight line? It was thus necessary to rethink the process of historical building conservation via a complete start-to-end digital design process.

The subject of Heritage Buildings and Digital Tectonic, a research project at the Singapore University of Technology and Design (SUTD) sponsored by the SUTD-MIT International Design Centre, the Yueh Hai Ching temple is situated at the centre of Singapore's business district. Constructed between 1895 and 1896, the extant building is currently being restored, having last undergone a programme of conservation in 1996–7. The goals for the Digital Heritage lab at SUTD are: in education, to create a contemporary learning experience for architectural history and theory through both archival research and empirical acquisition of information via digital technologies; in practice, to mitigate obstacles in traditional analogue methodology, a relatively slow and potentially costly

process, through an integrated process of precision measurement (3-D scanning), digital restoration (3-D modelling) and reconstruction (3-D printing); and in research, to explore concepts of a data-oriented version of digital design-computation and the advancement of the state-of-the-art practice of historical building conservation via development of computer-aided design (CAD) applications. While currently the time and costs associated with implementing digital design technology for building-scale conservation are prohibitive, it is envisioned that in the next decade or two it will become the predominant mode of work.

The field of historical conservation by digital design has been expanding over the past few decades. Surface reconstruction, global registration, and the visualisation of large data sets have been extensively studied by the computer graphics community, notably the Digital Michelangelo Project (1992).[6] There are also compelling architectural precedents such as the parametric design study of the Sagrada Família cathedral by Mark Burry, investigating the tectonic dimensions of Antoni Gaudí's architecture.[7] The SUTD study is situated at the intersection of these ideas in the light of now widely accessible mass sensing, parallel computing and rapid prototyping technologies. Digital tectonic thus denotes an interest in the discovery of the interplay between material, form and the construction methodology in historical architectural artefacts.

Yueh Hai Ching Temple, Singapore, 2010
The subject of the Heritage Buildings and Digital Tectonic research project, the Yueh Hai Ching Temple, is situated at the centre of Singapore's business district. The extant building, built between 1895 and 1896, is currently undergoing restoration since the last such exercise in 1996–7.

Dragon wall case study. The granite dragon carving previously mounted on the wall of Yueh Hai Ching Temple was installed in 1996–7. During the current restoration of the temple, the stone carving was removed in order to restore the wall to its original ceramic shards ornamentation. This provided the researchers with the opportunity to carry out trial experiments in the scanning of the dragon carving at close proximity without the need to take the precautionary measures usually necessary with historic artefacts.

Reconstructed geometry of dragon wall. Low-resolution (64,000 polygons/square metre) triangulated mesh geometry produced by structured-light 3-D scanning technology (approximately 10 gigabytes/hour). Original raw geometry measures at 3 million polygons/square metre, while rapid prototyping grade mesh counts 700,000 polygons/square metre.

Dragon wall prototype. A true scale reconstruction of the Yueh Hai Ching Temple dragon wall. The final object exhibits traces of the original stone-carving grain, polygonal geometry reconstruction and layered 3-D printing technique. The plaster-based prototype is infused with polymer adhesives to create a strong and lightweight (40-kilogramme/88-pound) composite surface.

The lessons learned from the domain of historical building conservation and digital design methodology throw up a few interesting topics for discussion.

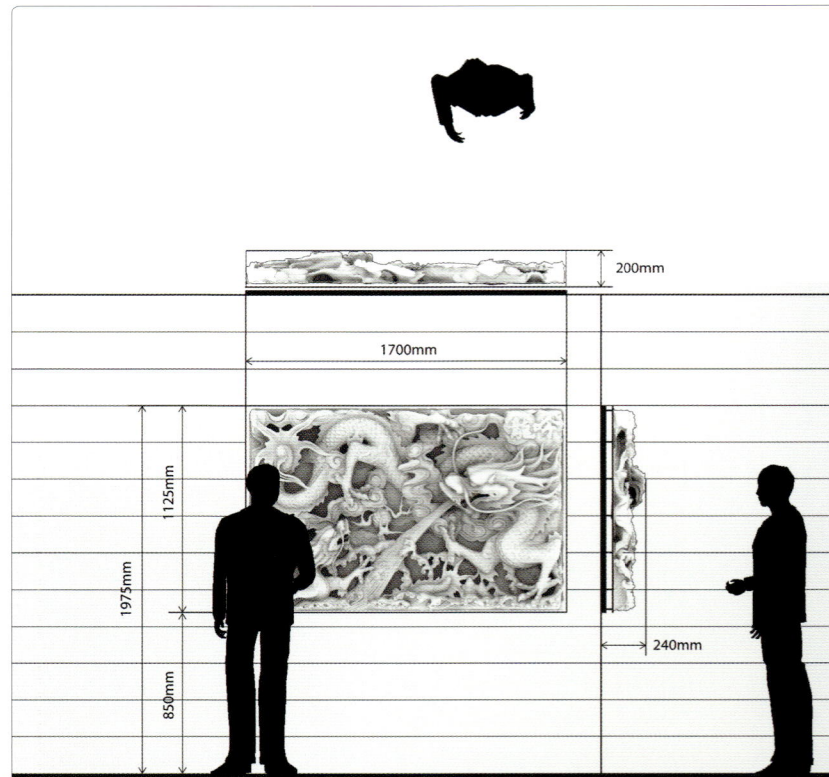

200mm

1700mm

1125mm

1975mm

850mm

240mm

right: Dragon-scale-one. Diagram of the first one-to-one prototype reproduction of the dragon wall using 3-D printing technology. The exhibit comprises 71 egg-shell (3 millimetres/0.1 inches thick) ceramic composite tiles assembled into the original size.

below top: Topographic laser detection and ranging (LIDAR). Architectural artefacts span a wide range of scales, from hundreds of metres to fractions of a millimetre. No technology exists that is capable of spanning the entire range of scales competitively and without shortcomings. Two architectural scales were identified: (a) building scale and (b) component scale. Building scale can best be captured using long-range professional topographic equipment such as LIDAR technology. Component scale is better captured by short-range equipment that allows one to physically reach within and around concave interior envelopes and complex geometry artefacts.

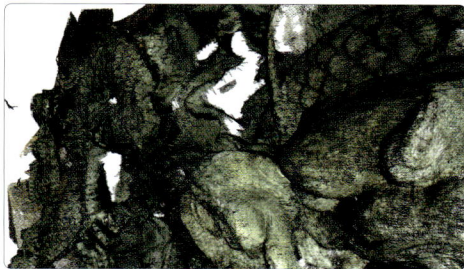

While methodologically it is tempting to revert to notions of reductionism or reverse engineering, it was decided to experiment with architectural large-data. Hundreds of gigabytes of point cloud and mesh geometry information was acquired, captured using a coupled strategy of laser detection and ranging (LIDAR) as well as structured-light 3-D scanning technology to span the vast range of architectural scales.[8] The design and computation applications developed as part of the SUTD study aim at piercing through surface information to discover something about the actual building tectonic: to infer material composition, identify architectural detail and understand the formation process. Rapid prototyping is being evaluated alongside the potential and limitations of current materials and technologies in building-part (such as decorative details) substitution by 3-D printing.

The lessons learned from the domain of historical building conservation and digital design methodology throw up a few interesting topics for discussion. For example, there is a surprisingly different kind of architectural complexity contrasting historical and contemporary form. While digital techniques are flexible, expressive and forgiving, their results are relatively straightforward, predictable and thoroughly rational. After all, the genotype of digital form is an excruciatingly descriptive process that invariably surfaces into the object itself. This is quite unlike historical form, which while indeed governed by principle, its formal expression is artisanal, improvisational and less divisible, due perhaps to the stronger bonds between geometry, material and craft. While it is arguable to what degree these processes and products are relevant in contemporary design praxis, the notion of progressively shorter spans between design and production via digital fabrication brings interesting potential for the near future. In one or two decades' time, when 3-D scanning may be performed using mobile phones, and prototypes may be 3-D printed at the nearest convenience store, it is debatable whether we will think and make in the same way we do today. ⊅

Notes
1. Branko Kolarevic and Kevin Klinger, *Manufacturing Material Effects: Rethinking Design and Making in Architecture*, Routledge (New York), 2008.
2. Mikael Johansson and Mattias Roupé, 'Real-Time Rendering of Large Building Information Models: Current State Vs State-of-the-Art', *CAADRIA 2012 – Beyond Codes & Pixels*, Chennai, India, 17, 2012, pp 647–56.
3. Jorge Luis Borges, *Collected Fictions*, Penguin (New York), 1998.
4. Seung-Jin Chung, 'East Asian Values in Historic Conservation', *Journal of Architectural Conservation*, Vol 11, No 1, 2005, pp 55–70.
5. Jeremy Wells, 'The Plurality of Truth in Culture, Context, and Heritage: A (Mostly) Post-Structuralist Analysis of Urban Conservation Charters', *City & Time*, Vol 3, No 2, 2007: www.ct.ceci-br.org.
6. Marc Levoy, 'The Digital Michelangelo Project', 1992: http://graphics.stanford.edu/projects/mich.
7. Mark Burry, *Expiatory Church of the Sagrada Familia: Antoni Gaudi*, Phaidon (London), 1992.
8. Stylianos Dritsas and Kang Shua Yeo, 'Dragon Scale One: Heritage Buildings and Digital Tectonic', 2012: http://ds1.jeneratiff.com.

above bottom: Short-range reconstruction of geometry. Representation of partial raw sensor data in the form of overlapping mesh surface fragments belonging to various scanning sessions, prior to geometric fusion into one coherent form. Overshadowed areas within deep undercut sculptural form – areas of the dragon wall not visible by the scanner's camera – appear as holes that require geometric CAD reconstruction.

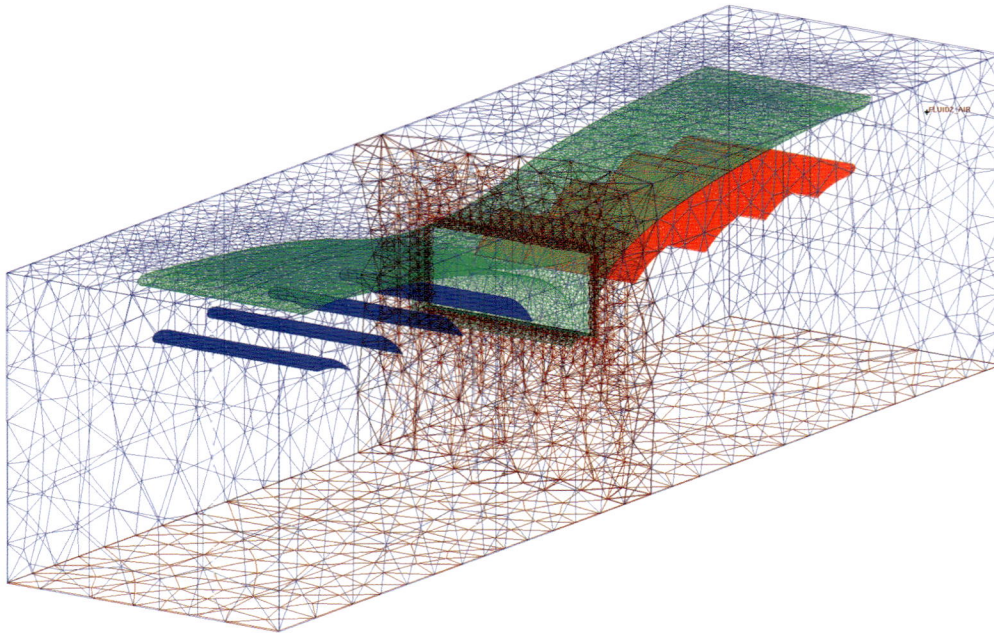

SAWAKO KAIJIMA, ROLAND BOUFFANAIS, KAREN WILLCOX   AND   SURESH NAIDU

There are many 'compelling possibilities' for computational fluid dynamics (CFD) in architecture, as demonstrated by its successful adoption in the aerospace, automotive and product manufacturing industries. **Sawako Kaijima, Roland Bouffanais, Karen Willcox and Suresh Naidu** of ARCH-CFD, a research initiative at the International Design Centre established by the Singapore University of Technology and Design (SUTD) and the Massachusetts Institute of Technology (MIT), explore CFD's potential.

COMPUTATIONAL FLUID DYNAMICS FOR ARCHITECTURAL DESIGN

ARCH-CFD, Bus-stop canopy, International Design Centre,
Singapore University of Technology and Design (SUTD) and
Massachusetts Institute of Technology (MIT), 2012
Hybrid mesh. Opposite top: Unstructured mesh around the geometry
of interest. Bottom: Structured mesh of the surrounding environment.

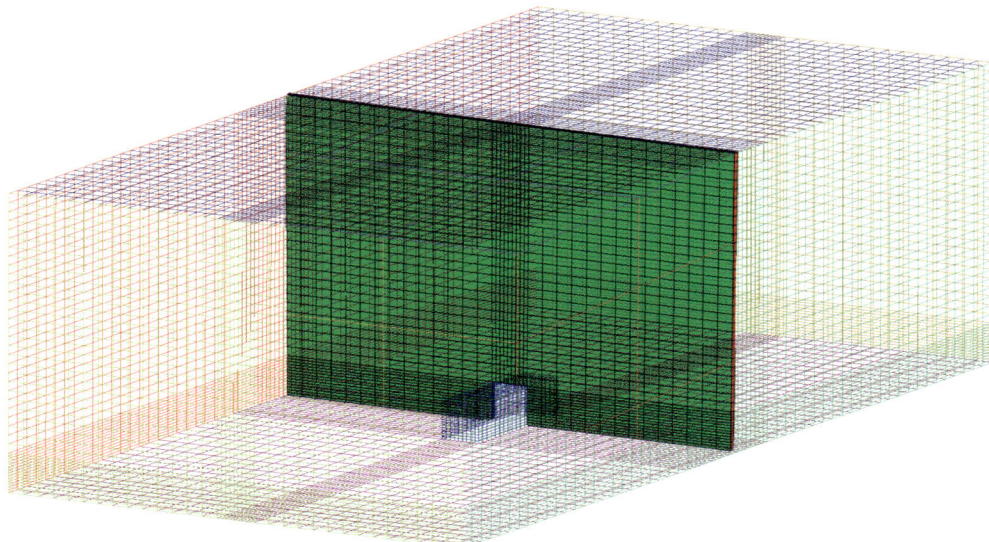

The understanding of natural phenomena in relation to buildings, and in particular internal and external air flow, is becoming increasingly important to architectural design. This is due to the increased complexity of contemporary buildings[1] and a growing interest in improving building performance in terms of environmental impact.[2]

Computational fluid dynamics (CFD) is a cost-effective technique widely employed in industrial design. While indoor analysis can be achieved via CFD, for outdoor studies wind tunnel testing (WTT) is still the prevailing mode of analysis. Moreover, WTT is often performed only a few times during the course of a building design/construction cycle for verification purposes. The CFD versus WTT debate has been around since the introduction of CFD several decades ago: both methods provide a certain degree of knowledge and understanding of the environment in which the design exists.

WTT, however, requires expensive setups and sophisticated instruments to measure field variables (wind velocity, pressure loads, turbulence intensity and temperature). Its main limitation is that these measurements are obtained at only a few discrete points within the test section, therefore severely restricting understanding of the evolutionary or transient processes of unsteady complex phenomena such as vortex shedding, turbulence wakes, thermal stratification, and the atmospheric boundary layer effects on urban landscape.

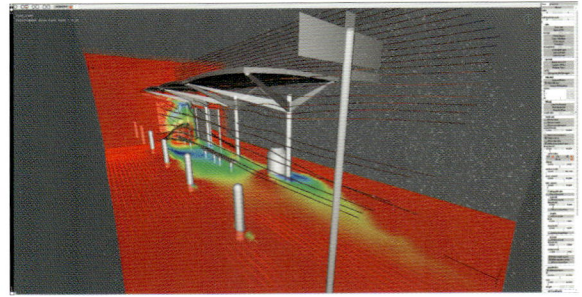

Computational fluid dynamics (CFD) is a cost-effective technique widely employed in industrial design. While indoor analysis can be achieved via CFD, for outdoor studies wind tunnel testing (WTT) is still the prevailing mode of analysis.

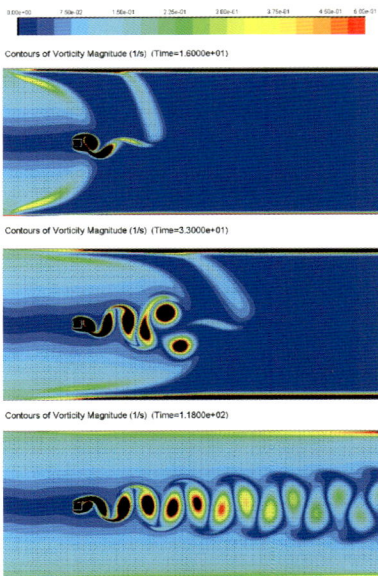

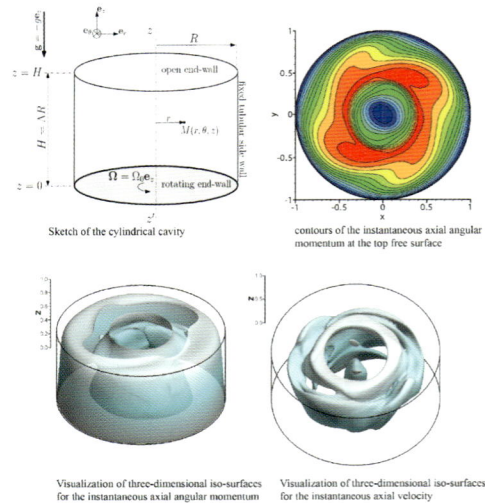

The use of CFD in engineering design
bottom right: Simulation of an open transitional swirling flow. Simulation of Shear-Driven Flows: Transition with a Free Surface and Confined Turbulence, Swiss Federal Institute of Technology, Lausanne, 2005–09.

bottom left: Vortex shedding. Simulation of the inversion of a von Kármán vortex street behind a confined cubical cylinder, Swiss Federal Institute of Technology, Lausanne, 2010–11.

top: CFD analysis and result visualisation of an existing bus stop.

CFD intrinsically overcomes this issue as the simulations yield instantaneous volume data. However, it suffers inherently from the discretisation of the governing equations of fluid dynamics combined with the modelling of the initial and boundary conditions. Some flow phenomena exhibit an extreme sensitivity to these conditions, often referred to as the so-called 'butterfly effect'.[3] These current limitations to using CFD are often misinterpreted as a major hurdle to its adoption as a standard practice in many industries. Yet CFD is used successfully in the aerospace, automotive and many product design industries; this fact alone stresses the compelling possibilities of CFD for architectural design.

THE ARCH—CFD PROJECT

ARCH-CFD is a cross-disciplinary research initiative at the International Design Centre established by the Singapore University of Technology and Design and the Massachusetts Institute of Technology (MIT), which aims to make CFD understandable and accessible to the architecture community. A particular interest is in the incorporation of CFD during the early stages of architectural design, when many of the critical decisions, including those pertaining to the general shape of buildings, are made. Access to wind/air-flow information during these early stages would help architects make responsible design decisions. As a first step in this research, a passive cooling bus-stop canopy has been designed based on a climatic condition of Singapore where wind/air-flow was a driving factor for geometry generation. Here, two bottlenecks were identified utilising CFD in this framework: mesh generation and result comprehension.

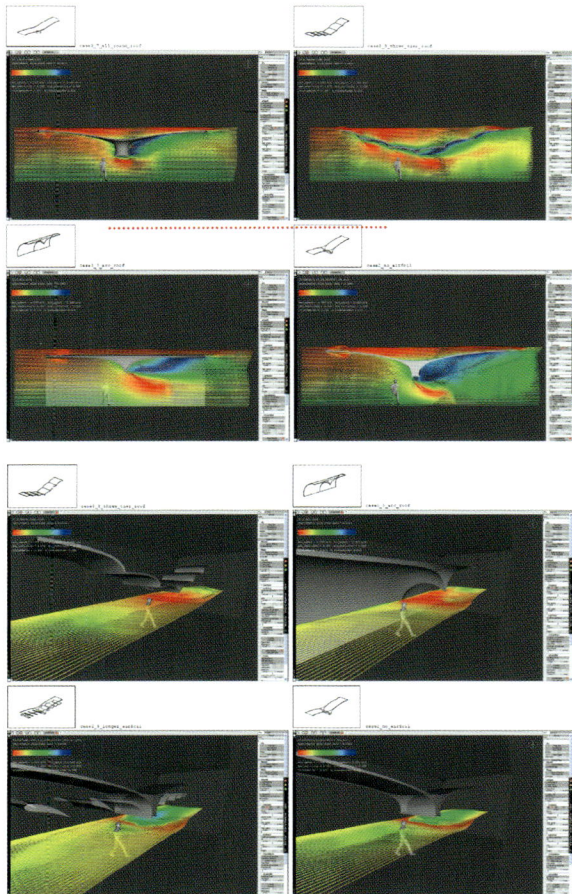

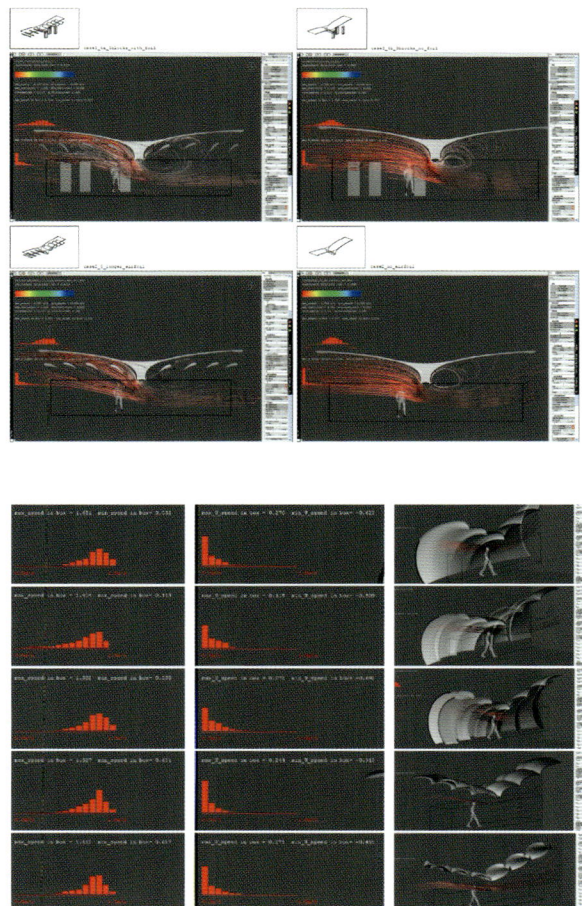

Design iterations. Screen captures of the visualisation toolkit.

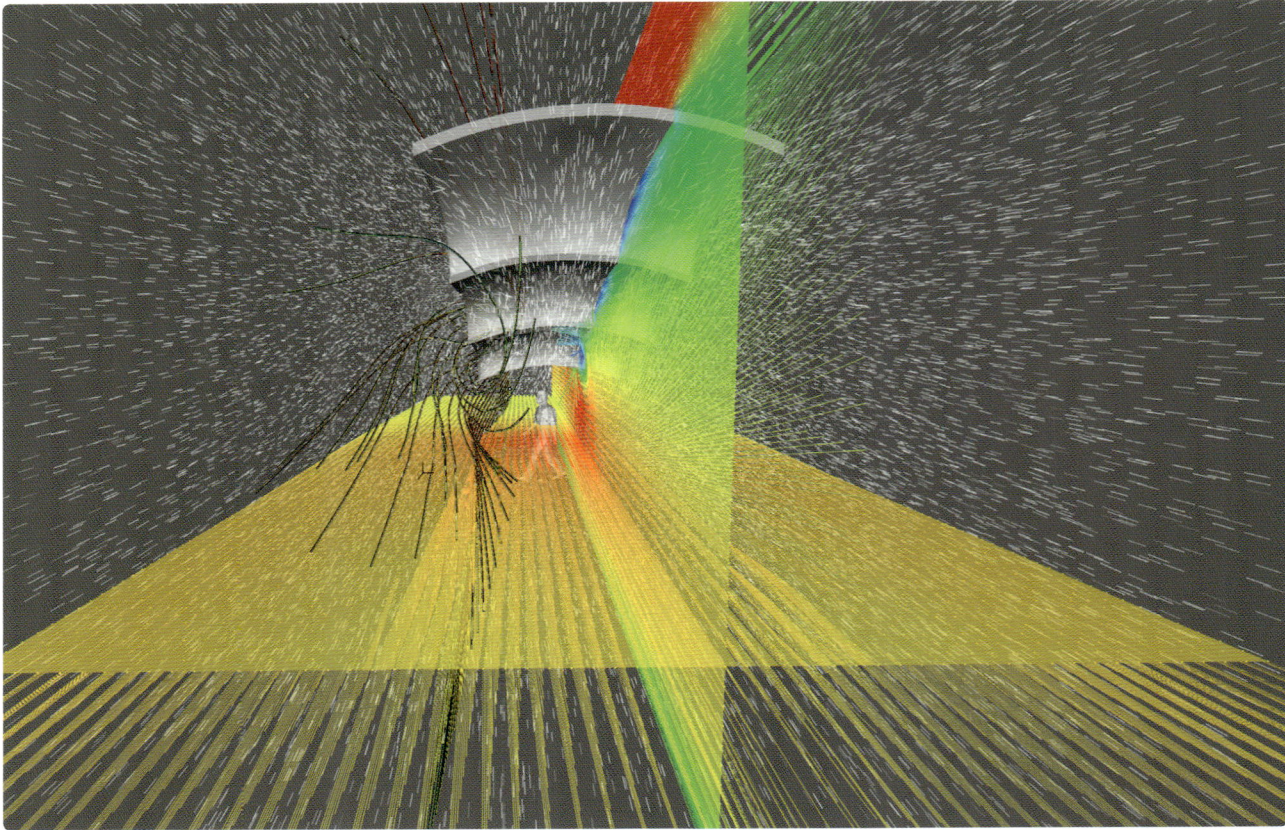

Computer simulations such as CFD have opened up new possibilities
for design and research by introducing environments in which we can
manipulate and observe. However, using such simulations in a meaningful
manner is not an easy task. The aim of the bus-stop canopy case study was to
build a platform that would facilitate domain knowledge exchange within
the existing framework as a first step of the ongoing research.

Visualisation of a CFD analysis result using the custom-
developed toolkit.

opposite: Visualisation of thermal comfort. Top: Proposed bus stop design.
Bottom: Existing bus stop. Orange colour indicates areas of discomfort.

MESH GENERATION

Running CFD requires the creation of a volumetric meshing of the geometry of interest and its surroundings. This step is critical and the most manually intensive. During the conceptual design phase, architects explore multiple geometries before arriving at a particular building design, which means that multiple meshing processes are required to run CFD. There are two aspects that need to be balanced when meshing: quality and quantity. Mesh quality affects the overall accuracy of the analysis, while the quantity of mesh nodes dictates the computational cost, which can easily become overwhelming for complex geometries.

In the Arch-CFD bus-stop canopy case study, hybrid mesh generation is employed to maintain an acceptable accuracy level with the flexibility of meshing various complex shapes. Hybrid mesh is the combination of structured mesh (surrounding environment) and unstructured mesh (geometry of interest). This enables simple and rapid iteration of a particular conceptual design while maintaining a reduced level of mesh cells, therefore increasing efficiency while reducing the computing cost. Here, a parametric model for geometry generation was developed that omitted details such as holes, fillets and sharp corners that are small in relation to the overall size of the domain. While these details may be important for architecture expression, they have very little effect on the overall airflow. The parametric model ensured the consistency of the model for data exchange from design to analysis, and was used by the architects as a means to improve communication with the engineers regarding the range of geometries under consideration.

RESULT COMPREHENSION

Subsequent to analysis is comprehension of the analysis results. Most architects are not familiar with CFD, and it is therefore difficult for them to observe images provided by CFD practitioners and to expand their understanding of wind/air-flow.

To make CFD results more intuitive for architects, an interactive visualisation toolkit, originally developed by Sawako Kaijima and Panagiotis Michalatos at Adams Kara Taylor, was adopted and further developed in the ARCH-CFD project. The toolkit takes analysis results in a text format containing position, wind speed, and turbulence kinetic energy and provides interactive 3-D visualisations of physical phenomena throughout the domain of interest. In addition to the more typical streamlines or sectional visualisations, capabilities to view thermal comfort and vorticity have been incorporated, as well as animated particle tracking to aid the user in understanding the often counterintuitive air-flow features throughout the domain. The toolkit helped not only the architects but also the engineers in grasping the flow field in relation to the architecture geometry, and overall greatly improved communication among the team, which ultimately resulted in an enhanced design.

Computer simulations such as CFD have opened up new possibilities for design and research by introducing environments in which we can manipulate and observe.[4] However, using such simulations in a meaningful manner is not an easy task. The aim of the bus-stop canopy case study was to build a platform that would facilitate domain knowledge exchange within the existing framework as a first step of the ongoing research. It is believed that the collective effort in this domain will soon make possible the use of CFD in the early stages of architecture, encouraging design decisions based on the underlying physics of air flow. ⌂

Notes
1. Christopher Alexander, *The Nature of Order: An Essay on the Art of Building and the Nature of the Universe*, Oxford University Press (New York), 1997.
2. Joana Carla Soares Gonçalves and Erica Mitie Umakoshi, *The Environmental Performance of Tall Buildings*, Earthscan (London), 2010.
3. Edward N Lorenz, 'Deterministic Nonperiodic Flow', *Journal of the Atmospheric Sciences*, Vol 20, No 2, 1963, pp 130–41.
4. Sherry Turkle, *Simulation and Its Discontents*, MIT Press (Cambridge, MA) 2009.

CUSTOMISING THE ARCHITECTURAL DESIGN ENVIRONMENT WITH SOFTWARE PLUG-INS

DESI
ECO-
SYST

DANIEL DAVIS AND BRADY PETERS

As a preface to this section dedicated to the rise of plug-ins, **Daniel Davis and Guest-Editor Brady Peters** describe the shift in architectural culture that has seen the adoption of scripting interfaces – once the preserve of CAD specialists – spread to designers using code to create geometry and find form.

They explain how this defines an entirely new landscape in which 'cathedrals' (monolithic applications) are challenged by 'bazaars' (generative-modelling editors) populated by animal-named plug-ins, where architects become the formulators rather than just the end users of programs.

GN SEMS

Design environments are undergoing a perceptible shift in authorship. Advances in scripting interfaces are empowering architects to create parts of their own design environments. The boundaries between end user and developer are falling down around a network of designers sharing their creations as part of an emerging design ecosystem.

While computer-aided design (CAD) software has included scripting interfaces for many years, and there have been select individuals who have used this functionality to develop digital tools, the number of designers now using these scripting interfaces is increasing. What they are using it for, as well as how they are using it, are also changing. It is no longer only the CAD specialist writing scripts to increase efficiency or manage construction data, but also the designer creating geometry and finding form through sketching with code.[1]

Through the introduction of better-performing scripting capabilities in CAD software, designers have been able to quickly generate large amounts of geometry using relatively simple scripts. For example, the Visual Basic for Applications (VBA) scripting interface included with Bentley Systems' MicroStation v8 in 2001 was vastly superior to the Basic scripting interface included with v7 (1998). These generative or analytical algorithms can be shared, either through computer code or through packaging the script with an easy-to-understand interface. Through a combination of using common geometric elements, and outputting data to simple formats such as text files or spreadsheets, these computational techniques allow a diverse range of design software, analysis techniques and fabrication methods to be linked.

Beyond the scripting interface, some designers are finding further potential to shape the design environment itself. A number of designers have been developing 'plug-ins' that function as core parts of existing CAD platforms. The process of development is similar to the computer-programming techniques of scripting, but unlike scripts these plug-ins are packaged as small pieces of software and themselves become part of the design environment. Each plug-in emerges to address a specific problem or opportunity that an architect has identified in their work, thus widening the digital design environment around the desires of the individual designer.

Not only are more and more architects computer programming, writing scripts and creating plug-ins, but these are increasingly being shared via the Internet, conferences and workshops.[2] This marks the formation of a new design ecosystem, one under constant evolution and catalysed by sharing at a scale never before seen, that is simultaneously a community of architects and a collection of related algorithmic concepts. This design ecosystem is probably growing in a CAD environment near you.

One way of structuring a CAD environment is to have it do everything: a single self-contained application that can take a design from massing to construction drawings, from positioning doors to producing schedules, from creating geometry to composing visualisations. By integrating all of these components, each part can make assumptions and guarantees about how the rest operate, saving the designer the indignity of converting CAD files into different data formats (if this is even possible) and from having to purchase many different standalone softwares. This monolithic process is the holy grail of project lifecycle management (PLM) and, arguably, its brethren building information modelling (BIM).

The self-contained design environments set up to support these monolithic processes belong to a software category that Eric Raymond calls 'cathedrals' – large applications crafted by a highly talented group working together in isolation.[3] Raymond contrasts the cathedral with the 'bazaar' – a marketplace in which the collective action of individuals contributes to the larger community. For architects, the dichotomy exposes the fact that for many decades design environments have almost exclusively consisted of cathedrals.

Breaking the norm, Robert McNeel & Associates' Grasshopper® is a bustling bazaar-type environment. Grasshopper is a graphical programming environment that runs within Rhinoceros® CAD software, where architects visually link together components that are conceived of, and created by, other architects rather than by a team of software engineers. Even McNeel's sole developer on the project, David Rutten, has an architectural background rather than a formal computer science education. While Rutten controls the core, he is joined by a community of architects who freely share the plug-ins that make up Grasshopper.

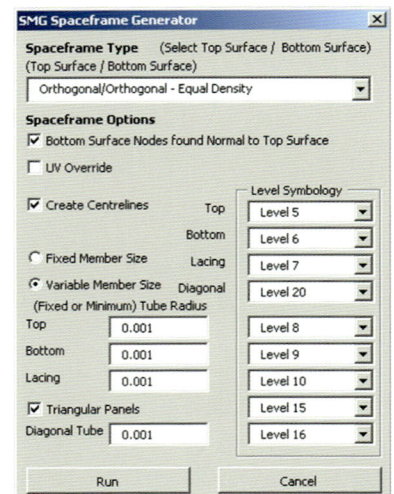

Foster + Partners, West Kowloon Canopy Masterplan, Kowloon, Hong Kong, 2003
right and previous spread: Using a script written in VBA in Bentley's MicroStation, the designers were able to quickly draw in 3-D a 1,500-metre (4,921-foot) long space-frame structure. The use of this technique made the design of this complex structure simple and intuitive. The script was written by Brady Peters and modified throughout the design process.

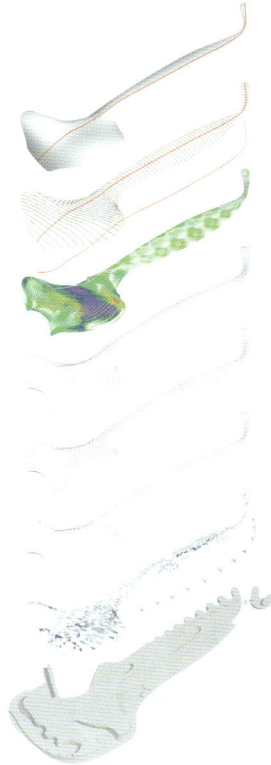

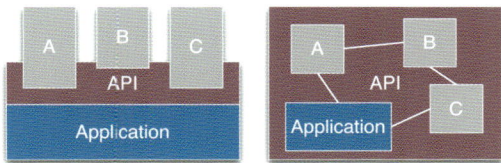

This section of the issue features the plug-ins: Galapagos, Kangaroo, Firefly, WeaverBird, GECO™ and Pachyderm Accoustical Simulation. Unlike the teams of specialist developers working on monolithic CAD applications, the creators of these Grasshopper plug-ins work alone or in pairs, and they are all end users. Significantly, their plug-ins are motivated by specific problems they have encountered in their own architectural practice. They also share their work, for free, through the sizeable online community. This 'bazaar-esque' community serves to shape the design ecosystem by implicitly encouraging or discouraging particular plug-ins. A traditional hierarchical structure does not apply since popularity is based on usability and functionality rather than on limitations of access, cost or compatibility. There is such a market for these plug-ins that one wonders whether, in future, they will be sold more formally as apps.

The focus of each plug-in on a particular niche problem follows what Doug McIlroy has termed the Unix philosophy of programming: to 'write programs that do one thing and do it well. Write programs to work together.'[4] It is the 'working together' that distinguishes the Grasshopper environment, for all the plug-ins within it can freely exchange data with one another. For instance, WeaverBird can panel a structure designed in Kangaroo without the designer manually converting the data, and without the authors of either plug-in needing to coordinate with each other. This is in large part due to the Grasshopper application programming interface (API) developed by David Rutten, which formalises the exchange of data around simple collections of basic geometric primitives. This 'geometric-content-based' data exchange is in opposition to BIM's 'assigned-attribute-based' data structures,[5] and is a simplification that enables plug-ins to easily work together.

There is a diverse range in what the plug-ins do, but each facilitates a translation of some kind. GECO and Firefly serve as translators between Grasshopper and other sources of data; GECO connects to the Autodesk® Ecotect® environmental analysis package, while Firefly sends and receives data from the Arduino microcontroller platform. The remaining plug-ins all translate research into accessible components. For instance, WeaverBird takes work done by computer scientist Edwin Catmull and others, and packages it for designers unfamiliar with the mathematics. As such, knowledge normally locked away in esoteric research is made accessible to the point where a designer can use it without needing to necessarily understand what he or she is designing with. Sherry Turkle describes this as 'Macintosh Transparency' (transparent because nothing gets in the way), which she places in opposition to 'Modernist Transparency' (transparent because you can see how everything works).[6] In Turkle's view, Macintosh Transparency risks producing designers who are 'drunk with code', designers so enamoured with the results that they fail to see that the plug-in translates a far more nuanced concept.[7]

**Center for Information Technology and Architecture (CITA) and
Spatial Information Architecture Laboratory (SIAL), Dermoid,
Royal Danish Academy of Fine Arts, Copenhagen, 2011**
The hierarchy of scripting modules that constitutes the Dermoid
design environment.

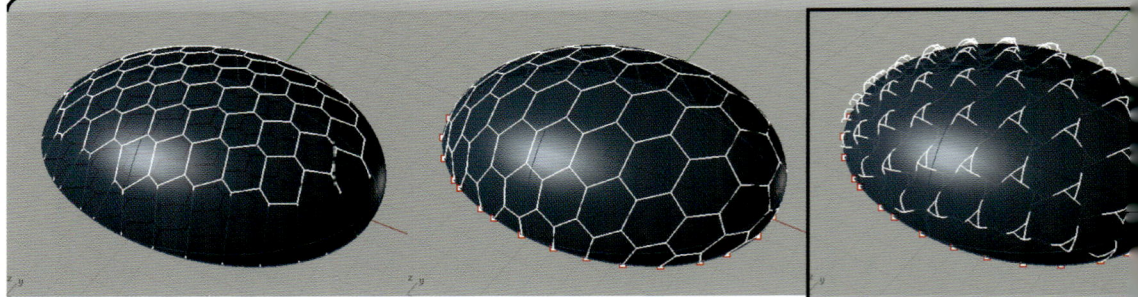

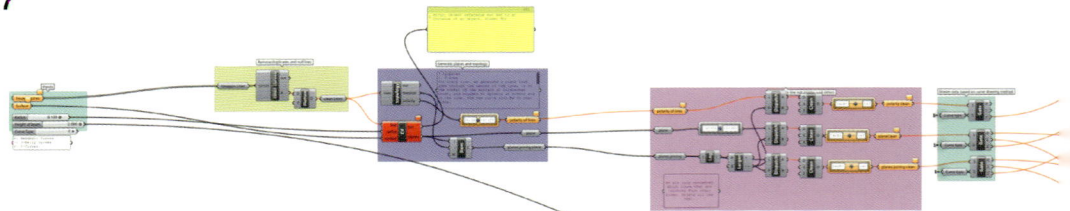

The coordination and creation of the design environment is itself becoming the domain of the designer. These are environments orchestrated by architects from core components created by architects, environments continually changing in dialogue not only with the project, but also with particular stages of it.

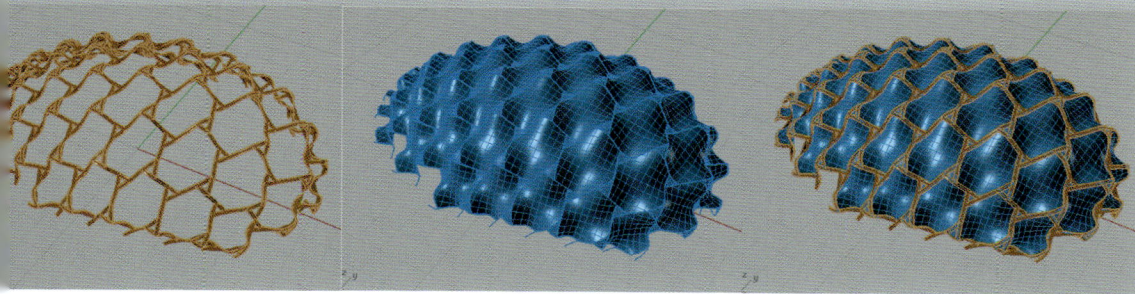

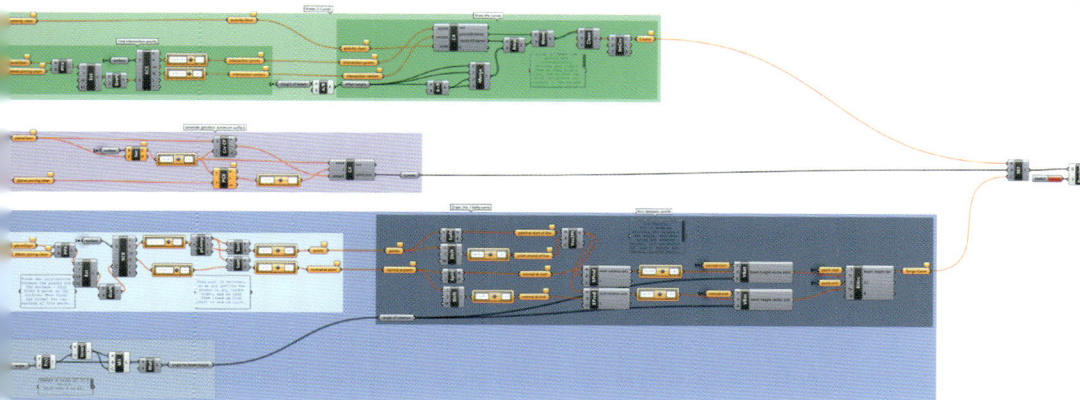

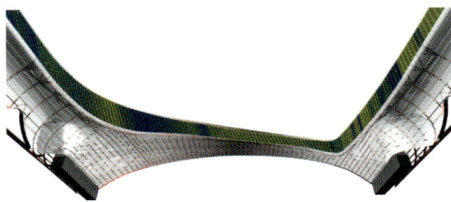

Center for Information Technology and Architecture (CITA) and Spatial Information Architecture Laboratory (SIAL), Dermoid, Royal Danish Academy of Fine Arts, Copenhagen, and RMIT University, Melbourne, 2011

top: The overall form of Dermoid was radically changed just days before its construction at the Royal Danish Academy of Fine Art's '1:1: Research by Design' exhibition – a change afforded by the flexibility of the design environment.

Foster + Partners, Kai Tak Cruise Terminal, Hong Kong, 2013

centre and bottom: Using Kangaroo, an initial set of non-planar panels (shown in yellow) were physically constrained while being allowed to slide along guide rails during the planarity optimisation process. As the steel structure is fixed, the optimisation is restricted to deviate < 30 millimetres (1.2 inches) from its original surface geometry. Towards the end of the optimisation process, most panels were improved from the original double curvature to achieve planar panelisation (shown in blue).

Architects are expert coordinators: of building projects, of different disciplines and building trades, and of bringing together the multitude of parameters and constraints that define the boundaries of a project. While there are inherent dangers in not knowing what lies within a black-box piece of code, it is part of the definition of the architect not to know everything, but to know enough; they alone understand the overall concept and hold together the project. As architects adopt the coordination of code in addition to the coordination of design and construction, their role diversifies.

The coordination and creation of the design environment is itself becoming the domain of the designer. These are environments orchestrated by architects from core components created by architects, environments continually changing in dialogue not only with the project, but also with particular stages of it.[8] In this sense, these continually evolving design environments are unlike any static design tool, and unlike any design environment architects have previously encountered.

It is this evolution of the design environment that provokes the designer's new role. For the environment to adapt easily, the designer must ensure the relationships between components are flexible enough to accommodate unexpected changes. If the designer fails to do so, writes Mark Burry, 'there is no solution other than to completely disassemble the model and restart'.[9] When such a moment of inflexibility occurs, in the best case it causes an unexpected delay to the project while the relationships are reorganised. However, in the worst case the designer is dissuaded from making the change and ends up with a design that was not so much created in their design environment as it was for the limitations of that environment. To avoid these difficulties, architects must take on a role of actively maintaining flexible relationships between components within the design environment.

The role of the architect as the creator of generative scripts or developer of plug-ins goes beyond the creation of conventional digital 3-D models. It also goes beyond that of tool-maker, as creation, modification and coordination of the design environment becomes an integrated part of the design product. The design environment of which the architect is now part-author must be flexible and have the ability to accommodate change, and this represents a significant shift in authorship away from isolated teams of highly talented programmers towards end users collaboratively shaping their own environment. ⌂

Notes
1. Mark Burry, *Scripting Cultures: Architectural Design and Programming*, John Wiley & Sons (Chichester), 2011.
2. Rob Woodbury, 'Design Flow and Tool Flux', in Brady Peters and Terri Peters (eds), *Inside Smartgeometry: Expanding the Architectural Possibilities of Computational Design*, John Wiley & Sons (Chichester), 2013.
3. Eric Raymond, *The Cathedral and the Bazaar: Musings on Linux and Open Source by an Accidental Revolutionary*, O'Reilly Media (California), 1999.
4. Peter Salus, *A Quarter Century of Unix*, Addison-Wesley (Boston, MA), 1994, p 52.
5. Andre Chaszar, 'Navigating Complex Models in Collaborative Work for Integrated (and Sustainable) Design', in Pierre Leclercq, Ann Heylighen and Geneviève Martin (eds), *Proceedings of the 14th International Conference on Computer Aided Architectural Design Futures*, Les Éditions de l'Université de Liège (Liege), 2011, p 625.
6. Sherry Turkle, *Simulation and its Discontents*, MIT Press (Cambridge, MA), 2009, p 44.
7. Ibid, p 7.
8. See Daniel Davis, Jane Burry and Mark Burry, 'Understanding Visual Scripts: Improving Collaboration Through Modular Programming', *International Journal of Architectural Computing*, Vol 9, No 4, 2011, p 372; and Brady Peters and Hugh Whitehead, 'Geometry, Form and Complexity', in David Littlefield (ed), *Spacecraft*, RIBA (London) 2008.
9. Mark Burry, 'Parametric Design and the Sagrada Familia', *Architectural Research Quarterly*, Vol 1, No 4, July 1996, p 78.

While there are inherent dangers in not knowing what lies within a black-box piece of code, it is part of the definition of the architect not to know everything, but to know enough; they alone understand the overall concept and hold together the project.

GALAPAGOS ON THE LOGIC AND LIMITATIONS OF GENERIC SOLVERS

DAVID RUTTEN

A graduate in architecture and urbanism from TU Delft, **David Rutten** works with software company Robert McNeel & Associates (RMN). The developer of Grasshopper®, he was recently awarded the ACADIA 2012 award for innovative research. The Galapagos plug-in, which Rutten has developed for Grasshopper®, implements two generic solvers (one using a genetic algorithm and one using a simulated annealing algorithm). A generic solver will find a solution to a problem that can be expressed in a mathematical way; however, as he explains here, while these solutions may not be exact, they will be very good.

Generic solvers, despite being called generic, can only be applied to a subset of all possible problems. To understand the limitations of a solver, one needs to understand both its underlying theory as well as the algorithmic representation of any given problem. These must necessarily remain somewhat abstract as the dimensionality of a problem is dependent on the chosen formulation, which is often far beyond what mere humans can visualise. It is, however, possible to explain some of the topologies of phase spaces through vernacular language by treating only low-dimensional cases, which fall within the realm of the imaginable. This article discusses the parallels between phase space topologies and computational terminology as well as how generic solvers arrive at their solutions.

Phase spaces and their fitness landscapes
The relationship between a two-dimensional phase space and the resulting three-dimensional fitness landscape.

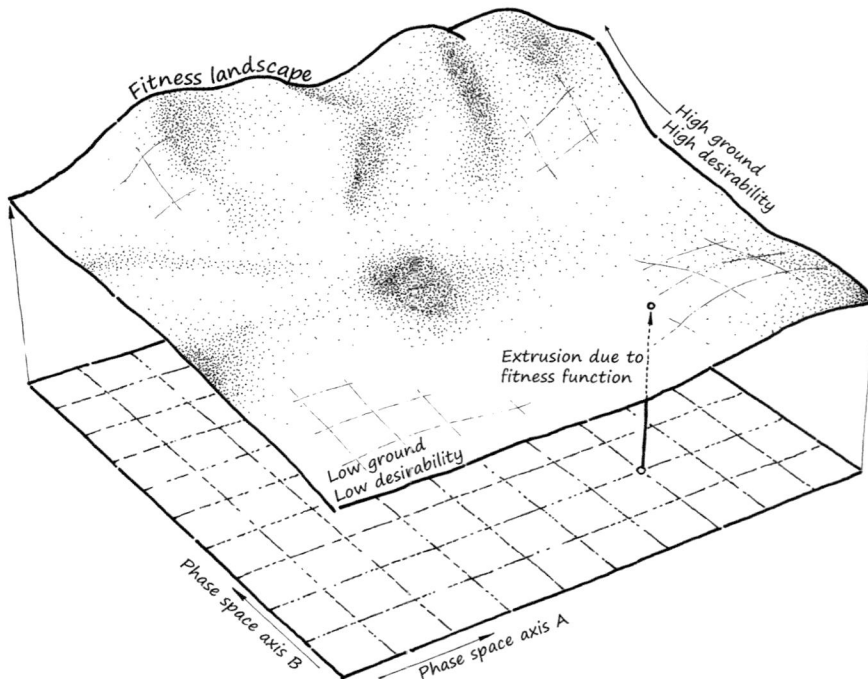

Fitness landscape

High ground
High desirability

Extrusion due to fitness function

Low ground
Low desirability

Phase space axis B

Phase space axis A

Problems come in many shapes and sizes. Some have an obvious solution, some have no possible solution, and some solve themselves if only we stop picking at them. There are well-defined mathematical classes of problems that categorise solvability: NL, NP-Hard, NP-Complete. Although these categories are of interest to complexity theorists, they are well beyond what the average person can make use of. Here, I will use the metaphor of landscape to explain the search for possible solutions. We are all familiar with the basic geometry of landscapes, which thus provides a good locus for a shared narrative.

So what exactly do we mean by 'problem' and 'solution'? A fairly hardcore definition of both would be that a problem is the extrusion of a system phase space, and a solution equals high ground in this newly created landscape. This sentence probably contains more unknowns than most are comfortable with, but I will do my very best to explain.

You may have heard the term 'phase space' before, perhaps even from someone who was trying to impress you. Mathematicians love to use 10-dollar words for two-cent notions, and this is no exception. A phase space is nothing more than the collection of all possible manifestations (states) of a given system. For example, let us imagine the system of a hanging chain. If the end points are fixed, then the only variable is the chain length. A system with a single variable is represented by a phase space with a single dimension. In one phase space corner we find short chains, and in the other, long chains. But if we allow the suspension points to move freely across the ceiling, the number of variables increases to five. Each suspension point can move in the X and Y directions, and of course the chain length also remains a variable. The phase space for this new system is a five-dimensional volume, which is not something you can imagine, nor is it something I can draw on a piece of paper. There is no theoretical upper limit to the dimensionality of a phase space,

and complicated problems can easily have thousands upon thousands of variables.

But a phase space merely contains all possible states, and does not award any significance to individual states. It is one thing to list all possibilities, but quite something else to have an opinion about them, and something else yet again to identify the best one. Before we can start to assay states, we must define a 'fitness function' that computes the desirability of any given state and expresses that desirability as a single number. The higher the number, the better we like that particular state. Once a fitness function has been defined, we can compare two states and favour one of them. Then, in theory, we can compare all states to all other states and find the one with the highest desirability. Such a brute-force search is often not practical, as the total number of distinct locations in a phase space of even moderate dimensionality is prohibitively large. We thus need better ways of finding quality locations in phase space.

Common fitness landscape topologies
Specific classes of problems result in specific landscape topologies. Problematic topologies can usually be repaired by adjusting the fitness function.

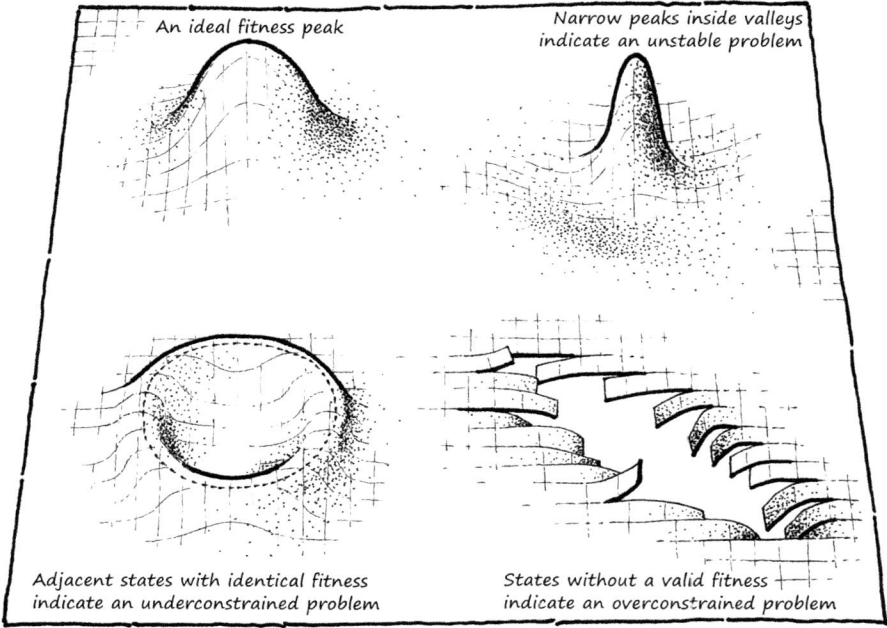

An ideal fitness peak

Narrow peaks inside valleys indicate an unstable problem

Adjacent states with identical fitness indicate an underconstrained problem

States without a valid fitness indicate an overconstrained problem

I still need to explain what exactly is meant by 'extrusion of a phase space'. We can unify a phase space and a fitness function into a single entity by evaluating all states and moving them according to their desirability. The direction in which we move states must be perpendicular to the phase space itself, which means we need one additional dimension to move them in. If our phase space happens to have two dimensions, it will be extruded into a third dimension, giving us a three-dimensional fitness landscape where the valleys represent low-quality states and peaks represent solutions, albeit local ones. But note that this landscape is a purely abstract concept, and at no point do we actually compute it, as that would often take far too long. We will have to content ourselves with only sampling a tiny minority of phase-space locations, but we also want these few samples to yield an acceptable solution. This is what generic solvers are supposed to be good at. They find high ground in uncharted fitness landscapes.

There is no guarantee that a solver will find the best solution in a finite amount of time. There could not be. The best we can hope for is a solution of acceptable quality in an acceptable amount of time. How well a solver performs (how many iterations it takes to find an acceptable solution) depends largely on the topology of the fitness landscape. Large horizontal plateaus tend to confuse a solver as it is not obvious in what direction it is smart to move. Areas that slope away from high peaks will give wrong directions, so to speak. Landscapes with gaps can trap solvers by restricting their movement. Rough or, worse, fractal terrain is bad as it scatters the solver momentum. The topology of the landscape is a direct result of the fitness function and is therefore at the mercy of whoever defined the said function.

Schematic representation of a simulated annealing run
The progression of an annealing solver can be represented as a series of converging jumps.

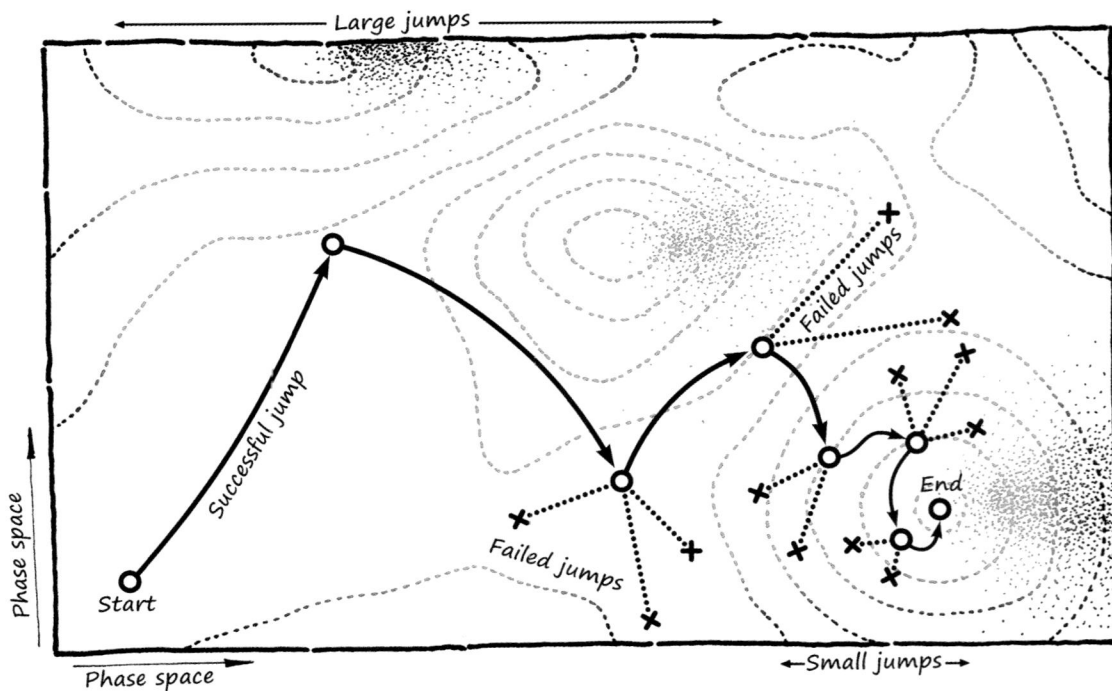

I would like to explain two very different generic solver classes, both of which I implemented in the Galapagos plug-in for Grasshopper®. This will necessarily be a very brief explanation that cuts many corners, but the basic idea behind each solver is not very complicated. Both are based on real-life processes: one physical, one biological.

Simulated annealing applies the theory of thermodynamics to search algorithms. More specifically, the process of crystalline matrix formation that occurs when molten metal is allowed to cool. When the atoms cool down, they start banding together into tiny crystals that grow larger as the temperature drops. This process can be described by a set of equations, which can in turn be employed to find peaks in a landscape. The way an annealing solver progresses is by jumping randomly across the landscape in ever-decreasing steps. If it does not accept the new location, perhaps because it is worse than before, it will revert to the previous one. Eventually, all jumps will be very small and it will be very picky about accepting new states. The lifetime of the solver can thus be divided into two parts: first it tries to find promising high ground, then it will fine tune its position in order to find the highest peak associated with this high ground.

Evolutionary algorithms apply the biological principles of mutation, selection and inheritance. They will populate the landscape with virtual individuals and then proceed to breed the highest ones in the hope that their offspring will be closer to a summit. Much decision-making is involved here regarding mate selection and various stochastic processes, but these are mere details.

Both solvers have their benefits and drawbacks. Annealing is better at navigating rough landscapes. Evolution is better at finding reliable intermediate solutions early on. To list all idiosyncrasies would take us far beyond the scope of this article. However, they are not something to be dismissive about if one intends to utilise generic solvers. ⌂

Both solvers have their benefits and drawbacks. Annealing is better at navigating rough landscapes. Evolution is better at finding reliable intermediate solutions early on.

Schematic representation of an evolutionary solver run
The progression of an evolutionary solver can be represented as a series of contracting boundaries that delineate the evolving population.

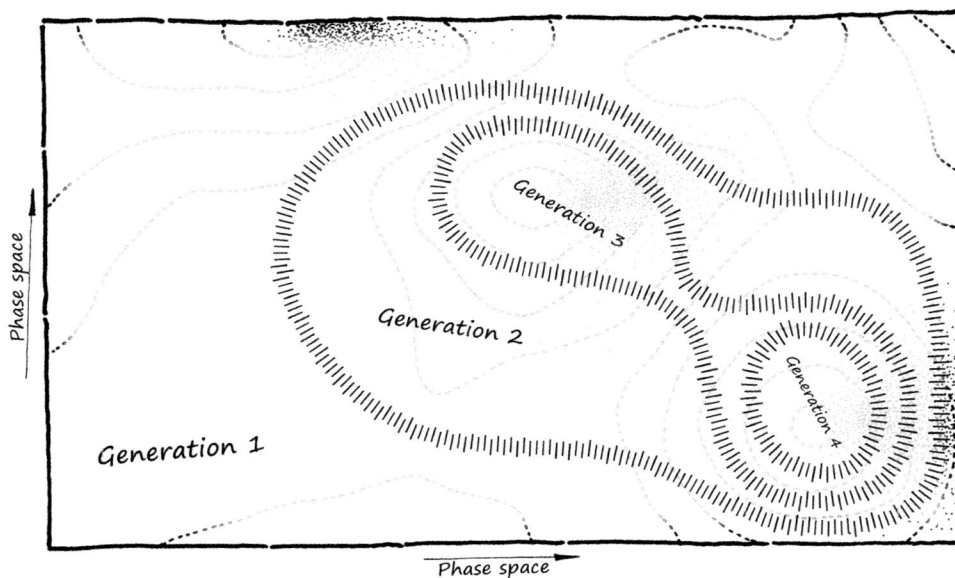

Generation 1
Generation 2
Generation 3
Generation 4

Phase space

Phase space

KANGAROO FORM FINDING WITH COMPU— TATIONAL PHYSICS

A trained architect, who works with the Specialist Modelling Group (SMG) at Foster + Partners, **Daniel Piker** is also the developer of the Kangaroo plug-in for Rhinoceros® and Grasshopper®. He explains how Kangaroo has been devised to simulate aspects of the behaviour of real-world materials and objects in order to modify designs in response to engineering analyses, engendering an intuitive sense of the material world.

From a young age we all develop a sense of certain predictable behaviours of the world around us,[1] things like interacting forces, momentum, elasticity and friction. This internal model allows us to effectively manipulate physical objects, because we can intuitively predict how they will react to forces we apply to them. There are many possible ways of manipulating digital geometry, but one great advantage of physically based methods is that we have a natural feel for them, and this intuitive quality lends itself well to the design process.

Kangaroo plug-in for Rhinoceros® and Grasshopper® is a collection of algorithms that enable a computer to simulate some aspects of the behaviour of real-world materials and objects, ie a 'physics engine'.[2] It is embedded directly in the computer-aided design (CAD) environment, enabling geometric forms to be shaped by material properties and applied forces and interacted with in real time. Modification of designs in response to engineering analyses is normally slowed

DANIEL PIKER

AHO Auxiliary Architectures Studio, Nested Catenaries, Oslo, 2010
A brick arch structure based on the same inverted hanging chain approach used by Antoni Gaudí to find structures acting in pure compression. The form was developed through a combination of actual and digitally simulated physical experimentation.

CODA BarcelonaTech, Jukbuin Gridshell, Barcelona, 2012
An experimental timber pavilion using an active-bending structural system developed from traditional basket weaving. Physical simulation in Kangaroo of bending and gravitational forces was used to find an effective form.

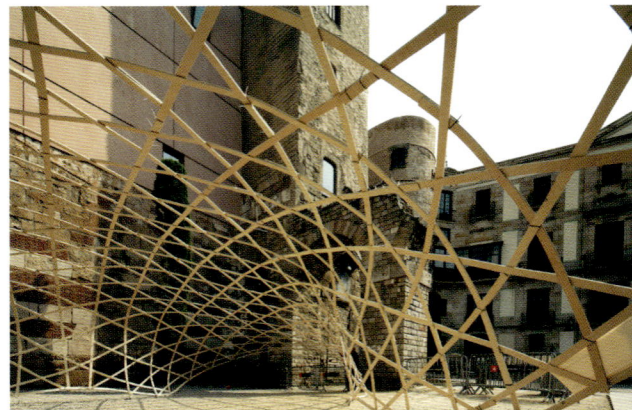

Just as a craftsman develops a sophisticated feel for a material through time spent working with it, if we can interact and play with virtual materials in our CAD programs then we can extend our intuition and develop a more sophisticated feel for their constraints and possibilities.

by calculation time and transfer between softwares.[3] By embedding rapid simulation in the early-stage design process, Kangaroo allows this feedback loop to be greatly accelerated.

Simulation in Kangaroo is nonlinear. This makes it particularly useful for the design of structures involving large deformations of material from its rest state, such as tensile membranes, bent-timber grid shells and inflatable structures. It enables digital form-finding, in the tradition of engineers/architects such as Frei Otto, Antoni Gaudí and Heinz Isler, where the physical response of a model (such as a hanging chain network or soap film) to a set of forces is used to generate an optimal form for resisting the design loads on the actual structure. However, Kangaroo can also be applied to the interactive optimisation of geometric and aesthetic qualities that may not themselves be intrinsically physical. Constraints such as the smoothness of a space-frame grid, or

the planarity of glazing panels on a curved surface, can be assigned physical energies that allow these problems to be solved within the same intuitive framework.

Just as a craftsman develops a sophisticated feel for a material through time spent working with it, if we can interact and play with virtual materials in our CAD programs then we can extend our intuition and develop a more sophisticated feel for their constraints and possibilities. Through the application of real-world physics we can make computational tools that really work *with* us to design in a way that is both creative and practical. ◁

Notes
1. Susan J Hespos, and Kristy vanMarle,'Physics for Infants: Characterizing the Origins of Knowledge About Objects, Substances and Number', *WIREs Cognitive Science*, Vol 3, No 1, 2012, pp 19–27.
http://onlinelibrary.wiley.com/doi/10.1002/wcs.157/abstract
2. Chris Hecker, 'Physics, the Next Frontier', *Game Developer Magazine*, October/November, 1996, pp 12–20.
3. Kirk Martini, 'Non-Linear Structural Analysis as Real-Time Animation: Borrowing from the Arcade', *Computer-Aided Architectural Design Futures 2001*, Kluwer Academic Publishers (Dordrecht), 2001, pp 643–56.

SOFTlab, Xtra Moenia, San Gennaro Gateway North, New York, 2011
In tensile structures the form must be closely linked to the stresses in the material in order to avoid wrinkling. Purely geometric CAD tools lack this physical behaviour, whereas traditional engineering approaches are slow and difficult to use for early exploration of design options. Kangaroo tackles these problems by embedding simulation directly in the modelling environment.

ID52/Wannes Lernout, Blaasstructuur, Hoboken, Antwerp, Belgium, 2011
The way inflatables are shaped by the interaction between air pressure and fabric tension makes their final form difficult to predict from the flat cutting pattern. Kangaroo allows the 'plug-and-play' combination of such forces, so that this shape formation can be easily simulated as part of the design process.

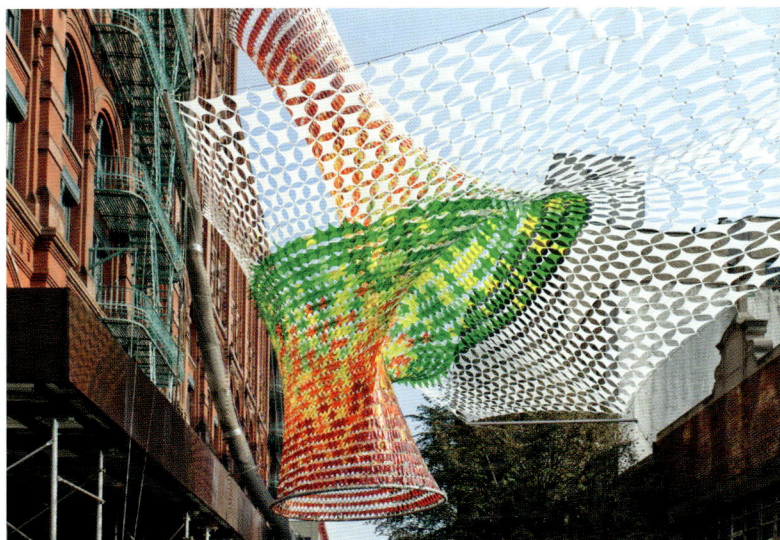

ARTHUR VAN DER HARTEN

PACHYDERM ACOUSTICAL SIMULATION
TOWARDS OPEN-SOURCE SOUND ANALYSIS

The creator of the Pachyderm Acoustical Simulation plug-in, **Arthur van der Harten** is an acoustician working in the Specialist Modelling Group (SMG) at Foster + Partners. Here he describes the flexible format of this plug-in and how open-source software aided the analysis of a negative distortion in the acoustics of Hamer Hall Arts Centre in Melbourne.

Understanding the sound qualities of a room often requires a more rigorous understanding than the analyses of reverberation and energy ratios alone can provide. Sound imperfections such as harshness and stridency can be associated with surface shapes that transform sound by emphasising high frequencies by diffracting energy in non-intuitive ways. Despite the iconic aesthetic of its faceted upper wall surfaces, Melbourne's Hamer Hall, a 2,380-seat performance venue in the city's Arts Centre, has suffered a negative acoustics reputation from its opening in 1982. In 2009, early in-situ studies by Kirkegaard Associates and Marshall Day Acoustics as part of a renovation effort implicated the facets as the source of a distortion caused by multiple audible diffuse reflections heard in succession.[1]

Pachyderm Acoustical Simulation, an acoustic analysis plug-in for Robert McNeel & Associates' Rhinoceros®,

Kirkegaard Associates, Faceted upper wall finish, Hamer Hall, Arts Centre Melbourne, Melbourne, Victoria, 2009
The original wall finish of the room was designed by Bolt, Beranek and Newman in 1982.

provided the acoustician with the capacity to generate convincing visualisations of the phenomenon. The tool was written to provide a flexible environment for acoustical simulation and is similar to many more expensive acoustic analysis tools. However, Pachyderm is unique in that it exposes the source code so that users can customise simulations either in the plug-in's native C#, or using Rhino's IronPython scripting interface. To date, it has been used for both acousticians' analyses performed on reduced versions of the architect's model, and for customised design experiments for academics in the fields of genetic algorithms[2] and experimental parameters.[3] In the case of Hamer Hall, Pachyderm helped prove that the harshness phenomenon in the venue was not produced by intuitively understood specular reflections. A useful supplement to these analyses came from the open-source boundary element modeling (OpenBEM) Mathworks®' MATLAB® toolkit,[4] which enabled the illustration of the scattering effects of the upper wall shapes and, even more importantly, predictions as to the effect of an absorptive treatment on various combinations of the facet surfaces and edges.

Altering the surface shaping turned out to be impossible due to the historical protection of the room aesthetic. A thin (high-frequency only) spray-on cellulose absorptive treatment was therefore recommended for specific facets in order to tame the distortion effects.[5] Critical reviews of the space were positive, acknowledging the increase in clarity of sound that the interventions provided, but also hinting at the unsolvable problem of lessened sound strength in very large rooms. Analysis tools should be offered in ways that enable users to become more informed. The more we invest ourselves in such tools, the more complete our understanding of the analysis. The Arts Centre Melbourne project demonstrates the benefits of the increased understanding provided by the detailed analysis made possible using open-source sound analysis techniques. ◬

Notes
1. Timothy E Gulsrud, Peter Exton, Arthur van der Harten and Larry Kirkegaard, 'Room Acoustics Investigations in Hamer Hall at the Arts Centre, Melbourne', *Proceedings of the International Symposium on Room Acoustics (ISRA)*, Melbourne, August 2010: www.acoustics. asn.au/conference_proceedings/ICA2010/cdrom-ISRA2010/Papers/P3c.pdf.
2. Tomás Mendez, Arianna Astolfi, Mario Sassone, Louena Shtrepi and Arthur van der Harten, 'Esplorazione Multi Obiettivo nella Progettazione Acustica Architettonica', *39 Convegno Nazionale dell'Associazione Italiana di Acustic*, Rome, 4–6 July, 2012.
3. Arthur van der Harten, 'Customized Room Acoustics Simulations Using Scripting Interfaces', *Proceedings of Meetings on Acoustics (POMA)*, Vol 12, June 2011: http://scitation.aip.org/getpdf/servlet/GetPDFServlet?filetype=pdf&id=PMARCW000012000001015001000001&idtype=cvips&prog=normal.
4. OpenBEM open-source MATLAB codes for the boundary element method by Peter M Juhl and Vicente Cutanda-Henriquez of the University of Southern Denmark.
5. Arthur van der Harten, Timothy Gulsrud, Larry Kirkegaard and Andy Kiel, 'A Multi-Faceted Study of Sound Diffusing Elements in an Auditorium', *Proceedings of Meetings on Acoustics (POMA)*, Vol 12, June 2011: http://scitation.aip.org/getpdf/servlet/GetPDFServlet?filetype=pdf&id=PMARCW000012000001015006000001&idtype=cvips&doi=10.1121/1.3633211&prog=normal.

Kirkegaard Associates, Ray Diagram, Hamer Hall, Arts Centre Melbourne, Melbourne, Victoria, 2010
The specular reflections shown in the diagram were created by a modified command in Pachyderm and illustrate the extent to which multiple audible specular reflections could be responsible for the multiple audible diffuse reflections heard in succession at Hamer Hall.

Kirkegaard Associates, OpenBEM Reflection Plot, Hamer Hall, Arts Centre Melbourne, Melbourne, Victoria, 2010
The exact scattering pattern was calculated in OpenBEM. The plot here illustrates that significant reflections at Hamer Hall occur in regions outside of the specular reflection zone.

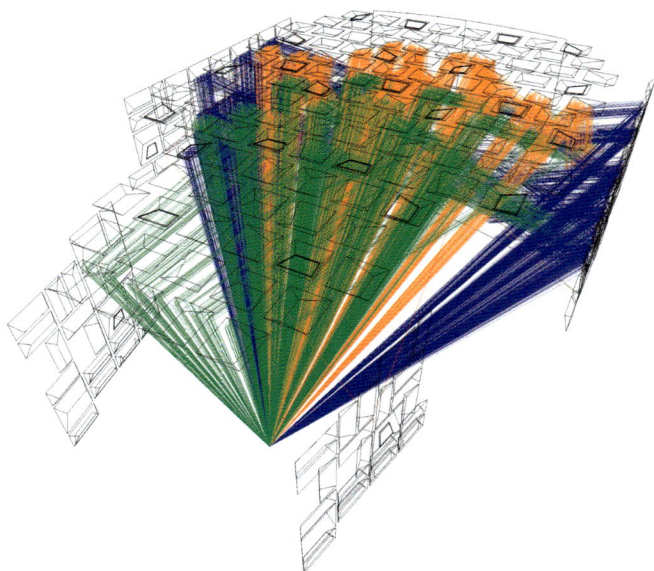

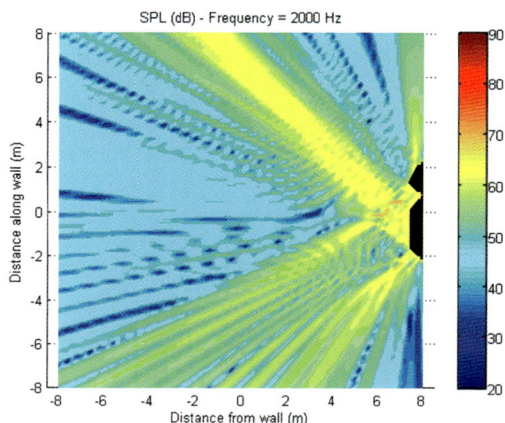

SPL (dB) - Frequency = 2000 Hz

WEAVERBIRD TOPOLOGICAL MESH EDITING FOR ARCHITECTS

Design and computation consultant **Giulio Piacentino** is the developer of WeaverBird. Here he describes how the plug-in 'gives architects more geometric control and allows them to create complex surface structures that join in orderly ways, yet in arbitrary configurations'.

WeaverBird is a topological editor that contains many of the well-known surface subdivision and transformation operators, and makes these accessible to architects and designers. Instead of doing the work repeatedly, or sometimes using complicated scripts, this plug-in reconstructs the shape, creates an infinitely defined, continuous surface from any mesh, and helps prepare the model for fabrication.

Its conception began when I was graduating in architecture with a winery project. The structure was partially underground and consisted of a complex arrangement of tubular paths and spaces. But it was difficult to model the junctions between tubes. I conducted tests with various tools; however, these were mostly developed with films, graphics or mathematics in mind. I discovered that there was a need for architectural tools to model organic complexity.

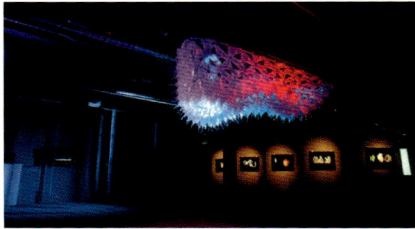

GIULIO PIACENTINO

SURFACE GENERATION

Andrea Graziano, Alessio Erioli, Davide del Giudice, Mirco Bianchini and Alessandro Zomparelli, Convoluted Inferences, MIGZ Festival, Moscow, 2011
above, below: The Italian Co-de-it group used WeaverBird to help in the construction of the Convoluted Inferences installation, a collaborative project where polypropylene tiles are arranged on a surface that is iteratively subdivided.

First step /
3 mesh faces

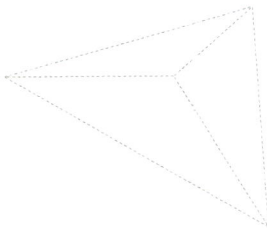

Second step /
quads subdivision 2 iterations /
32 mesh faces

Remove faces

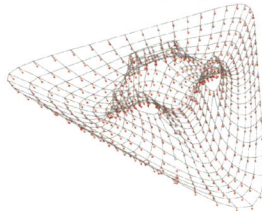

Third step /
Catmull-Clarck subdivision 2 iterations /
528 mesh faces

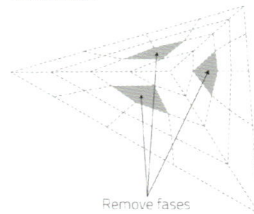

Fourth step /
relax mesh and sorted mesh face

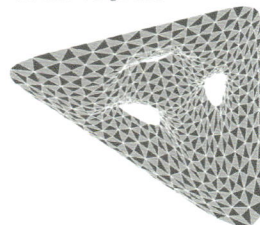

Fifth step /
evaluation triangle faces

Sixth step /
selection triangular faces

I started the WeaverBird project to help designers conceive hard-to-draw shapes and to go beyond established tiling patterns. The program operates as a plug-in in Robert McNeel & Associates' Rhinoceros® and Grasshopper®. Elements available in Rhino are usually non-uniform rational basis spline (NURBS) patches, and these are inherently rectangular, so WeaverBird expands this available toolset with industry-proven and applicable low-level algorithms.

WeaverBird gives architects more geometric control and allows them to create complex surface structures that join in orderly ways, yet in arbitrary configurations. As opposed to what happens with some form-finding tools, the designer has the advantage of being able to choose the position of surfaces. The development plan of WeaverBird is to implement all polyhedral operators, often named 'Conway's operators', defined in studies dating back at least to Johannes Kepler.[1]

The model need not be solid or enclosable: open and manifold cases are correctly handled. For example, WeaverBird contains the Catmull–Clark subdivision first described in 1978[2] and used in many motion picture pipelines. Another subdivision algorithm, adapted to terrains, is triangular and was first discussed by Charles Loop in 1987.[3] Several other operators are available in the editor. ⌂

Notes
1. Johannes Kepler, 'Harmonice Mundi', *Opera Omnia*, Vol 5, 1864.
2. Edwin Catmull and James Clark, 'Recursively Generated B-Spline Surfaces on Arbitrary Topological Meshes', *Computer-Aided Design*, Vol 10, No 6, 1978, pp 350–5.
3. Charles Loop, 'Smooth Subdivision Surfaces Based on Triangles', MS Mathematics thesis, University of Utah, Salt Lake City, 1987.

WeaverBird gives architects more geometric control and allows them to create complex surface structures that join in orderly ways, yet in arbitrary configurations.

Wieland Schmidt, Side lamp, Munich, 2011
German architect designer Wieland Schmidt used Picture Frames, another operator in WeaverBird, to help in the conception of some of his furniture pieces, such as this partly transparent side lamp with a smooth, irregularly pierced body.

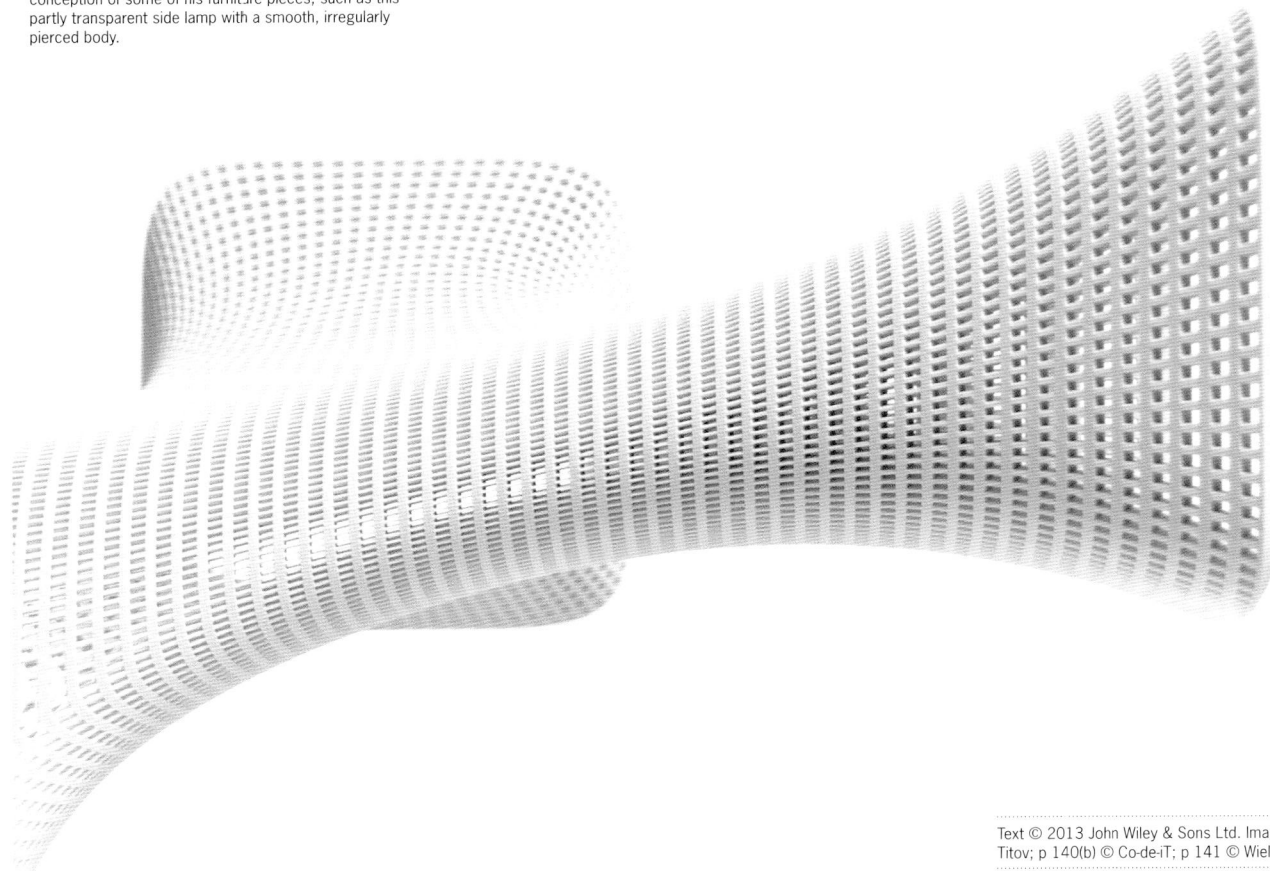

Daylight autonomy displays the areas of the project that can be lit without any additional artificial light. Areas that achieve 100 per cent of their target light level are shown in yellow, while those outside of the target are blue.

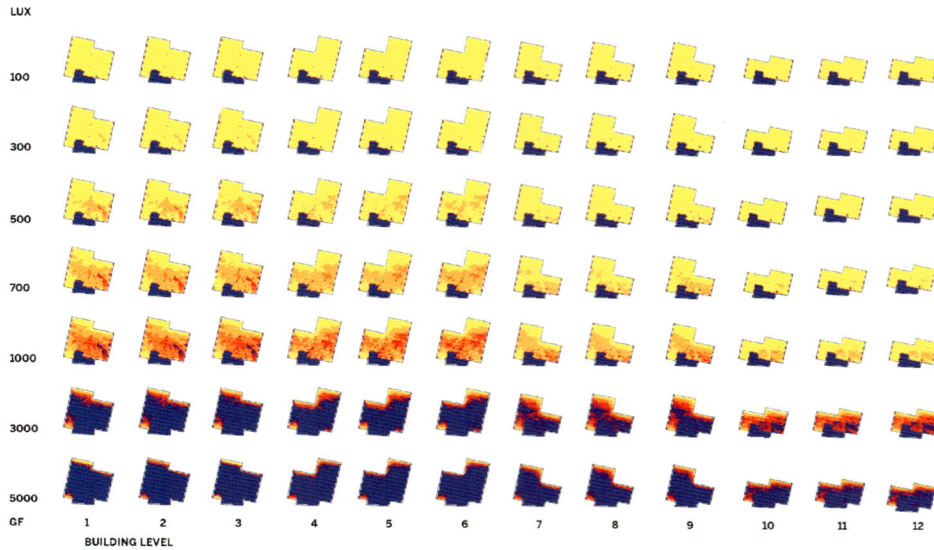

THOMAS GRABNER AND URSULA FRICK

GECO™
ARCHITECTURAL DESIGN
THROUGH ENVIRONMENTAL
FEEDBACK

Built By Associative Data, 1234, Beirut, Lebanon, 2011
This corporate building design utilised GECO to optimise the interior office spaces within for daylight autonomy.

In recent years there has been a disconnect between the early stages of design and the power of evolving analysis tools. **Thomas Grabner and Ursula Frick**, the founding directors of design research and development consultancy [uto], explain how their plug-in GECO™ creates essential connections between modelling and analysis software, providing the opportunity to restructure conceptual design.

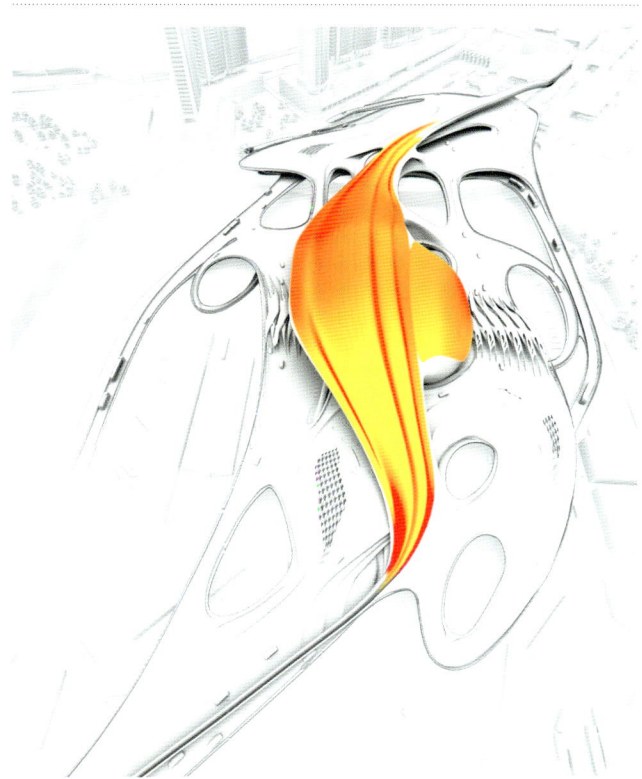

SPAN (Matias del Campo and Sandra Manninger with Federico La Piccirella and Filippo Nassetti), Hong Kong Shenzhen Border station competition entry, Hong Kong, China, 2011
left: The architects used GECO here to perform a solar access analysis of the roof design over a time period of one year to develop the roof openings and their relationship to the form of the overall design. The feedback is accessible as vertex colour or watt-hours per square metre, and can be translated into an algorithm for the definition of the openings.

below: Rendering demonstrating the results of integrating GECO within the design process: the dynamic application of roof openings finely tuned to the environmental conditions of the project.

GECO allows the user to export complex geometries, evaluate the design's performance in Ecotect, and import the results back into Grasshopper, without reworking the model repeatedly.

Generative modelling tools are increasingly popular in architectural practice as they enable the user to iteratively create and evaluate multiple models to explore design potentials and inform architectural decisions. However, many current ways of working cannot fully utilise this capacity, as there is no direct link between the power of iterative modelling and analysis. In practice, multiple models are independently generated for the purposes of visualisation and analysis. This requires time-consuming efforts and often generates a pattern of degradation in data, as models must be exported from their native format. It is therefore necessary to rethink the structure of this digital workflow and narrow the gap between modelling and analysis. [uto] has therefore developed GECO, a plug-in for Robert McNeel & Associates' Grasshopper®, to explore the potential of creating live linkages between 3-D modelling software and analysis platforms.

Autodesk®'s Ecotect® Analysis sustainable design analysis software evaluates environmental performance and is used in the early stages of design. However, it is limited by the necessity to export and restructure models for analysis. GECO allows the user to export complex geometries, evaluate the design's performance in Ecotect, and import the results back into Grasshopper, without reworking the model repeatedly. This can be performed as a single process or set up as an iterative loop. Through iterative analysis and geometry modification, the performance of a building can be maximised in the context of its environment. As Ecotect works on the principle of 'progressive data input', whereby visual feedback can be generated with very little data provided, analysis can become an integral part of the early stages of design. Creating this live link improves workflow and consolidates data, maintaining the native file format and preserving the integrity of the original geometry. Results generated in Ecotect using GECO are applied and saved directly to the original geometry, allowing values to be assessed locally or globally. As a result, the original model geometry is enriched, becoming a dynamic catalogue of information rather than a geometric base file that must be exported and revised for analysis and visualisation in other settings.

GECO has been used successfully in practice, for example in Built by Associative Design's project for a fully day-lit corporate office building in Lebanon, and in academia where it is used as a research and teaching tool at the Institute of Urban Design (ioud) at the University of Innsbruck. These projects have shown that GECO has the potential to improve current practice, particularly in the earliest phases of design, to identify strong concepts that can have the greatest impact on the final design. ∆

Andrew O Payne/LIFT architects, Air Flow(er) facade prototype, 2009
The Air Flow(er) is a heat-sensitive facade system that responds to changes in temperature using shape memory alloy wires to open and close the facade panels without the need for electricity. The project focuses on simplicity, employing specifically calibrated shape memory alloy wires to act as a sensor, processing system and actuator all in one. It is designed to behave like 'thermonastic' flowers whose 'petals' naturally open wide when exposed to warmer temperatures.

ANDREW O PAYNE AND JASON KELLY JOHNSON

FIREFLY INTERACTIVE PROTOTYPES FOR ARCHI-TECTURAL DESIGN

Andrew O Payne of LIFT architects and **Jason Kelly Johnson** of Future Cities Lab describe the Firefly plug-in for Grasshopper® they have developed, which extends geometric control beyond the virtual parametric model to the real world of machines and mechanisms. Firefly also enables communication to flow in the other direction, allowing virtual building models to be informed by, and interact with, data from the real world.

Prototyping has always been integral to the architectural design process. Prototypes give designers the ability to test and simulate how a particular design will perform under a range of conditions. Following the latest trends, architects in the future will be increasingly called upon to create building systems, spaces and landscapes that are computationally enhanced and interconnected.[1] Our environments will also demand some form of intelligent adaptability – a recognition of evolving external environmental parameters, user demands and feedback systems.[2] We are therefore currently developing a new set of tools that allow a more integrative and fluid approach to prototyping. The tools are intended to enhance the design process for interactive and responsive architectures and enable a move towards 'interactive prototyping environments' (IPEs),[3] which will allow new creative and technical opportunities for architects and improve the design and prototyping process.

The typical design process for interactive prototypes often requires the use of several disparate software applications and programming languages, and demands a variety of highly specialised skill sets. It is evident that a new integrated approach towards design and prototyping is required,

Following the latest trends, architects in the future will be increasingly called upon to create building systems, spaces and landscapes that are computationally enhanced and interconnected.

Seen here in a double-skin facade application, other variations of the design included prototypes for a single-skin ventilation system and a roof vent. While the original design intent was to be entirely self-regulating, these prototypes have the capacity to respond to other environmental stimuli (light, movement, wind) when connected to other sensors using Firefly's IPE.

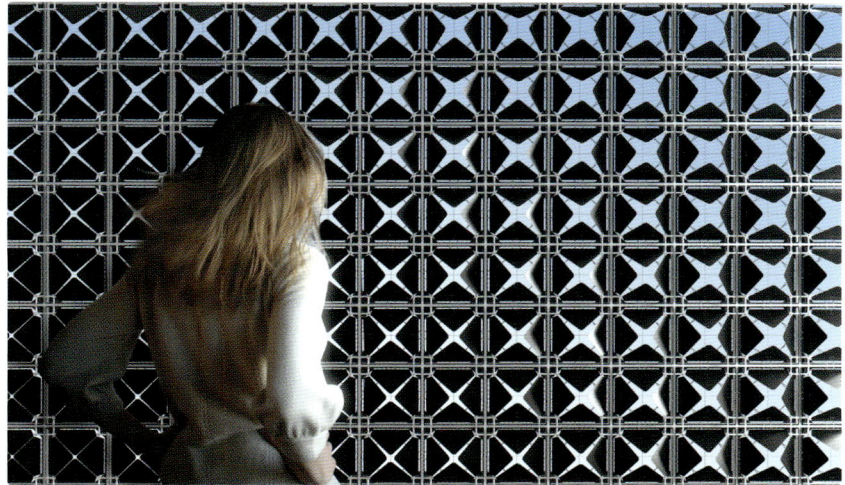

Firefly's IPE gives the designer the ability to quickly test various configurations and designs using real-world data to drive interactive, or 'live', digital models.

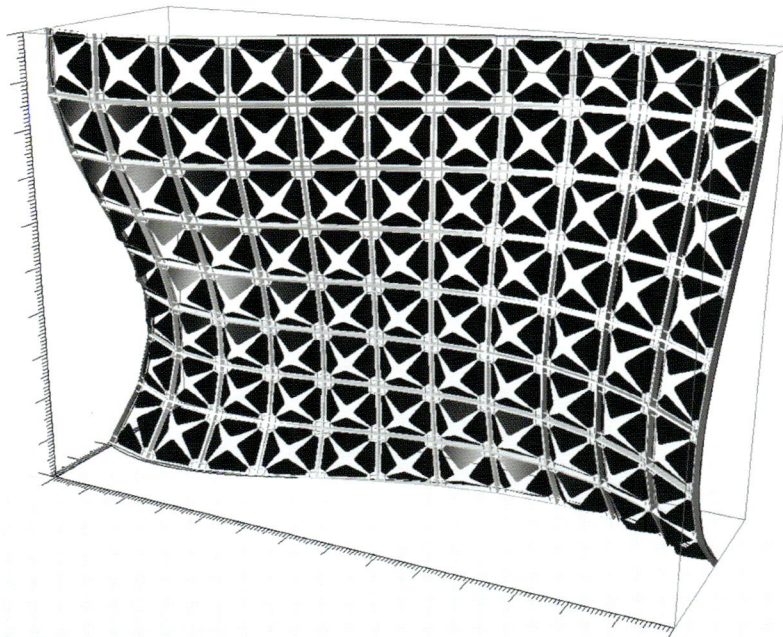

Jason Kelly Johnson/Future Cities Lab, Cirriform responsive facade, Seattle, Washington, 2012
top: Detail view of the Cirriform physical prototype. The final full-scale prototype used Firefly and Grasshopper to iterate through many design possibilities, fluidly working back and forth between the digital and the physical realms with ease.

bottom: Facade and plan drawing illustrating Cirriform's sensing envelope and overall geometric configuration. As visitors walk towards the facade, their proximity triggers the rotation of hundreds of small illuminated crystalline components. Firefly was first connected to proximity sensors to simulate pedestrian point attractors as they moved across the site.

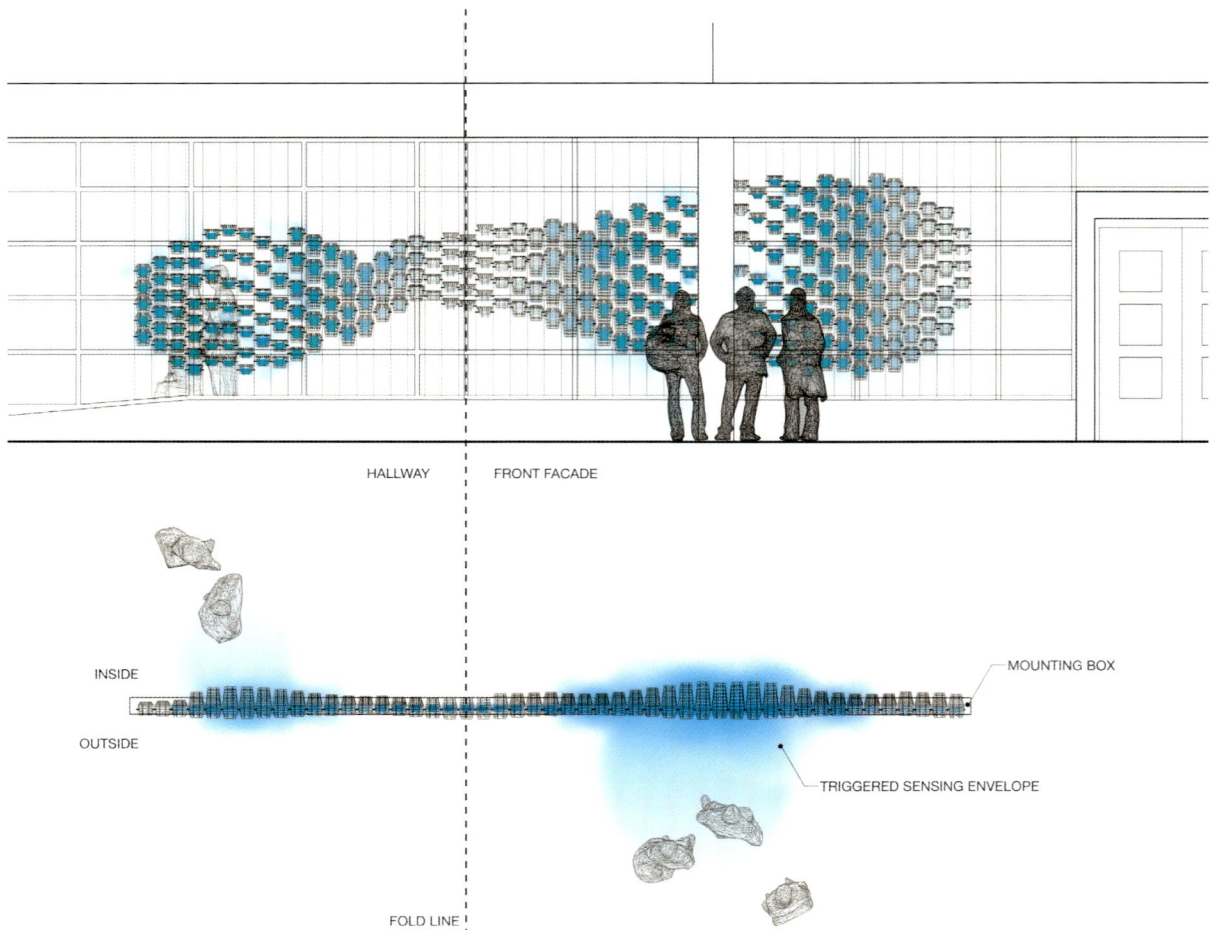

HALLWAY | FRONT FACADE

INSIDE

OUTSIDE

MOUNTING BOX

TRIGGERED SENSING ENVELOPE

FOLD LINE

Cirriform used both Grasshopper and the Firefly interactive prototyping environment (IPE) as tools to explore the project from concept to simulation, fabrication, and interaction design. Cirriform is a site-specific installation that activates a building facade responding to the proximity of pedestrians using sensors, LEDS and small stepper motors. Grasshopper/ Firefly was used to generate a real-time taxonomy of digital algorithmic patterns that could be simulated in real time using the physical prototype.

and the proposed solution is a visually oriented IPE called Firefly,[4] which is an extension to Robert McNeel & Associates' Grasshopper® plug-in for Rhinoceros®.

Firefly bridges the gap between the digital and physical worlds and simplifies the prototyping process for interactive and responsive architectures. It combines a specialised set of components with a novel communication protocol (called the Firefly Firmata), which together enable real-time feedback between hardware devices such as the well-known Arduino microcontroller and the Rhino/Grasshopper modelling environment. Since it is tightly integrated into this robust CAD application, real-world data acquired from various types of sensors (light, touch, proximity, accelerometers) or other input devices (video cameras, Internet feeds or mobile phone devices) can be used to explicitly define relationships within a parametric model to drive 3-D geometry.

Firefly's toolset gives the designer the ability to quickly test how well a design will perform when confronted with different real-world environmental conditions, saving on physical prototyping costs and time. It also opens up the possibility to control digital prototypes using a range of real-time data – creating 'live models'[5] whose

parameters can be iteratively tested until a desired set of outcomes is achieved. Firefly completes the communication feedback loop by allowing users to send information from Grasshopper back to hardware devices to incite real-world actuations (controlling lights, a variety of motors, valves, etc). It leverages Grasshopper's visual programming environment as a new model for microcontroller programming, making it ideal for visually oriented professionals such as architects and designers who prefer creating programs by manipulating elements graphically rather than by specifying them textually.

While we are just at the beginning of understanding how new interactive prototyping tools such as Firefly will open up new possibilities for designers, some exciting possibilities are already becoming apparent. As architectural designers gain knowledge and expertise in these new tools and technologies, they will have an increased capacity to explore building systems, spaces and landscapes in a more robust and cross-disciplinary way. When IPE tools such as Firefly are used in combination with the rich ecology of available hardware and software extensions, plug-ins and apps, a whole new and exciting set of interactive prototypes will emerge. ∆

Notes
1. See Mark C Taylor, *The Moment of Complexity: Emerging Network Culture*, University of Chicago Press (Chicago, IL), 2001, and William J Mitchell, *Me++: The Cyborg Self and the Networked City*, MIT Press (Cambridge, MA), 2003.
2. Patrik Schumacher, 'On Systemic Architecture', in Marco Poletto and Claudia Pasquero, *Systemic Architecture: Operating Manual for the Self Organizing City*, Routledge (London), 2012, pp 15–17.
3. Andrew Payne, 'IDE vs IPE: Toward an Interactive Prototyping Environment', in Jörg Petruschat and Julian Adenauer (eds), *Prototype!*, Form + Zweck Verlag (Berlin), 2012, pp 172–82.
4. www.fireflyexperiments.com.
5. Jason Kelly Johnson and Nataly Gattegno, 'Experiments in Live Modeling', *PRAXIS 13: Ecologics*, December 2011, pp 45–7.

Alessandro Beghini works as a structural project engineer at Skidmore, Owings & Merrill (SOM) where he is involved in all aspects of the design process. He is responsible for conducting research in the field of optimal structural topologies and development of innovative methodologies for structural analysis. He maintains collaborations with academic institutions, including the University of Illinois at Urbana-Champaign. He serves as an Adjunct Professor at Northwestern University. He has co-authored several technical publications on a variety of structural engineering topics, including topology optimisation, the behaviour of fibre composites and fibre-reinforced concrete.

Bruce Bell is the designer and founding partner of Facit Homes. He studied interactive arts at Manchester Metropolitan University before completing an MA in design products at the Royal College of Art in 2004. Prior to founding Facit, he worked with a number of leading architects and artists including Foster + Partners, Olafur Eliasson and Antony Gormley, and was Creative Director of Willson & Bell architects.

Keith Besserud is a director of BlackBox, a research-oriented computational design resource within the Chicago office of Skidmore, Owings & Merrill (SOM). With design partner Ross Wimer, he set up the BlackBox studio in 2007 to lead the development and integration of advanced computational concepts within the multidisciplinary design processes of the office. The group is interested in exploiting various types and sources of data to guide form-finding design processes. It relies on parametric frameworks built with scripting expertise and parametric software, as well as a variety of simulation and search optimisation tools, including commercially available tools as well as those custom-developed by the team.

Roland Bouffanais is an assistant professor in the Engineering & Product Development Pillar at the Singapore University of Technology and Design (SUTD). His research efforts aim at understanding some of nature's most awe-inspiring phenomena in order to devise novel engineering techniques; for example, the hydrodynamics of cell-to-cell mechanical signalling for cell migratory control, and blind cave fish distant touch through a fluid.

Daniel Cardoso Llach is a designer and multidisciplinary researcher interested in the social and cultural aspects of design technologies. He recently completed his PhD as a Presidential Fellow at the Massachusetts Institute of Technology (MIT) with a dissertation examining the politics of representation, participation and authorship in technological discourses concerning design. With a background in architecture, he is active as a designer, educator and critic, and more recently as an assistant professor in the Stuckeman School of Architecture at the Pennsylvania State University.

Daniel Davis lives in Melbourne where he spends his time writing code and writing his PhD thesis. His research at RMIT University's Spatial Information Architecture Laboratory (SIAL) focuses on the crossovers between methodologies of programming and architectural design.

Christian Derix co-founded the Research & Development group (Aedas|R&D) at Aedas Architects in 2004. He directs the Computational Design Research Group (CDR), which develops computational design applications for generative and analytical design processes in architecture and urban design with an emphasis on spatial configuration and human occupation. He has taught design computation since 2001 at various universities in the UK and Europe,

and was recently a visiting professor for emergent technologies at the Technical University Munich.

Stylianos Dritsas is an assistant professor in architecture and sustainable design at the Singapore University of Technology and Design (SUTD). Prior to joining SUTD he was an associate principal at Kohn Pedersen Fox Associates in London. He has taught at the Architectural Association (AA) in London and the École Polytechnique Fédérale in Lausanne.

Seth Edwards is a computational designer at Grimshaw, working within the office's Design Technology Group deploying advanced geometric systems, analysis and custom scripting for a range of current projects. He holds a degree in architecture from the University of Virginia, and is a volunteer at the Smartgeometry organisation. His professional interests lie in the ability to effectively use advanced technology to both further the design process and create interactive environments in which to learn.

Al Fisher joined Buro Happold's SMART Solutions team in 2007 following his PhD at the University of Bath. As a structural engineer with a research background in computational design and analysis, he has interests covering a range of specialist problems including geometric, structural and environmental optimisation. He has a particular interest in freeform geometries where the structural and architectural forms are inextricably linked. He has also been developing novel conceptual design tools such as SMART Form and SMART Solar to optimise building forms.

Ursula Frick and Thomas Grabner are the founding directors of [uto], based in Innsbruck, Austria. Their research and consultant work focuses on the development of formal strategies, generation and analysis of complex geometries, and the relationship between the part and the whole. They have taught and held workshops around the world, in locations including the Advances in Architectural Geometry 2010 (AAG10) symposium in Vienna, Tamkang University in Taipei and, recently, at the University of Pennsylvania and the Southern California Institute of Architecture (SCI-Arc). They are also recognised for their development of digital tools, namely GECO™, Flowlines, and MeshEdit, which seek to improve workflow in a parametric environment. Both graduated with distinction from the University of Innsbruck, with degrees in architecture, and are currently working as teaching and research associates at the Institute of Urban Design, headed by Peter Trummer.

David Hines is a senior associate at Populous. He joined the global design practice in 2005 and worked on the development of the Aviva Stadium in Dublin, being involved with all aspects from design to completion. He leads the parametric and advanced geometry group within Populous, developing in-house tools and applications, and has lectured on this topic at several universities and conferences around the world.

Jethro Hon is an architect and an associate partner at Foster + Partners. As a member of the Specialist Modelling Group (SMG), he has worked on international projects as an in-house consultant specialising in computational methods in the optimisation of complex geometry, fabrication and building performance. Since receiving his education from the Architectural Association (AA) in London, he has taught at the Bartlett, University College London (UCL), the University of Nottingham and Syracuse University.

Åsmund Izaki is a senior designer and researcher in the Computational Design Research (CDR) group of Aedas|R&D since 2007, investigating and creating new forms of furniture design, architecture and urban planning through code. He has taught courses and seminars for design students on robotics, nanotechnology and responsive environments at Konstfack University College of Arts, Crafts and Design, and for architecture students on generative techniques, algorithms and representation at the KTH School of Architecture in Stockholm.

Jason Kelly Johnson is a design principal of Future Cities Lab in San Francisco and an assistant professor at the California College of the Arts (CCA). His design research is focused on robotic architectures and interactive technologies. After receiving his MArch degree from Princeton University, he was awarded the Young Architect's Prize from the Architectural League of New York, the Oberdick Fellowship from the University of Michigan, and the New York Prize from the Van Alen Institute.

Kristoffer Josefsson received his education in mathematics in Sweden and Berlin. After pursuing mathematical research in discrete differential geometry, he turned his interest to architecture and to the intersection of form finding in freeform architecture and mathematics. He has taught workshops for architects in Melbourne, Berlin and Istanbul, and has co-authored several articles on these topics. He currently works as a specialist geometer for Foster + Partners.

Sawako Kaijima is an assistant professor in architecture and sustainable design at the Singapore University of Technology and Design (SUTD) and a director of Sawapan Design. Her research focuses on the integration of engineering knowledge

into the architectural domain through computation. Along with her partner Panagiotis Michalatos, she has developed a range of software applications for intuitive and creative use of structural engineering methods in design.

Bas Kalmeyer studied fine arts, advertising and architecture at the Willem de Kooning Academy in Rotterdam, and architecture at the Academy of Architecture and Urbanism, also in Rotterdam. He worked as an architect at MVRDV on several large-scale projects before switching to The Why Factory, the think tank and research/masters programme at Delft University of Technology, to work as a researcher, editor and tutor.

Neil Katz is an architect with Skidmore, Owings & Merrill (SOM). He uses a computational design approach in exploring models and for analysing and designing in response to many project, including environmental and sustainability, goals. He has worked in the New York and Chicago offices of SOM, focusing on projects including the WTC Tower One, JFK Airport International Arrivals Building and Oakland Cathedral of Christ the Light, and also on research in, and development of, computational processes and tools.

Jan Knippers is the founder and partner of Knippers Helbig Advanced Engineering. He is particularly intrigued by complex shapes and parametrically generated structures, as well as by structures composed of membranes and plastics. He heads the Institute of Building Structures and Structural Design (ITKE) at the Faculty of Architecture and Urban Planning at the University of Stuttgart. He is the author of numerous books and publications, and a speaker at international conferences and congresses.

Michael Meredith is a principal of MOS Architects and an assistant professor at Princeton University School of Architecture.

Suresh Naidu is a research assistant at the Singapore University of Technology and Design (SUTD). His research consists of using computational fluid dynamics (CFD) to enhance architectural design methodologies and visualisation. His professional career with aerospace and wind energy companies focused on using simulations to enhance product design and test innovative concepts.

Andrew O Payne is a registered architect and founder of LIFT architects located in Cambridge, Massachusetts. He is currently pursuing his doctoral degree at Harvard's Graduate School of Design where his research focuses on creating architectural systems that are personalised, intelligent and responsive. He has recently published work on embedded computation, robotics, fabrication methodologies and parametric design, and has taught extensively throughout the US, Canada and Europe.

Giulio Piacentino uses his passion for geometry and his architecture degree from the Delft University of Technology to combine design and computation with the same care he exercises when looking after his vines. After working for some offices in the Netherlands, including the Rotterdam-based NIO Architekten, he served as the architecture specialist at Robert McNeel & Associates' office in Barcelona. He now provides custom consultancy and shares his advances with the community.

Daniel Piker is a researcher on the use of computation in the design and realisation of complex forms and structures. After studying architecture at the Architectural Association (AA) in London, he worked as part of the Advanced Geometry Unit (AGU) at Arup, and later the Specialist Modelling Group (SMG) at Foster + Partners. He has taught numerous studios and workshops, including the AA Design Research Lab (AADRL) and a cluster at Smartgeometry, and presented his work at conferences around the world. He is the creator of Kangaroo, the widely used form-finding physics engine software, which he continues to develop independently as well as consulting and collaborating with a wide range of practices and researchers.

Dusanka Popovska is a design system analyst in the Specialist Modelling Group (SMG) at Foster + Partners. She graduated as an engineer and architect from the Faculty of Architecture of St Kiril and Methodius University in Skopje, Macedonia, in 2002. She received an Advanced Master of Architecture in 2006 from the postgraduate laboratory for architecture at the Berlage Institute in Rotterdam. She joined Foster + Partners the same year and has since worked on various projects of different scale and function. Her main involvement is based on parametric modelling, rationalisation and construction of complex geometries and environmentally driven design.

Clemens Preisinger is a structural engineer at Bollinger + Grohmann Engineers. He contributed to the Algorithmic Generation of Complex Space-Frames research project at the University of Applied Arts Vienna. Since 2010 he has been developing the parametric, interactive finite element program Karamba as a freelancer. He holds a PhD in structural engineering from the Technical University Vienna.

Armando Ramos has more than 16 years' experience in architecture, development, marketing and building information modelling (BIM) coordination. His expertise lies in managing the design and execution of large-scale projects worldwide. Before joining Fernando Romero EnterprisE (FREE), he was Director of Business Development at Gehry Technologies, and was responsible for establishing the firm in Latin America. Prior to this he ran his own studio, designing and building projects in Mexico and the US.

Fernando Romero is the founder and CEO of Fernando Romero EnterprisE (FREE). The visionary architect behind the Soumaya Museum, he works between FREE's offices in New York and his native Mexico City. In the last 10 years he has designed and built more than a million square feet spanning across more than 100 projects. He has produced several books including *Translation: LAR/Fernando Romero* (Actar, 2000), *Hyper-Border: The Contemporary US–Mexico Border and Its Future* (Princeton Architectural Press, 2007) and *Simplexity* (Hatje Cantz, 2010), which embody his approach of translating crucial moments in society into works of architecture.

David Rutten graduated in architecture and urbanism at TU Delft, where he taught himself programming after it became painfully obvious he was never going to be a famous architect. He began his programming career at the Le Bihan Partnership in Turku, Finland, where he worked on projects for Robert McNeel & Associates, most notably the RhinoScript101 primer and the Monkey Script Editor. In late 2007 he began working on a visual programming platform that was eventually to become Grasshopper®.

Shrikant Sharma leads SMART Solutions, Buro Happold's specialist service that offers advanced computational solutions to support architectural design, engineering, construction and operations of buildings and urban spaces. He has a PhD in Engineering and over 15 years' experience in the development and application of novel modelling and analysis tools. He is a leading consultant in people movement, and has led several major crowd-flow consultancy projects in a variety of sectors. He is actively engaged in rigorous research and development of rapid crowd-simulation tools.

Dennis Shelden is a founder and Chief Technology Officer of Gehry Technologies, and an associate professor of practice in computation and design at the Massachusetts Institute of Technology (MIT). He joined Gehry Partners in 1997 and became Director of Computing in 2000. Prior to joining Gehry he performed structural and energy systems engineering and technology research at firms including Arup, the Consultants' Computation Bureau and Cyra Systems. He is a licensed architect in the state of California.

Sarah Simpkin is a writer who is currently based in the Foster + Partners studio. She has contributed to a number of publications and books, including the *Norman Foster Works* series and two editions of the Catalogue, both published by Prestel. She studied interactive arts with Bruce Bell at Manchester Metropolitan University, and has collaborated with Facit Homes since the company was first founded.

Kai Strehlke studied architecture at the Swiss Federal Institute of Technology (ETHZ) in Zurich. Since 2005 he has been working for Herzog & de Meuron in Basel, Switzerland, where he built up and now directs the Digital Technologies Department. In this role he is responsible for integrating new geometrical and technical methods into the work of the office using digital and parametric design as well as different CNC fabrication technologies. In 2008 he submitted his PhD with the theme of 'The Digital Ornament in Architecture; its Generation, Production, and Application using Computer-Controlled Technologies'.

Ben van Berkel is the co-founder and principal architect of UNStudio in Amsterdam and Shanghai. UNStudio is a network of specialists in architecture, urban development and infrastructure. Current projects include restructuring the station area of Arnhem, the Raffles City mixed-use development in Hangzhou, a dance theatre for St Petersburg, and the design and restructuring of the Ponte Parodi harbour project in Genoa. Van Berkel is Professor of Conceptual Design at the Staedelschule in Frankfurt am Main, and was recently awarded the Kenzo Tange Visiting Professor's Chair at Harvard University Graduate School of Design. Central to his teaching is the inclusive approach of architectural works integrating virtual and material organisation and engineering constructions.

Sanne van der Burgh is senior project leader and architect at MVRDV. She is involved in many international competitions and commissions, and also heads the Parametric Design Taskgroup that researches, develops and applies parametric design technologies within the office. She graduated from Delft University of Technology, where she has also been developing and teaching 3-D parametric technologies.

Arthur van der Harten is an acoustician working in the Specialist Modelling Group (SMG) at the Foster + Partners London office. Prior to this he worked in the Kirkegaard Associates Chicago office on many types of acoustically sensitive spaces. He manages the open-source initiative Pachyderm Acoustic, which seeks to disseminate knowledge of sound through the provision of working open-source acoustical simulation algorithms for Rhinoceros®.

Karen Willcox is a professor of aeronautics and astronautics in the Aerospace Computational Design Laboratory at the Massachusetts Institute of Technology (MIT). She is also a co-director of the MIT Center for Computational Engineering, and Associate Head of the Department of Aeronautics and Astronautics. She holds a Bachelor of Engineering degree from the University of Auckland, and masters and PhD degrees from MIT.

Kang Shua Yeo is an assistant professor of architectural history, theory and criticism at the Singapore University of Technology and Design (SUTD). He has published in both local and international journals on theory of architecture, conservation and history. He won the 2005 and 2010 UNESCO Asia-Pacific Heritage Awards for Culture Heritage Conservation, the Award of Excellence for the Singapore Lam Ann Association's Hong San See Temple Restoration Project, and the Jury Commendation for Innovation inaugural heritage award for the Yuhu Elementary School Project in Lijiang, China.

Jeroen Zuidgeest is a project manager and architect at MVRDV. He is responsible for the development of many design and research projects, including the headquarters of the DNB bank in Oslo, the Paris Plus Petit vision for the Grand Paris region, and the 2022 Floriade vision for future growth of the new town of Almere. He has worked as a writer and editor, teaches at the Berlage Institute and The Why Factory, and has lectured at various institutions.

What is *Architectural Design*?

Founded in 1930, *Architectural Design* (△) is an influential and prestigious publication. It combines the currency and topicality of a newsstand journal with the rigour and production qualities of a book. With an almost unrivalled reputation worldwide, it is consistently at the forefront of cultural thought and design.

Each title of △ is edited by an invited guest-editor, who is an international expert in the field. Renowned for being at the leading edge of design and new technologies, △ also covers themes as diverse as architectural history, the environment, interior design, landscape architecture and urban design.

Provocative and inspirational, △ inspires theoretical, creative and technological advances. It questions the outcome of technical innovations as well as the far-reaching social, cultural and environmental challenges that present themselves today.

For further information on △, subscriptions and purchasing single issues see: www.architectural-design-magazine.com

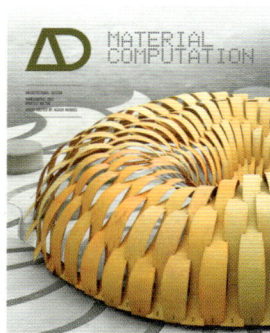

Volume 82 No 2
ISBN 978 0470 973301

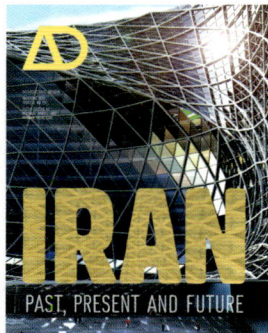

Volume 82 No 3
ISBN 978 1119 974505

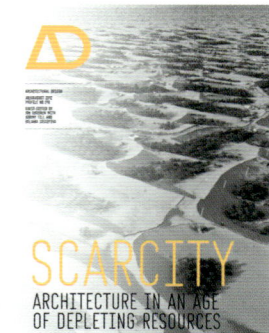

Volume 82 No 4
ISBN 978 1119 973621

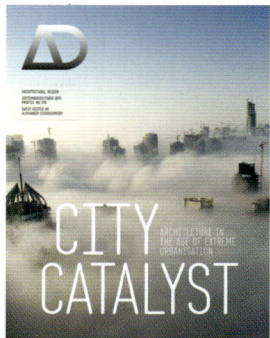

Volume 82 No 5
ISBN 978 1119 972662

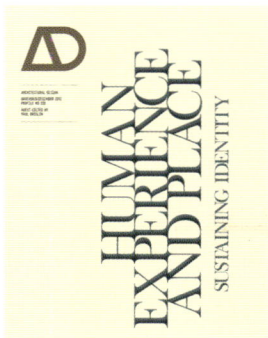

Volume 82 No 6
ISBN 978 1118 336410

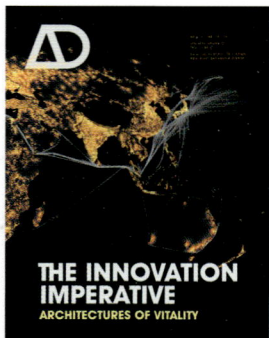

Volume 83 No 1
ISBN 978 1119 978657